The Laura Secord

Canadian Cook Book

The Laura Secord

PREPARED BY THE CANADIAN HOME ECONOMICS ASSOCIATION

Canadian Cook Book

M&S

© 1966 by Laura Secord Candy Shops

Reprinted 1990.

All rights reserved. The use of any part of this publication reproduced, transmitted in any form or by any means, electronic, mechanical, photocopying, recording or otherwise, or stored in a retrieval system, without the prior consent of the publisher is an infringement of the copyright law.

Canadian Cataloguing in Publication Data
Main entry under title:

The Laura Secord Canadian cook book

Issued also in French under title: Recettes canadiennes de Laura Secord. Montréal: Éditions de l'homme, c1984. Includes index. ISBN 0-7710-4084-9

1. Cookery, Canadian.   I. Canadian Home Economics Association.

TX715.L39 1984   641.5971
    C85-011067-X

Printed and Bound in Canada by Gagné Printing Ltd.

McClelland & Stewart Inc.
The Canadian Publishers
481 University Avenue
Toronto, Ontario
M5G 2E9

Credits

The photography for this book is by Dennis Colwell. Illustrations interspersed with the text are by Robert Daignault, Hedda S. Johnson, and Don Fernley. The historical paintings which appear in the photographs are by Robert Daignault.

Beef chart photographs are from *Meat: How to Buy – How to Cook,* Consumer Section, Marketing Service, Canada Department of Agriculture, Publication No. 971, by permission of The Queen's Printer.

The illustration for *Yeast Breads and Tea Breads* was photographed at the Black Creek Pioneer Village, Toronto, Ontario.

Art Direction	Frank Newfeld
Layout	Don Fernley
Type	Optima
	set by Mono Lino
	Typesetting Company Ltd.

Contents

List of Illustrations

SECTION 6

Desserts and Sauces

Fur traders dining in state at the Beaver Club of the North West Company in Montreal would certainly have enjoyed these St. Lawrence Maple Dumplings, the traditional "grands-pères" of Quebec.

SECTION 7

Cookies and Candy

Antigonish Brownies are a typical recipe of Nova Scotia. The seagoing heritage of this province is recalled by the objects in the background which include a representation of the *Bluenose*, Queen of the Grand Banks fishing fleet.

SECTION 8

Preserves and Vegetables

The arrival of the United Empire Loyalists at Saint John in 1783 left an indelible stamp on the province of New Brunswick. Home preserving must certainly have been one of the arts they brought with them to their new country.

SECTION 9

Soups, Snacks and Specialties

During the time of their deliberations at Charlottetown the Fathers of Confederation may well have had the opportunity to savour this delicious P.E.I. Potato Soup.

SECTION 10

Pastries

Against the background of a typical quiet outport of the "Oldest Colony" we have illustrated Newfoundland Berry Pie together with equally delicious peach and cherry pies.

Foreword

HOW DID THIS COOK BOOK HAPPEN?

It's all because two groups of people had the same good idea.

Several years ago, we arrived at what we thought was a unique idea. Why shouldn't Laura Secord sponsor the first truly Canadian cook book? After all, we've been associated with fine foods for over half a century. By now, we have quite a fund of knowledge about Canadian cooking. Why not share this knowledge with all the Canadians who are interested in fine foods?

But Laura Secord wasn't the only one with this idea. The Canadian Home Economics Association had also thought of an all-Canadian cook book as a Centennial project. The matchmaker was the publishers McClelland and Stewart Limited. At their suggestion, we reached the happy agreement that we would sponsor this first truly Canadian cook book if the Association compiled and approved all the recipes.

Then the work began. The representatives of the Canadian Home Economics Association deserve more credit than we can ever show them. First, they had to gather authentic Canadian recipes from every province, every region in this vast country. Then, teams of professional home economists spent almost a year researching, testing, and perfecting these recipes to make sure each one met their high standards of quality.

We are delighted with the result!

LAURA SECORD CANDY SHOPS

Introduction

IT REALLY *WAS* WORTH ALL THE WORK!

This cook book turned out to be one of the most fascinating projects any of us has ever worked on!

One thing we did prove conclusively: there *is* a Canadian cuisine, and it is unique in all the world.

To find out, we had our representatives scouring every province to find recipes distinctive to different regions. They collected well over a thousand. The story that goes with each recipe tells, in essence, the history of the region from which it comes.

Some recipes, brought from the Old Country generations ago, are still made exactly as they were in Europe. Others have been adapted to the foods and the way of life in Canada. We found recipes that are the result of several Canadian-European alterations. And there are many dishes, "born in Canada," that had never been served in any other country!

But all these recipes are truly Canadian. And all the recipes we have chosen are absolutely delicious! You'll enjoy trying them. We certainly did.

CANADIAN HOME
ECONOMICS ASSOCIATION

Sally Henry
Lorraine Swirsky
Carol Taylor

12

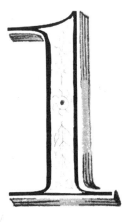

Yeast Breads

Since many Canadians depend for their livelihood on wheat, the chief farm product of the Prairies, and since bread has a traditional and religious aspect throughout our land, one can understand the importance of this basic food.

All recipes have been designed for use with or without a mixer. For convenience, the first amount of flour may be beaten in with a mixer to fully develop the elastic quality of the dough. Gradually stir in the second amount of flour with a spoon until the dough is so stiff it must be blended by hand. Knead until the dough feels smoothly stretched and springy and does not stick to the board, (exception: some doughs containing molasses will have a tendency to stick to the board even when fully kneaded).

Cover bowl and pans with greased wax paper and a damp cloth before setting in a warm place to rise. The rising times will vary depending on the temperature of "the warm place" and the stated times resulted when the dough was kept at a temperature of 90°F.

York County Corn Bread

This corn bread recipe, from Ontario, must date back to an earlier era, but its delicious flavour merits a modern day revival. For a special treat try a toasted back bacon sandwich made with this golden bread.

Scald
1½ cups milk

Pour into a large bowl and add
¼ cup granulated sugar
1 tablespoon salt
¼ cup shortening
¾ cup water
1 cup cornmeal

Stir until shortening melts.
Cool to lukewarm.

Meanwhile, dissolve
1 teaspoon sugar
in
½ cup lukewarm water (100° F.)

Over this, sprinkle
1 envelope active dry yeast

Let stand for 10 minutes. Then stir briskly with a fork. Add softened yeast to lukewarm milk mixture. Stir.

Beat in
3 cups all-purpose flour

Add another
3 to 3½ cups all-purpose flour

Work in last of flour with a rotating motion of the hand. Turn dough out on a lightly floured surface and knead 8 to 10 minutes. Shape into a smooth ball and place in a greased bowl, rotating dough to grease surface. Cover and let rise until doubled (about 1½ hours). Punch down and shape into 2 loaves. Place in 8½ x 4½-inch loaf pans that have been greased and sprinkled with cornmeal. Grease tops of loaves and let rise again until doubled (about 1¼ hours). Bake in preheated 425°F. oven for 30 minutes.

Makes 2 loaves.

Dutch Kringle Bread

The Dutch brought to Canada a special bread for Christmas time. Some versions call for a puff pastry shaped into a Christmas wreath and filled with almond paste, but we especially liked this almond-filled yeast bread from Winnipeg, Manitoba.

We understand that it originated in a local bake shop.

Scald
1 cup milk

Pour into a large bowl and add
½ cup granulated sugar
1 teaspoon salt
¼ cup butter

Stir until butter melts. Cool to lukewarm.

Meanwhile, dissolve
1 teaspoon sugar
in
½ cup lukewarm water (100° F.)

Over this, sprinkle
1 envelope active dry yeast

Let stand for 10 minutes. Then stir briskly with a fork. Stir softened yeast into lukewarm milk mixture.

Beat in
2 cups all-purpose flour
1 slightly beaten egg
1 teaspoon almond flavouring

Combine and blend in
¾ cup all-purpose flour
1 cup blanched sultana raisins
1 cup currants
¼ cup chopped candied cherries
¼ cup chopped citron peel

Beat well.

Add another
2 cups all-purpose flour

Work in last of flour with a rotating motion of the hand. Turn dough out on a lightly floured surface and knead 8 to 10 minutes. Shape into a smooth ball and place in greased bowl, rotating dough to grease surface. Cover and let rise until doubled (about 1½ hours). Punch down and divide in half. Flatten each into an oblong about ¾ inch thick.

Shape into two bars, each 1 inch in diameter
1 can (8 ounces) almond paste

Place almond paste lengthwise on dough and roll up in dough like a jelly roll, but carefully folding in ends before rolling.

Place seam side down in two greased 8½ x 4½-inch loaf pans. Cover and let rise until doubled (about 1 hour).

Bake in preheated 375° F. oven for 45 to 50 minutes.

Makes 2 loaves.

French Bread

14

This crusty classic came to Canada with the early French settlers and today has won favour from coast to coast.

Scald together
½ cup milk
¾ cup water

Pour into a large bowl and add
1 tablespoon granulated sugar
2 teaspoons salt
2 tablespoons shortening

Stir until shortening melts. Cool to lukewarm.

Meanwhile, dissolve
1 teaspoon granulated sugar
¼ teaspoon ginger
in
½ cup lukewarm water (100° F.)

Over this, sprinkle
1 envelope active dry yeast

Let stand for 10 minutes. Then stir briskly with a fork. Add softened yeast to lukewarm milk mixture. Stir.

Beat in
2½ cups all-purpose flour

Add another
2 cups all-purpose flour

Work in last of flour with a rotating motion of the hand. Turn dough out on a lightly floured surface and knead for 8 to 10 minutes. Shape into a smooth ball and place in a lightly greased bowl, rotating dough to grease surface. Cover with a damp cloth and let rise in a warm place until doubled (about 1½ hours).

Punch down the dough and turn out on a lightly floured surface. Divide dough in three, forming each portion into a smooth ball. Cover and let rise for 15 minutes. Knead and shape each ball into a narrow 12-inch-long loaf. Place well apart on a greased baking sheet. With scissors, slash tops diagonally. Cover with a damp cloth and let rise in a warm place until doubled (in unheated oven with a pan of boiling water underneath improves crustiness).

Bake in preheated 400°F. oven for 15 minutes, then reduce heat to 350° for 25 minutes. Brush with 1 egg white mixed with 2 tablespoons water twice during baking.

Makes 3 loaves.

Greek Easter Bread

Almost every country possesses traditional breads for religious occasions. This clover-leaf shaped loaf from Manitoba has a particularly festive appearance.

Dissolve
1 teaspoon sugar
in
½ cup lukewarm water (100° F.)

Over this, sprinkle
1 envelope active dry yeast

Let stand for 10 minutes. Then stir briskly with a fork.

Meanwhile, cream together
2 tablespoons shortening
¼ cup granulated sugar
¾ teaspoon salt

Add, and beat well
1 egg
1 egg yolk

(Batter will be curdled.)

Stir in softened yeast with
2 tablespoons skim milk powder
1 cup all-purpose flour

Beat until smooth.

Add another
½ to ¾ cup all-purpose flour

Work in last of flour with a rotating motion of the hand. Turn dough out on a lightly floured surface and knead 8 to 10 minutes. Shape into a smooth ball and place in a greased bowl, rotating dough to grease surface. Cover and let rise until doubled (about 2¼ hours).

Combine
¼ cup seedless raisins
¼ cup slivered citron peel
2 tablespoons chopped candied orange peel

Punch down dough, turn out on a lightly floured surface and spread with fruits. Knead to distribute fruit. Divide dough in three, forming each into a smooth ball. Arrange, just touching, in clover leaf shape on greased baking sheet. Grease tops, cover, and let rise again until doubled. Bake in preheated 375° F. oven for 25 to 30 minutes. While still warm brush with Icing Sugar Glaze (see page 107). Decorate with blanched almonds, citron and candied cherries.

Makes 1 loaf.

Hot Cross Buns

Originally available only on Good Friday, hot cross buns predate all other traditional English cakes and buns. In Canada they are served throughout the Lenten season, usually halved and toasted.

Scald
¾ cup milk

Pour into a large bowl and add
½ cup granulated sugar
1 teaspoon salt
¼ cup butter

Stir until butter melts. Cool to lukewarm.

Meanwhile, dissolve
1 teaspoon sugar
in
½ cup lukewarm water (100°F.)

Over this, sprinkle
1 envelope active dry yeast

Let stand for 10 minutes. Then stir briskly with a fork. Add softened yeast to lukewarm milk mixture together with
1 egg, beaten
1 egg yolk
1 teaspoon cinnamon
½ teaspoon cloves
¼ teaspoon nutmeg

Beat in
2 cups all-purpose flour

Add another
1¾ to 2 cups all-purpose flour

Work in last of flour with a rotating motion of the hand. Turn dough out on a lightly floured surface and knead 8 to 10 minutes.

Knead in
½ cup raisins or currants

Shape into a smooth ball and place in a greased bowl, rotating dough to grease surface. Cover, and let rise until doubled (about 1½ hours). Punch down, and shape into 18 to 20 buns. Arrange 2 inches apart on greased baking sheets. Cover, and let rise until doubled (about 45 minutes).

Combine and brush on buns.
1 slightly beaten egg white
1 tablespoon water

Slash top of bun in the form of a cross. Bake in preheated 400° F. oven for 15 to 18 minutes.

Drizzle with Icing Sugar Glaze (see page 107).

Makes 18 to 20 buns.

Makiwnyk

From Winnipeg we received this recipe for *makiwnyk*, a sweet-dough bread traditionally served at Christmas by those of Ukrainian origin. We liked the dough so much that we used it in the recipes for Chelsea Buns, Cinnamon Ring and Hungarian Coffee Cake.

Scald
2 cups milk

Cool to lukewarm.

Meanwhile, dissolve
1 teaspoon sugar
in
½ cup lukewarm water (100° F.)

Over this, sprinkle
1 envelope active dry yeast

Let stand for 10 minutes. Then stir briskly with a fork. Add softened yeast to lukewarm milk. Stir.

Beat in
3 cups all-purpose flour

Cover bowl. Let stand in warm place until light and full of bubbles (about 1 hour).

Stir in
1 cup granulated sugar
½ teaspoon salt
½ cup butter, melted
1 tablespoon grated lemon rind

Beat with a fork
3 eggs } OR
3 egg yolks } **4 whole eggs**

Stir into batter.

Add
2 cups all-purpose flour

Beat vigorously. Add another
4 to 4½ cups all-purpose flour

Work in last of flour with a rotating motion of the hand. Turn dough out on a lightly floured surface and knead 8 to 10 minutes. Shape into a smooth ball and place in a greased bowl, rotating dough to grease surface. Cover and let rise until doubled (about 1½ hours). Punch down and divide into three parts. Roll each into a ½-inch-thick rectangle. Spread with Poppy Seed Filling (p. 16). Roll up each rectangle like a jelly roll. Pinch seams to make edges secure. Place on greased baking sheet. Cover, let rise until doubled. Brush with cream.

Bake in preheated 350° F. oven for 1 hour.

Makes 3 loaves.

POPPY SEED FILLING

Scald with boiling water
1 pound poppy seeds
Let stand for 1 hour.

Drain and dry thoroughly, preferably overnight.

Grind in poppy seed grinder or through finest blade of food chopper.

Stir in
½ cup granulated sugar

Beat until stiff
3 egg whites

Fold into poppy seed mixture along with
1 tablespoon grated lemon rind

Maple Syrup Buns

From Quebec, the Canadian home of maple syrup, comes the recipe for these delicately spiced raisin buns glazed with this native syrup. It effectively proves the adage that "Almost any good recipe is better with maple sugar or syrup added".

Scald
1 cup milk

Pour into a large bowl and add
½ cup granulated sugar
2 teaspoons salt
¾ cup shortening
1 cup mashed cooked potatoes (2 medium)
1 cup all-purpose flour
2 eggs, well beaten
1 tablespoon cinnamon

Stir until shortening melts. Cool to lukewarm.

Meanwhile, dissolve
1 teaspoon sugar
in
½ cup lukewarm water (100° F.)

Over this, sprinkle
1 envelope active dry yeast

Let stand for 10 minutes. Then stir briskly with a fork. Add softened yeast to lukewarm milk mixture. Stir. (Mixture will be liquidy.)

Cover with wax paper and a damp cloth.

Let stand in warm place for 2 hours.

Cover with boiling water, allow to plump, then drain
1½ cups raisins

Stir raisins into batter with
2 cups all-purpose flour

Add another
2 cups all-purpose flour

Work in last of flour with a rotating motion of the hand. Turn dough out on a lightly floured surface and knead 8 to 10 minutes. Shape into a smooth ball and place in a greased bowl, rotating dough to grease surface. Cover and let rise until doubled (about 2 hours). Roll dough out ½ inch thick and cut with 2-inch cookie cutter. Place on greased baking sheet.

Cover, and let rise 15 minutes.

Bake in preheated 400° F. oven for 15 to 18 minutes, or until light golden brown.

Boil together until it forms a thread (230° F. on a candy thermometer).
½ cup maple syrup
1 tablespoon granulated sugar

Drizzle on buns while they are still hot.

Makes about 4 dozen buns.

Mary's Polish Bread

Mary and her husband are Canadians by choice arriving in Canada not so very long ago. Now they, too, contribute to the New Brunswick way of life as indicated by this flavourful, open-textured bread, frequently served at the Magnetic Hill dining room near Moncton.

Dissolve
1 teaspoon sugar
in
¼ cup lukewarm water (100° F.)
Over this, sprinkle
1 envelope active dry yeast
Let stand for 10 minutes. Then stir briskly with a fork.
Stir softened yeast into
2 cups lukewarm water
Beat in
1 cup all-purpose flour
1 cup rolled oats
1 tablespoon salt
Add
3 cups graham flour
2 tablespoons caraway seeds

Work in last of flour with a rotating motion of the hand. Turn dough out on a lightly floured surface and knead 8 to 10 minutes. Shape into 2 loaves. Place in greased 8½ x 4½-inch loaf pans, grease tops of loaves, cover with damp cloth and let rise until doubled. Bake in preheated 375° F. oven for 55 to 65 minutes.

Makes 2 loaves.

Paska

This rich Ukrainian bread features a cross surrounded by fancy dough ornaments. It is taken to church on Easter morning in a small basket, along with other foods to be blessed by the priest, while the choir sings the traditional Easter hymn *Christ is Risen.*

Scald and then cool to lukewarm
1½ cups milk

Meanwhile, dissolve
1 teaspoon sugar
in
½ cup lukewarm water (100° F.)
Over this, sprinkle
1 envelope active dry yeast

Let stand for 10 minutes. Then stir briskly with a fork.
Combine lukewarm milk with
2½ cups all-purpose flour
Stir in softened yeast and beat until smooth. Cover with damp cloth and let rise until light (about 1½ hours).

Beat together until thick and lemon coloured
5 egg yolks
3 whole eggs
¼ cup granulated sugar
1 teaspoon salt
Stir in
½ cup butter, melted

Blend egg mixture into risen batter.
Beat in
2 cups all-purpose flour
Beat in another
4 to 4½ cups all-purpose flour

Work in last of flour with a rotating motion of the hand. Turn dough out on a lightly floured surface and knead 8 to 10 minutes. Shape into a smooth ball, rotating dough to grease surface. Cover and let rise until doubled (about 1 hour). Punch down. Remove about one third of dough. Shape remaining dough into 2 round loaves. If desired, knead into 1 loaf candied fruit and plumped raisins. (To plump, cover with boiling water and let stand 2 to 3 minutes.) With palm of hand, shape reserved dough into four 1-inch-wide rolls. Press rolls on top of dough to form cross. Trim and tuck ends underneath. Shape trimmed dough into swirls and rosettes and arrange around cross. Cover and let rise again until doubled.

Beat together with a fork
1 egg
1 tablespoon water
Brush over dough.

Bake in preheated 400° F. oven for 15 minutes. Reduce heat to 350° and bake for 35 to 40 minutes longer.

Makes 2 loaves.

Oatmeal Brown Bread

Top prize for a Maritime specialty could well be awarded to this oatmeal brown bread, or porridge bread. It seemed we received a recipe from every county, many suggesting that the bread be served with baked beans on Saturday night.

Combine in a large bowl
1 cup rolled oats
2 teaspoons salt
3 tablespoons butter or shortening
Pour over top
2 cups boiling water
Stir until shortening melts. Cool to lukewarm.
Meanwhile, dissolve
1 teaspoon sugar
in
½ cup lukewarm water (100° F.)
Over this, sprinkle
1 envelope active dry yeast
Let stand for 10 minutes. Then stir briskly with a fork. Add softened yeast to lukewarm mixture, together with
½ cup molasses
Beat in
1 cup whole wheat flour
Then
2 cups all-purpose flour
Add another
2 to 3 cups all-purpose flour

Work in last of flour with a rotating motion of the hand. Turn dough out on a lightly floured surface and knead 8 to 10 minutes. Shape into a smooth ball and place in a greased bowl, rotating dough to grease surface. Cover and let rise until doubled (about 1½ hours). Punch down and shape into 3 loaves. Place in greased 8½ x 4½-inch loaf pans, grease tops and let rise again until doubled.

Bake in preheated 375° F. oven for 60 to 65 minutes.

Makes 3 loaves.

Pulla

When the United States purchased Alaska in 1867, some of the Finnish people left that region and moved to southern British Columbia, which perhaps explains why this delicious Finnish coffee bread recipe came from Haney, British Columbia.

Scald
¾ cup milk
Pour into a large bowl and add
½ cup granulated sugar
1 teaspoon salt
⅓ cup butter
½ teaspoon ground cardamom
Stir until butter melts. Cool to lukewarm.
Stir in
2 eggs, beaten
Meanwhile, dissolve
1 teaspoon sugar
in
½ cup lukewarm water (100° F.)
Over this, sprinkle
1 envelope active dry yeast

Let stand for 10 minutes. Then stir briskly with a fork. Add softened yeast to lukewarm milk mixture. Stir.
Beat in
2 cups all-purpose flour
Add another
3 to 3½ cups all-purpose flour

Work in last of flour with a rotating motion of the hand. Turn dough out on a lightly floured surface and knead 8 to 10 minutes. Shape into a smooth ball and place in a greased bowl, rotating dough to grease surface. Cover and let rise until doubled (about 2 hours). Punch down, and divide into 3 parts. Shape each part into three 15-inch rolls and braid together. Place braided loaf on greased baking sheet. Repeat to make 3 loaves. Cover and let rise again until doubled (about 1¼ hours).

Bake in preheated 375° F. oven for 30 to 35 minutes. As soon as bread is removed from oven, brush with a glaze of
2 tablespoons sugar
dissolved in
1 tablespoon hot coffee
Sprinkle with
granulated sugar
After bread is several days old it makes delicious toast — just slice ¾ inch thick and toast in preheated 350° oven for 15 to 20 minutes.

Makes 3 loaves.

Sweet Dough

From Makiwnyk dough three delicious breads may be prepared which portray the international aspect of Canadian food. For a Maritime variation place slices of the unbaked cinnamon roll in a pan with a thin layer of molasses, allow to rise, bake, and you have Annapolis Valley "Lick me Fingers".

Chelsea Buns

Prepare Makiwnyk dough (see page 15) and let rise until doubled. This is enough dough to make next three recipes.

In a 13 x 9-inch cake pan melt
½ cup butter

Stir in
1⅓ cups lightly packed brown sugar
1½ tablespoons corn syrup

Blend until smooth.

Sprinkle with
⅔ cup coarsely chopped pecans

Allow to cool.

Roll out slightly more than one third of dough on a lightly floured surface into a rectangle 24 x 9 inches.

Spread with
3 tablespoons soft butter

Sprinkle with a mixture of
1 cup lightly packed brown sugar
1 teaspoon cinnamon
¾ cup seedless raisins

Distribute as evenly as possible over top. Roll up like a jelly roll and cut into pieces about 1 inch long. Arrange close together in prepared pan, cut side up. Cover and let rise until doubled (about 1¼ hours).

Bake in preheated 375° F. oven for 30 to 35 minutes, or until golden brown. Turn pan upside down on rack immediately. Allow syrup to run over rolls for several minutes before removing the pan.

Makes about 24 buns.

Cinnamon Roll

Roll out one half of remaining two thirds of Makiwnyk dough into a 12-inch square.

Brush generously with
melted butter

Mix together and sprinkle over dough
½ cup granulated sugar
1½ teaspoons cinnamon

Roll up like a jelly roll. Place on a greased cookie sheet, sealing the two ends together to form a circle. Slash with scissors ¾ of the way through the dough in 1-inch slices. Turn each slice carefully on its side. Cover, and let rise until doubled (about 1 hour). Bake in preheated 375° F. oven for 25 to 30 minutes, or until golden brown.

Makes 1 roll.

Hungarian Coffee Cake

Using the palm of the hand, roll remainder of Makiwnyk dough into a rope about 24 inches long. Cut into 25 equal pieces and form into balls.

Dip each in
melted butter

Then roll in a mixture of
⅓ cup granulated sugar
1 teaspoon cinnamon

Arrange the coated balls in layers in a greased 9-inch tube pan so that they barely touch.

Sprinkle with
¼ cup chopped nuts

Place maraschino cherries and raisins between each ball using
⅓ cup raisins
⅓ cup halved maraschino cherries

Cover and let rise until doubled (about 1½ hours).

Bake in preheated 375° F. oven for 30 to 35 minutes.

Invert at once on serving plate. Break apart to serve.

Makes 1 coffee cake.

20

Capilano Rye Bread

Capilano brings to mind the picturesque canyon and primitive suspension bridge of that name in the Vancouver area, and seems most appropriate for this nourishing bread recipe, submitted by a Vancouverite. It is an adaptation of a rye bread popular during the First World War, when homemakers were encouraged to use a variety of meals and flours, and thus increase the amount of wheat flour available for sending overseas to the troops and besieged peoples.

Scald
   2 cups milk

Pour into a large bowl and add
   ¼ cup granulated sugar
   1 tablespoon salt
   ¼ cup shortening

Stir until shortening melts. Cool to lukewarm.
Meanwhile, dissolve
   1 teaspoon sugar
in
   1 cup lukewarm water (100° F.)

Over this, sprinkle
   2 envelopes active dry yeast

Let stand for 10 minutes. Then stir briskly with a fork. Add softened yeast to lukewarm milk mixture. Stir.

Beat in
   ¼ cup wheat germ
   3 cups rye flour

Add
   1 cup graham flour
   3 to 4 cups all-purpose flour

Work in last of flour with a rotating motion of the hand. Turn dough out on a lightly floured surface and knead 8 to 10 minutes. Shape into a smooth ball and place in a greased bowl, rotating dough to grease surface. Cover and let rise until 1½ times its original volume (about 1 hour). Punch down and shape into 3 loaves. Place in greased 8½ x 4½-inch loaf pans, grease tops and let rise again until doubled (about 45 minutes).

Bake in preheated 375° F. oven for 55 to 65 minutes.

Makes 3 loaves.

Trapper's Bread

Each fall the women of Labrador bake this bread for their husbands before they leave for their traplines. The original recipe called for warming the flour, which is understandable since the hundred-pound bags are generally stored in a cool place. The larger amount of molasses will give a heavier loaf, but one that will keep moister for a long journey; for a lighter yet still flavourful bread we recommend the smaller amount.

Cover with boiling water, allow to plump and then drain
   1½ cups raisins
   1½ cups currants

In a large bowl combine
   2¾ cups hot water
   1 cup lightly packed brown sugar
   1 tablespoon salt
   1 cup butter
   ⅔ to 1 cup molasses

Stir until butter melts. Cool to lukewarm.
Meanwhile, dissolve
   2 teaspoons sugar
in
   1 cup lukewarm water (100° F.)
Over this, sprinkle
   2 envelopes active dry yeast

Let stand for 10 minutes. Then stir briskly with a fork. Add softened yeast to lukewarm mixture. Stir.
Beat in
   6 cups all-purpose flour
Mix plumped fruit with
   6 cups all-purpose flour
Stir into dough.

Work in last of flour mixture with a rotating motion of the hand. Turn dough out on a lightly floured surface and knead 8 to 10 minutes. Shape into a smooth ball and place in a greased bowl, rotating dough to grease surface. Cover with damp cloth and let rise until doubled (about 2 hours). Punch down and shape into 4 loaves. Place in greased 8½ x 4½-inch loaf pans, cover, and let rise again until doubled (about 1 hour).

Bake in preheated 375° F. oven for 1 hour.

Brush tops with butter while still hot.

Makes 4 loaves.

Sourdough Bread

Standard supplies for Canada's first settlers included yeast starter for making breads. Later, during the Klondike Gold Rush, miners and prospectors were nicknamed "Sourdoughs" because they kept the starter next to their bodies for warmth. We've modernized this recipe for sourdough bread in that the starter is prepared from commercial yeast rather than trusting to the flavour of the wild yeasts in the air.

In a large bowl dissolve

1 teaspoon granulated sugar

in

½ cup lukewarm water (100° F.)

Over this, sprinkle

1 envelope active dry yeast

Let stand for 10 minutes. Then stir briskly with a fork.

Stir in

3 cups lukewarm water
1 tablespoon salt
1 tablespoon sugar
3 cups all-purpose flour

Cover. Let stand at room temperature for 3 days, stirring down batter daily.

On third day, scald

1 cup milk

Stir in

¼ cup granulated sugar
2 tablespoons shortening

Cool to lukewarm. Blend in 3 cups yeast mixture. (To remainder add 2 cups lukewarm water and 2 cups all-purpose flour. Let stand at room temperature 1 day then pour into glass jar, seal and refrigerate. Use for next batch of bread.)

Beat in

3 cups all-purpose flour

Add another

3½ to 4 cups all-purpose flour

Work in last of flour with a rotating motion of the hand. Turn dough out on a lightly floured surface and knead 8 to 10 minutes. Shape into a smooth ball and place in a greased bowl, rotating dough to grease surface. Cover, and let rise until doubled (about 1¼ hours). Turn out on lightly floured board and knead until smooth. Divide in three. Roll out each portion and shape into loaves. Place in greased 8½ x 4½-inch loaf pans. Grease tops and let rise again until doubled (about 45 minutes).

Bake in preheated 400° F. oven for 30 to 35 minutes.

Makes 3 loaves.

100% Whole Wheat Bread

To be light and yet fine textured, bread must be made from flour with sufficient protein or gluten. Whole wheat flour does not possess sufficient protein for perfect bread, but many people prefer the more compact bread that results, especially when toasted.

Scald

2¾ cups milk

Pour into a large bowl and stir in

⅓ cup molasses
4 teaspoons salt

Cool to lukewarm.
Meanwhile, dissolve

2 teaspoons sugar

in

1 cup lukewarm water (100° F.)

Over this, sprinkle

2 envelopes active dry yeast

Let stand for 10 minutes. Then stir briskly with a fork. Add softened yeast to lukewarm mixture. Stir.
Beat in

4 cups whole wheat flour

Add another

4 to 5 cups whole wheat flour

Work in last of flour with a rotating motion of the hand. Turn dough out on a lightly floured surface and knead 8 to 10 minutes. Shape into a smooth ball and place in a greased bowl, rotating dough to grease surface. Cover, and let rise until doubled (about 2 hours). Punch down, and shape into 3 loaves. Place in greased 8½ x 4½-inch loaf pans, grease tops and let rise again until doubled (about 1 hour).

Bake in preheated 350° F. oven for 40 to 45 minutes.

Makes 3 loaves.

Tea Breads

With some two million Canadians of Scottish descent, we have understandably adopted the tremendous variety of quick breads, biscuits, scones, and muffins of the celebrated Scottish tea table. Rich moist loaves, thinly sliced and buttered, still accompany afternoon tea, and their use has expanded to include breakfast, morning coffee, lunch, and our fourth meal in the evening.

We have welcomed the foods of other lands — the German and Hungarian coffee cakes, spicy and warm, the golden, rich doughnuts designed for dunking in coffee — and combined them with native foods such as pumpkin, cornmeal, whole wheat flour and maple syrup, to produce Canadian tea breads.

Tantalizing Beer and Nut Loaf

Most quick breads, no matter how delectable, lack the haunting aroma of freshly baked yeast bread. This loaf, from Quebec City, merges the best of both — speedy stir-and-bake technique coupled with a yeasty fragrance and flavour.

Preheat oven to 350° F.
Grease a 9 x 5 x 3-inch loaf pan.
Sift or blend together
   2¼ cups all-purpose flour
   4 teaspoons baking powder
   1 teaspoon salt
   1 cup granulated sugar
With a pastry blender or two knives cut in
   ⅓ cup shortening
Beat together with a fork
   2 eggs
   1 cup beer
Add liquid to dry ingredients and stir only until combined (batter will be lumpy).
Fold in
   ½ cup chopped walnuts
   1 cup finely chopped dates
Turn into prepared loaf pan.
Bake in 350° oven for 55 to 60 minutes, or until toothpick inserted in centre comes out clean.

Remove from pan and allow to cool.
Wrap and store in canister. Serve thinly sliced, spread with cream cheese.
Makes 1 loaf.

Shediac Brown Bread

Steamed molasses or brown breads find favour throughout the Canadian Maritime Provinces and along both banks of the St. Lawrence River. Whether Boston possesses clear title to the origin of this bread (as some claim) seems debatable but none deny the well-known partnership of this moist and tangy bread with baked beans.

Grease thoroughly two 28-ounce tins or three 19-ounce tins.
Sift or blend together
   1 cup all-purpose flour
   1½ teaspoons salt
   1 teaspoon baking powder
   1 teaspoon baking soda
Stir in
   1 cup cornmeal
   1 cup whole wheat flour
   2 tablespoons brown sugar
Beat together with a fork
   ¾ cup molasses
   1¼ cups water
   2 tablespoons shortening, melted
Add liquids to dry ingredients and stir only until combined (batter will be lumpy).
Fill prepared tins ⅔ full. Cover with wax paper and foil and tie securely.
Steam for 2 hours on a rack in a pan with water to half the height of the tins. Unmould.
Serve warm or cold, sliced and spread with butter.
Makes 2 or 3 loaves.

Raisin Brown Bread
Stir in 1 cup raisins before filling tins.

Bonavista Fruit Bread

Because they keep well, becoming more moist with time, fruit breads prove popular throughout the country. This particular recipe came from Newfoundland where homemakers like to have it on hand at Christmas time.

Preheat oven to 350° F.

Grease thoroughly a 9 x 5 x 3-inch loaf pan.

Sift or blend together
   2 cups all-purpose flour
   3½ teaspoons baking powder
   ¾ teaspoon salt
   ¾ cup granulated sugar

Mix in
   ¼ cup diced candied pineapple
   ¼ cup raisins
   ½ cup chopped candied cherries
   ½ cup chopped walnuts

Beat together with a fork
   2 eggs
   1 cup milk
   3 tablespoons butter, melted

Add liquids to dry ingredients and stir only until combined (batter will be lumpy).

Fill prepared loaf pan and let stand 30 minutes.

Bake in 350° oven for 55 to 65 minutes, or until toothpick inserted in centre comes out clean.

Remove from pan and allow to cool.

Serve plain or buttered.

Makes 1 loaf.

Paradise Lemon Bread

Although not grown in Canada, lemons enjoy national popularity in cooking as indicated by this recipe received from Paradise Valley, Alberta, Moncton, New Brunswick, and Montreal, Quebec.

Preheat oven to 350° F.

Grease thoroughly an 8½ x 4½-inch loaf pan.

Sift or blend together
   1½ cups all-purpose flour
   ¼ teaspoon salt
   1 teaspoon baking powder

Cream
   ½ cup butter

Gradually blend in
   1 cup granulated sugar
   2 eggs

Beat until light and fluffy.

Add dry ingredients to creamed mixture alternately with
   ½ cup milk

Combine lightly after each addition.

Fold in
   2 tablespoons grated lemon rind
   ½ cup chopped nuts

Turn into prepared loaf pan.

Bake in 350° oven for 55 to 60 minutes, or until cake springs back when lightly touched. Cool 5 minutes.

Combine and pour over top
   2 tablespoons granulated sugar
   2 tablespoons lemon juice

Remove from pan when cool.

This may be served plain as cake or buttered as a sweet bread.

Makes 1 loaf.

Sherry Date Loaf

From Winnipeg comes this modern tea bread with an elusive flavour that wins loud acclaim — and much embarrassment when it was accidentally sliced and buttered for a church social.

Preheat oven to 350° F.

Grease a 9 x 5 x 3-inch loaf pan.

Bring just to boiling point
   1 cup sherry

Pour over
   2 cups chopped dates

Stir and allow to cool.

Sift or blend together
   2 cups all-purpose flour
   1 teaspoon baking powder
   1 teaspoon baking soda
   ¼ teaspoon salt

Cream
   ¼ cup shortening

Gradually blend in
   1 cup lightly packed brown sugar
   1 egg

Beat until light and fluffy.

Add dry ingredients to creamed mixture alternately with date mixture.

Combine lightly after each addition.

Blend in
   ½ cup chopped candied cherries
   ½ cup chopped walnuts

Turn into prepared loaf pan.

Bake in 350° oven for 50 to 60 minutes, or until toothpick inserted in centre comes out clean.

Remove from pan and allow to cool.

Keep in tightly covered tin. Allow to mellow a day before serving.

Makes 1 loaf.

24

Blueberry Oatmeal Muffins

Known as whortleberries or hurtleberries by the early English settlers, Canadian blueberries with their misty sky-blue colour and sweet flavour have found their place in cooking. Many varieties thrive in rocky and somewhat barren areas from Newfoundland to Vancouver Island.

This Scotch muffin recipe, from Newfoundland, adapts to the inclusion of this native fruit.

Preheat oven to 400° F.

Grease thoroughly 16 medium-sized muffin cups.

Sift or blend together

- **1 cup all-purpose flour**
- **2 teaspoons baking powder**
- **½ teaspoon salt**
- **½ teaspoon cinnamon**

Stir in

- **¾ cup rolled oats**
- **½ cup lightly packed brown sugar**

Beat together

- **1 egg**
- **1 cup milk**
- **¼ cup shortening, melted**

Add liquids to dry ingredients and stir only until combined (batter will be lumpy).

Fold in *+ ¼ c flour*

- **¾ cup fresh or frozen blueberries**

Fill prepared muffin cups ⅔ full.

Bake in 400° oven for 20 to 25 minutes, or until golden brown.

Remove from pans and serve warm.

Makes 16 muffins.

12

Buttermilk Oatmeal Muffins
Replace baking powder with ½ teaspoon baking powder and ½ teaspoon baking soda. Use buttermilk or sour milk in place of milk and increase shortening to ⅓ cup. Omit blueberries.

Cavendish Bran Muffins

Bran muffins could undoubtedly bear the title of the most truly national muffin, but recipes vary incredibly. Maritimers prefer them a rich brown molasses colour and studded with raisins or chopped dates. Others select a lighter, milder flavour and colour (for these, reduce the molasses to ¼ cup). We simply had to name these muffins after Cavendish Beach, P.E.I., near the farmhouse home of Lucy Maud Montgomery, the author of *Anne of Green Gables*.

Preheat oven to 400°F.

Grease thoroughly 12 medium-sized muffin cups.

Sift or blend together

- **1⅓ cups all-purpose flour**
- **1 teaspoon baking soda**
- **½ teaspoon salt**

Blend in

- **1 cup bran or bran flakes**

Cream

- **¼ cup shortening**

Gradually blend in

- **2 tablespoons brown sugar**
- **1 egg**
- **½ teaspoon vanilla**
- **½ cup molasses**

Beat until light and fluffy.

Add sifted dry ingredients to creamed mixture alternately with

- **⅔ cup buttermilk or sour milk**

Combine lightly after each addition.

If desired, fold in

- **½ cup seedless raisins**

Fill prepared muffin cups ⅔ full.

Bake in 400° oven for 15 to 18 minutes.

Remove from pans and serve warm.

Makes 12 muffins.

Maritime Cornmeal Muffins

Cornmeal in cooking indicates a North American recipe, and in Canada homemakers prefer the golden yellow cornmeal rather than the white. Throughout most of our country, the sunny yellow version of these muffins proves more popular, but our Maritimers like a dash of molasses.

Serve piping hot with butter and jam, syrup or molasses.

Preheat oven to 425°F.

Grease thoroughly 14 medium-sized muffin cups.

Combine and set aside for 20 minutes
- **1 cup cornmeal**
- **1¼ cups buttermilk or sour milk**

Sift or blend together
- **1 cup all-purpose flour**
- **1 teaspoon baking powder**
- **1 teaspoon baking soda**
- **1 teaspoon salt**
- **⅓ cup granulated sugar**

Beat slightly with a fork
- **1 egg**

and stir into cornmeal mixture together with
- **¼ cup molasses**
- **¼ cup shortening, melted**

Add cornmeal mixture to dry ingredients and stir only until combined (batter will be lumpy).

Fill prepared muffin cups ⅔ full.

Bake in 425° oven for 20 to 25 minutes.

Remove from pans and serve warm.

Makes 14 muffins.

Golden Cornmeal Muffins

Omit molasses and reduce cornmeal to ¾ cup.

Jack-O'-Lantern Muffins

In late October the markets across the country overflow with small, medium and giant sized pumpkins. After Halloween they vanish from sight because these days farmers sell pumpkins direct to the canning companies except for those that are hollowed out to make jack-o'-lanterns — meanwhile mothers seek ways to use the scooped-out flesh, as in these delicately flavoured pumpkin muffins.

Preheat oven to 400°F.

Grease thoroughly 12 medium-sized muffin cups.

Sift or blend together
- **1½ cups all-purpose flour**
- **3 teaspoons baking powder**
- **½ teaspoon salt**
- **½ teaspoon cinnamon**
- **½ teaspoon nutmeg**

Stir in

- **⅓ cup lightly packed brown sugar**

Beat together with a fork
- **1 egg**
- **¾ cup milk**
- **½ cup canned or cooked pumpkin**
- **¼ cup shortening, melted**

Add liquids to dry ingredients and stir only until combined (batter will be lumpy).

Fill prepared muffin cups ⅔ full.

Bake in 400° oven for 20 to 25 minutes, or until golden brown.

Remove from pans and serve warm.

Makes 12 muffins.

The Queen's Muffins

During the October, 1957 visit of Queen Elizabeth to Canada, chefs across the land prepared these muffins for Her Majesty's afternoon tea. We understand that Royal Canadian Air Force dietitians standardized the large-quantity recipe from which this version was derived. On many occasions the Press Corps assigned to the tour ate the muffins so fast that it was necessary to have a few in reserve for the Queen.

Preheat oven to 375° F.

Grease thoroughly 16 medium-sized muffin cups.

Sift or blend together
- **1⅔ cups all-purpose flour**
- **2½ teaspoons baking powder**
- **½ teaspoon salt**

Cream
- **⅝ cup butter (½ cup plus 2 tablespoons)**

Gradually blend in
- **½ cup granulated sugar**
- **2 eggs**

Beat until light and fluffy.

Add dry ingredients alternately with
- **1¼ cups milk**

Make 3 dry and 2 liquid additions, combining lightly after each.

Stir in
- **¾ cup wheat germ**
- **1 cup raisins, cut in half**

Fill prepared muffin cups ⅔ full.

Bake in 375° oven for 15 to 20 minutes, or until golden brown.

Remove from pans and serve warm or cold.

Makes 16 muffins.

25

Versatile Muffins

Two charming English words, muffin and gem, refer to the same little cake. Serve these puffy little morsels piping hot from the oven with butter — and don't overlook the quick-change ideas.

Preheat oven to 400° F.

Grease thoroughly 12 medium-sized muffin cups.

Sift or blend together
1¾ cup all-purpose flour
3½ teaspoons baking powder
½ teaspoon salt
¼ cup granulated sugar

Beat together with a fork
1 egg
1¼ cups milk
¼ cup shortening, melted

Add liquids to dry ingredients and stir only until combined (batter will be lumpy).

Fill prepared muffin cups ⅔ full.

Bake in 400° oven for 20 to 25 minutes, or until golden brown.

Remove from pans and serve warm.

Makes 12 muffins.

Blueberry Muffins
Fold ¾ cup fresh blueberries into batter.

Bacon Muffins
Chop and crisply cook 4 strips of bacon. Stir bacon and drippings into liquid ingredients instead of shortening.

Cranberry Muffins
Reduce milk to 1 cup. Fold ½ cup cranberry sauce into batter.

Maplewood Doughnuts

Oh for the days when maple sugar was both plentiful and economical! Now the maple sugar version of these light-as-a-feather doughnuts must await a visit to friends with a sugar bush, possibly near Maplewood, New Brunswick.

Preheat deep fat to 375° F.

Cream together
¼ cup butter
1 cup maple sugar or lightly packed brown sugar
¼ teaspoon maple flavouring (if using brown sugar)

Blend in
2 eggs

Sift or blend together
2¾ cups all-purpose flour
1 tablespoon baking powder
¼ teaspoon salt
½ teaspoon nutmeg

Stir dry ingredients into creamed mixture alternately with
¾ cup milk

Chill dough until stiff enough to roll out.

Divide dough in four. Roll out each portion ⅓ inch thick on a lightly floured surface. Cut with floured doughnut cutter. Lift with wide spatula and slide into hot fat. Turn doughnuts as they rise to the surface. Fry until golden brown on both sides.

Drain on absorbent paper.

Roll in maple sugar.

Makes 2 dozen doughnuts.

Old-Fashioned Doughnuts

This recipe comes from a descendant of one of the Scottish families who settled in Compton County, in the Eastern Townships of Quebec, about 1840. During the early years, this section of the border between the United States and Canada proved almost nonexistent, with families travelling back and forth quite freely. Doughnuts such as these are often served for breakfast on both sides of the border in this region.

Preheat deep fat to 375° F.

Add (from deep fat fryer)
¼ cup melted shortening or lard
to
1 cup granulated sugar

Blend in
2 eggs
½ teaspoon vanilla

Sift or blend together
4½ cups all-purpose flour
2 teaspoons baking powder
1 teaspoon baking soda
1 teaspoon salt
1 teaspoon nutmeg

Stir dry ingredients into sugar mixture alternately with
1½ cups buttermilk or sour milk

Chill dough until stiff enough to roll out.

Divide dough in four. Roll out each portion ⅓ inch thick on a lightly floured surface. Cut with floured doughnut cutter. Lift with wide spatula and slide into hot fat. Turn doughnuts as they rise to the surface. Fry until golden brown on both sides.

Drain on absorbent paper.

Serve plain, or drizzle with chocolate icing.

Makes 3 dozen doughnuts.

Sour Cream Coffee Cake

A winning recipe in a national contest sponsored by the Toronto *Star Weekly*, this spicy coffee cake well deserves its continuing popularity.

Preheat oven to 350° F.

Grease thoroughly an 8-inch square cake pan. Dust lightly with flour.

Sift together
1⅓ cups pastry (soft wheat) flour
2 teaspoons baking powder
1 teaspoon baking soda

Blend together
½ cup butter
1 cup granulated sugar

Beat in
2 eggs
1 teaspoon vanilla

Beat until light and fluffy.

Add sifted dry ingredients to creamed mixture alternately with
1 cup thick dairy sour cream

Combine lightly after each addition.

Spread half the batter in prepared pan

Sprinkle with half of a mixture of
¼ cup lightly packed brown sugar
1 tablespoon cinnamon
2 tablespoons finely chopped nuts

Cover with remaining batter. Sprinkle with remainder of topping. Bake in 350° oven for 45 to 50 minutes. Serve warm. May be wrapped in foil and reheated.

Makes 1 coffee cake.

Bannock

Bannock was made on the trail by the Selkirk settlers and has become a favourite bread of our northern fur trappers. Originally a very heavy unleavened bread made with whole grain or whole wheat flour, today's bannock contains baking powder and sometimes egg. Every year at the winter carnivals in Northern Manitoba, such as at Flin Flon and The Pas, trappers compete in a bannock baking contest.

Preheat oven to 450° F.

Grease lightly a heavy cast-iron frying pan or baking sheet.

Sift or blend together
2¾ cups all-purpose flour
2 teaspoons baking powder
½ teaspoon salt

With a pastry blender or two knives, cut in finely
3 tablespoons lard

Stir in gradually
⅔ cup water

Stir with a fork to make a soft, slightly sticky dough.

Turn dough out on a lightly floured surface and knead gently 8 to 10 times.

Roll out or pat ½ inch thick, or flatten dough to fit frypan.

Cook in frypan on hot ashes over open fire (turn bannock to brown both sides), or on baking sheet in 450° oven for 12 to 15 minutes, or until light golden brown.

Cut and serve hot, with butter.

Makes 1 bannock.

Scotch Graham Scones

An authentic recipe found in the hand-written cookbook of a Zorra township homemaker whose forbears were among the Scottish settlers who pioneered in this area near Woodstock, Ontario in the early nineteenth century.

Originally baked on a girdle (griddle), scones cook perfectly in today's modern skillets.

Preheat oven to 450° F.

Sift or blend together
- **1 cup all-purpose flour**
- **2 teaspoons baking powder**
- **½ teaspoon salt**

Stir in
- **1 cup graham flour**
- **⅓ cup granulated sugar**

With a pastry blender or two knives, cut in until crumbly
- **½ cup shortening**

Break into a measuring cup and beat with a fork
- **1 egg**

Pour off about 1 tablespoon of egg into a saucer. Fill measuring cup to ⅔ mark with
- **water**

With a fork, stir this liquid into flour mixture to make a soft, slightly sticky dough.

Turn dough out on a lightly floured surface and knead gently 8 to 10 times. Roll out or pat ½ inch thick. Cut into wedges. Brush tops with reserved egg. Bake on ungreased baking sheet in 450° oven for 12 to 15 minutes, or until light golden brown.

Serve warm, with butter and home-made jam or jelly.

Makes 8 to 10 scones.

Mandel Bread

This unusual quick bread that closely resembles a cookie came from Toronto and is German in origin. Mandel is the German word for almond, which explains the name.

Preheat oven to 350° F.

Grease a baking sheet lightly.

Sift or blend together
- **3½ cups all-purpose flour**
- **1½ teaspoons baking powder**
- **½ teaspoon salt**

Mix together
- **3 eggs**
- **1 cup granulated sugar**
- **1 cup vegetable oil**
- **1 teaspoon vanilla**

Blend in about 1 cup of dry ingredients together with
- **1 cup ground almonds**

Gradually add remaining dry ingredients to make a stiff dough.

Shape dough into 4 or 5 loaf-like pieces (2 inches wide, 1 inch high, 7 inches long). Brush with vegetable oil and roll each little loaf in a mixture of
- **¼ cup granulated sugar**
- **¼ teaspoon cinnamon**

Bake on prepared baking sheet in 350° oven for 25 minutes. Slice while still hot and place pieces flat on baking sheet. Return to oven to dry and brown slightly, about 10 minutes longer.

Serve plain or buttered.

Abegweit Oatcakes

We've named these Scotch oatcakes after Prince Edward Island, (called "Abegweit" by the Micmac Indians) where the recipe originated. The Scots who settled on the island during the first half of the nineteenth century brought their oatcake recipe, which is very similar in appearance to packaged graham wafers.

Preheat oven to 375° F.

Mix together
- **2 cups all-purpose flour**
- **1½ cups rolled oats**
- **⅓ cup granulated sugar**
  OR
- **½ cup lightly packed brown sugar**
- **1 teaspoon salt**
- **½ teaspoon baking soda**

With a pastry blender or two knives, cut in
- **¾ cup shortening or lard**

With a fork, stir in
- **½ cup water or milk**

(Dough should just cling together.) Divide in three portions. Roll out each very thin on a lightly floured surface. Cut into 2-inch squares with a knife or pastry cutter. Place 1 inch apart on ungreased baking sheet.

Bake in 375° oven for 10 to 15 minutes.

Makes 4 to 5 dozen oatcakes.

Salt Pork Buns

From Newfoundland we received this recipe for salt pork buns, which reminds us of recipes from the days when, in other parts of the country, pork was pickled in barrels to last the winter. In Canada's tenth province when finely chopped salt pork is cooked until all the fat has melted out, the crispy bits in the bottom of the pot are called "scrunchions".

Preheat oven to 425° F.

Fry until crisp
1 cup finely chopped salt pork

Drain well.

Sift or blend together
3¾ cups all-purpose flour
2 tablespoons baking powder
½ teaspoon salt

With a pastry blender or two knives, cut in until crumbly
¼ cup butter

Stir in cooked salt pork (scrunchions).

Combine and add
½ cup molasses
1½ cups water

Stir with a fork to make a soft, slightly sticky dough.

Turn dough out on a lightly floured surface and knead gently 8 to 10 times. Roll out or pat ½ inch thick. Cut with floured 3-inch cutter.

Place 1 inch apart on ungreased baking sheet and bake in 425° oven for 12 to 15 minutes, or until brown.

Serve hot, with butter.

Makes 30 biscuits.

Early Ontario Sour Cream Biscuits

These rich biscuits reflect the German predeliction for sour cream in cooking, which has influenced many of our recipes. Germans form the largest ethnic group in Canada after the two founding peoples — British and French.

Preheat oven to 450° F.

Sift or blend together
2¼ cups all-purpose flour
1 teaspoon salt
1 teaspoon baking powder
½ teaspoon baking soda

With a pastry blender or two knives, cut in until crumbly
¼ cup shortening

Stir in
1½ cups thick dairy sour cream

Mix lightly with a fork to make a soft, slightly sticky dough.

Turn dough out on a lightly floured surface and knead gently 8 to 10 times. Roll out or pat ½ inch thick. Cut with floured 1¾-inch cutter.

Bake on ungreased baking sheet in 450° oven for 12 to 15 minutes, or until light golden brown.

Makes 16 to 20 biscuits.

Traditional Tea Biscuits

The baked scones of the Scots and the baking powder biscuits of our American neighbours appear as tea biscuits on our menus. Knead the dough gently to give the flaky layers that become visible when the biscuits are halved for spreading with butter and jelly. 'Crusty-sided' biscuit devotees separate the little rounds on the baking sheet and 'soft-siders' know to snuggle them up closely before baking.

Preheat oven to 450° F.

Sift or blend together
2¼ cups all-purpose flour
4 teaspoons baking powder
1 teaspoon salt

With a pastry blender or two knives, cut in until crumbly
½ cup shortening

Stir in
1 cup milk

Mix lightly with a fork to make a soft, slightly sticky dough.

Turn dough out on a lightly floured surface and knead gently 8 to 10 times.

Roll out or pat ½ inch thick. Cut with floured 1¾-inch cutter.

Bake on ungreased baking sheet in 450° oven for 12 to 15 minutes, or until light golden brown.

Serve hot or cold, with butter and jam.

Makes 18 to 20 biscuits.

Eier Kuchen

30

This is a traditional Good Friday luncheon dish brought from Germany about 1860 to the (then) wilds of the Muskoka district in Ontario. No doubt the preserved blueberries served on these light fluffy pancakes are a Canadian addition.

Preheat griddle or heavy frypan. If necessary grease with unsalted fat.

Sift or blend together
   1¾ cups pastry (soft wheat) flour
   3 teaspoons baking powder
   ¼ teaspoon salt

Beat until very light
   4 egg yolks

Blend in
   ½ cup granulated sugar
   1 tablespoon soft butter

Add sifted dry ingredients alternately with
   1 cup milk

Beat until stiff
   4 egg whites

Fold into batter.

Pour batter onto preheated griddle, using about ¼ cup batter for each pancake. Turn when bubbles break on surface.

Serve hot, with butter and preserved blueberries or maple syrup.

Makes 14 to 16 pancakes.

NOTE: *May also be used to make small Scotch tea pancakes.*

French Pancakes

The French word *crêpes* means pancakes, not the puffy variety, but rather the wafer thin and tender ones that are lacey around the edges. Their size varies with the size of frypan used and the bigger the family the larger the pancakes. In reality this recipe unites many Canadians of different heritages — the French and English, as well as many Europeans who use these pancakes to make blintzes and nalysnyky.

Preheat heavy 6-inch frypan and brush with melted butter.

Sift or blend together
   1 cup all-purpose flour
   1 teaspoon sugar
   ¼ teaspoon salt

Beat together with a rotary beater
   3 eggs
   2 cups milk

Stir in dry ingredients, beating until almost smooth. Blend in
   2 tablespoons melted butter

Cover and chill for 1 hour.

Pour batter onto preheated pan, using about 2 tablespoons batter for each pancake, and tip to coat with a thin layer. When brown, turn to brown other side.

Roll up and serve hot, with butter, maple syrup or molasses.

Makes about 2½ dozen pancakes.

Perfect Popovers

In pioneer days in Upper Canada, the dash across the yard from the cookhouse to the dining room table proved the worth of a good popover or Yorkshire pudding recipe. This one pours scorn on all warnings about draughts, to stand tall and proud on the table for all to admire.

Preheat oven to 450° F.

Pour ½ teaspoon beef drippings in each of 8 medium-sized muffin cups. Keep warm in oven.

Blend together
   1 cup all-purpose flour
   ½ teaspoon salt

Beat together with mixer or rotary beater
   2 eggs
   1 cup milk
   1 tablespoon beef drippings or melted butter

Add flour mixture and beat 2 minutes.

Pour into prepared pans.

Bake in 450° oven for 20 minutes and serve immediately.

To keep for reheating — slit each popover once to allow steam to escape. Turn oven off and leave popover in another 20 minutes. Cool in pan and reheat before serving.

Yorkshire Pudding

Use 8-inch square pan (heated with 1 tablespoon drippings) and bake for 35 to 40 minutes.

Traditional Pancakes

Naturally enough, considering their convenience for pioneer cooks, pancakes in English speaking Canada adapted to any meal, and became bigger and better than ever to cope with hearty appetites. Familiarly called flapjacks, or hearth cakes, pancakes are now frequently served for breakfast.

Preheat griddle or heavy frypan. If necessary grease with unsalted fat.

Sift or blend together
  1½ cups all-purpose flour
  3 teaspoons baking powder
  ½ teaspoon salt
  1 tablespoon granulated sugar

Beat together with a rotary beater
  1 egg
  1¾ cups milk
  2 tablespoons melted shortening or vegetable oil

Stir in dry ingredients, beating until almost smooth.

Pour batter onto preheated griddle, using about ¼ cup batter for each pancake. Turn when bubbles break on surface.

Serve hot, with butter and maple syrup.

Makes 12 to 14 pancakes.

Blueberry Pancakes
Stir into batter ¾ cup fresh blueberries.

Apple Pancakes
Stir into batter ¾ cup finely diced peeled apples.

Potato Flour Waffles

From time to time we receive requests for recipes for those on restricted diets. This one was developed by a Vancouverite for a wheat-free diet and the results were so good that now it has a broader scope.

Preheat oven to 250° F., then turn off heat. Preheat waffle iron. If necessary grease with unsalted fat.

Sift or blend together
  1 cup potato flour
  2 teaspoons baking powder
  ¾ teaspoon salt

Beat until stiff
  2 egg whites

Beat until thick and lemon-coloured
  2 whole eggs

Blend in
  1 cup heavy cream

Stir in dry ingredients, beating until mixture is thickened.
Fold in egg whites.

Pour batter onto preheated waffle iron using 1½ cups batter for each 9-inch square waffle. Bake until waffle iron stops steaming.

Place on oven rack to dry for 30 to 40 minutes. When cool, store in a covered container. These waffles may be kept for 1 month, and reheated in a toaster.

Makes 8 to 10 waffles.

Pumpkin Nut Waffles

From the Indians we learned to value the native-grown pumpkin and added it to familiar foods or created new ones. Cinnamon and nutmeg enhance the pumpkin flavour of these waffles which should be served with a generous dab of golden butter and lots of Canadian maple syrup.

Preheat waffle iron. If necessary grease with unsalted fat.

Sift or blend together
  2 cups all-purpose flour
  3½ teaspoons baking powder
  1 teaspoon salt
  ¾ teaspoon cinnamon
  ¼ teaspoon nutmeg

Beat with a rotary beater
  3 egg yolks
  1¾ cups milk
  ⅓ cup vegetable oil

Blend in
  ½ cup canned pumpkin

Stir in dry ingredients, beating until almost smooth.

Beat until stiff and fold in
  3 egg whites

Pour batter onto preheated waffle iron using 1½ cups batter for each 9-inch square waffle.

Sprinkle with
  chopped pecans or walnuts

Bake until waffle iron stops steaming.
Serve hot, with butter and Canadian maple syrup.

Makes 8 to 10 waffles.

Meat

Knowing how to buy meat is just as important as knowing how to cook it. The charts included in this chapter are to help you choose the right cut for your needs and to help you cook it to the best possible advantage.

Canadians have a marked preference for beef and pork, perhaps attributable to the exceedingly high quality of that produced. Most of the meat sold in Canada has been government inspected and identified by the Federal Government Inspection stamp on the outside fat. Wise buyers look for the purple stamp on the meat they buy.

Beef is graded for the consumer: Canada 1 Choice (Red Brand), Canada 2 Good (Blue Brand), Canada 3 Standard, and Canada 4 Commercial. One must know the grade purchased in order to choose the most suitable method of cooking. The less tender meats should be cooked with liquid to improve tenderness: pot roasting, braising, stewing. The beef cuts in the less tender column, regardless of grade, should be cooked with liquid. The medium-tender cuts should be cooked with liquid when of either Standard or Commercial grade. Tender meat should be oven roasted, broiled, fried or barbecued or, in other words, cooked without liquid.

Fresh or smoked Canadian pork can be kept frozen for up to two months, because the scientific feeding of Canadian hogs bred for high meat quality ensures a more stable fat.

Since lamb and veal represent a much smaller share of meat sold, we have included only a few representative recipes.

Beef Cooking Chart

Tender Cuts	Size
Steaks	**Thickness in inches**
Sirloin Steak	$1/2$ to $3/4$ $1^1/4$
Porterhouse or T-Bone Steak	$1/2$ to $3/4$ 1 to $1^1/4$
Wing or Club Steak	$1/2$ to $3/4$ 1 to $1^1/4$
Tenderloin	1 to $1^1/4$
Roasts	**Weight**
Standing Rib	7 to 8
Rolled Rib	6 to 8
Rump (high quality)	5 to 7
Sirloin	5 to 6
Porterhouse and Wing	5 to 6
Round (high quality)	5 to 6
Less Tender Cuts	**Weights lb.**
Shoulder	5 to 6
Chuck	5 to 6
Blade	5 to 6
Rolled Plate	5 to 6
Rump	5 to 6
Brisket	4 to 5
Swiss Steak	$1^1/2$ to 2
Short Rib	$2^1/2$ to 3
Round Steak	2
Brisket	2
Neck — Boneless	$1^1/2$ to 2
Shank Meat	$1^1/2$ to 2
Stewing Beef	$1^1/2$ to 2
Brisket	$1^1/2$ to 2
Flank	$1^1/2$

Cooking Time Rare — Medium	Directions
Minutes	**BROIL** — Slash fat edge of meat to prevent curling. Place meat on cold rack, 4 to 5 inches below heat source, in an oven preheated to 325°F. Broil for half prescribed time on one side, season with salt and pepper. Using tongs, turn meat and broil other side until meat is done.
10 to 12 14 to 16 15 to 20 20 to 25 9 to 10 12 to 15 14 to 16 18 to 20 5 6 to 7 9 to 10 12 9 to 10 12	**PANBROIL** — Slash fat edge of meat to prevent curling. Lightly grease a heavy frypan and set over moderate heat. Place meat in pan and cook, turning frequently to insure even cooking. Pour off excess fat as it accumulates.
min. per lb.	**ROAST** — Place meat on rack in open pan, fat side up. Cook, uncovered, in an oven preheated to 300°F. Do not sear the meat or add water. Cook till meat thermometer registers internal temperatures:
18 to 20 22 to 24 32 to 34 36 to 38 20 to 22 25 to 30 20 to 22 25 to 30 18 to 20 22 to 24 20 to 22 25 to 30	Rare 140°F. Medium 160°F. Well Done 170°F.

Cooking Time min. per lb.	Directions
30 to 35 10 min. extra per lb. for rolled cuts	**POT ROAST** — Rub meat with well seasoned flour. Brown in a heavy pan or Dutch oven with a small amount of fat. Add 1 cup water, tomato juice, soup stock or other liquid. Cover pan tightly and cook slowly in a 300°F. oven or on top of the stove until tender. More liquid should be added as required.
2 to 2½ hours (total time)	**BRAISE** — Dip meat in well seasoned flour. Brown on both sides in a heavy frypan with a small amount of fat. Add ½ cup water, tomato juice, soup stock, or other liquid. Cover pan tightly and cook slowly in a 300°F. oven or on top of the stove until tender. More liquid should be added as required.
3 hours (total time)	**STEW** — Cut meat in small pieces. Dip in seasoned flour and brown quickly in fat. Cover meat with warm water. Simmer until tender. Do not boil. Measure the time from the moment the liquid begins to simmer. Add vegetables and seasonings about 30 minutes before the meat is done. The gravy may be thickened with flour, if desired.

Beef Chart

Tender Cuts

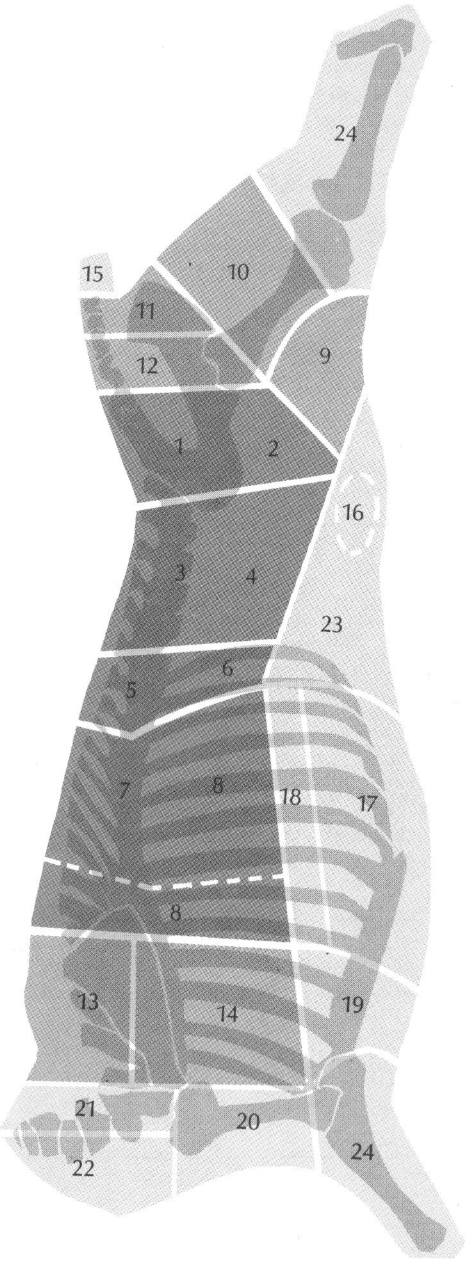

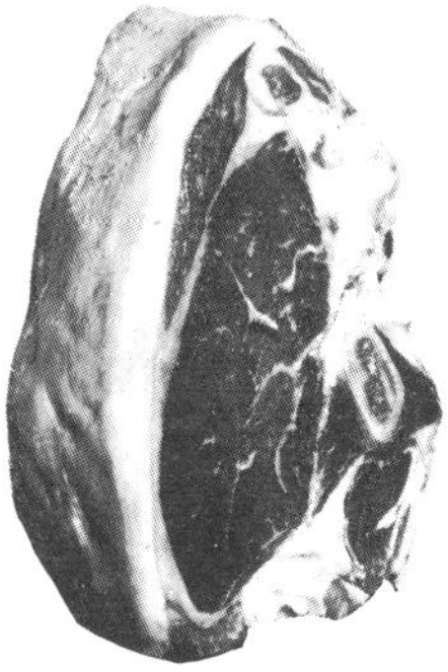

1. **Sirloin Roast**

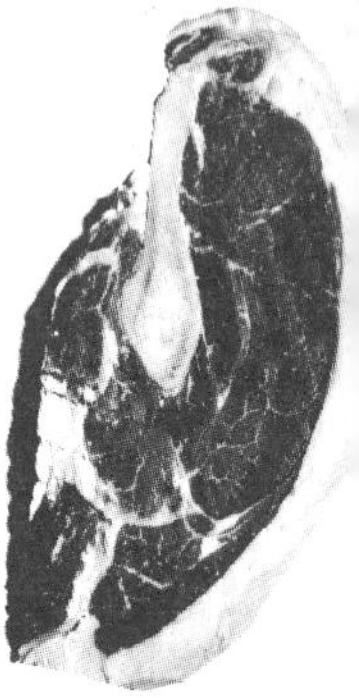

2. **Sirloin Steak**

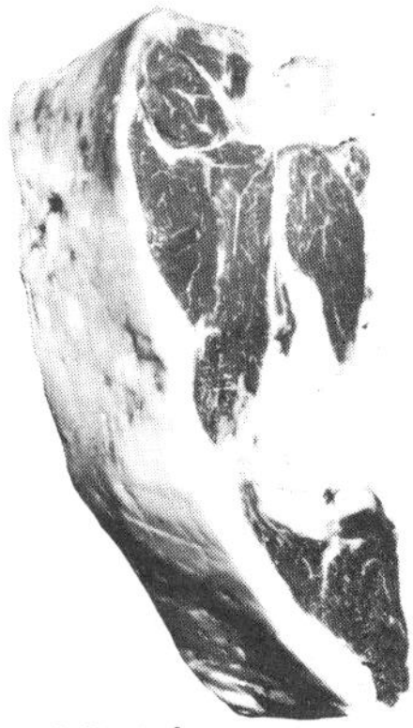

3. **Porterhouse** or **T-Bone Roast**

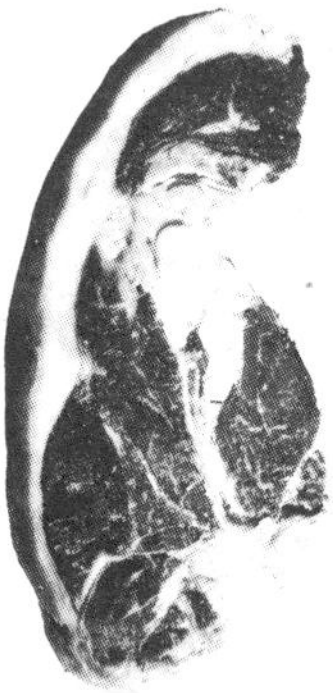

4. **Porterhouse** or **T-Bone Steak**

5. **Wing** or **Club Roast**

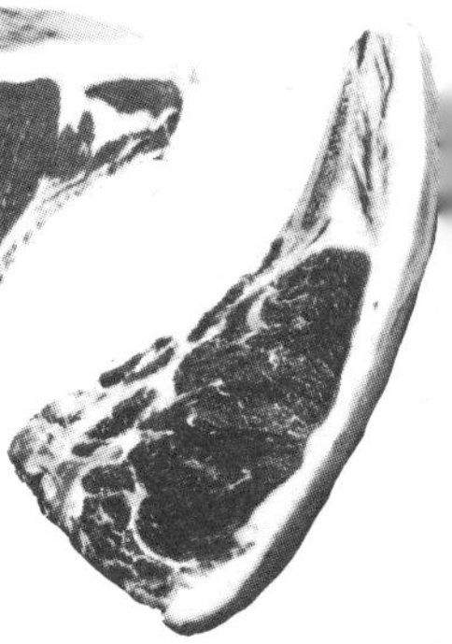

6. **Wing** or **Club Steak**

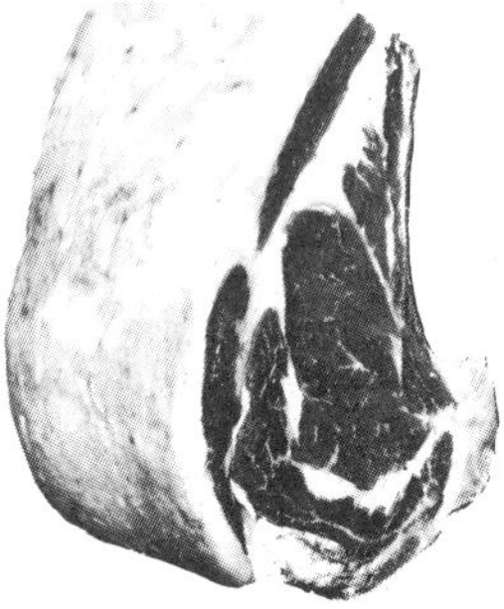

7. **Standing Rib Roast**

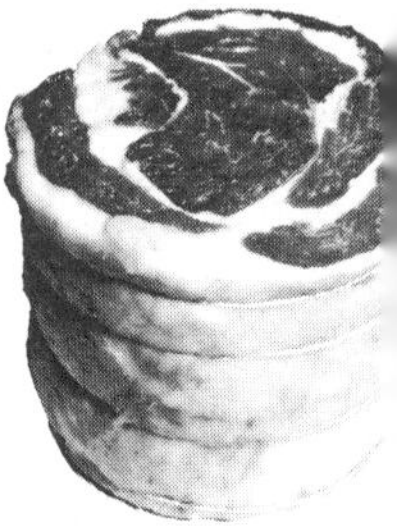

8. **Rolled Rib Roast**

Medium Tender Cuts	Less Tender Cuts

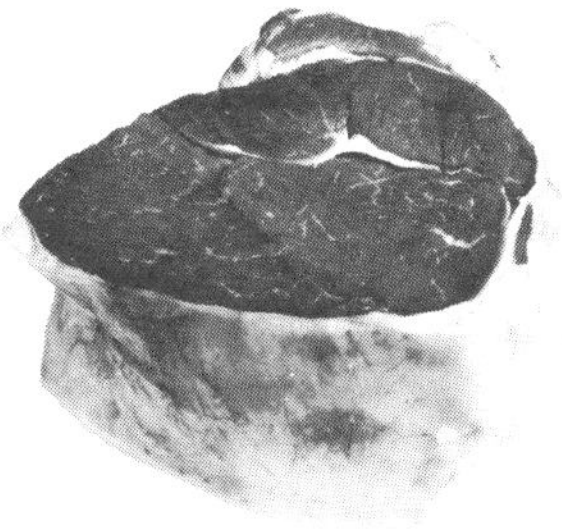

9. Sirloin Tip Roast

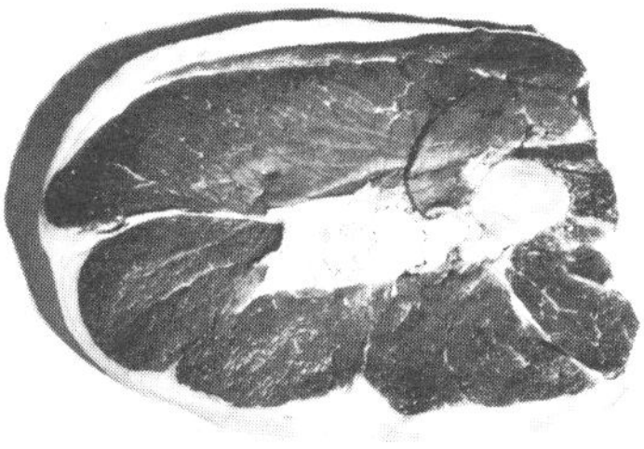

10. Round Steak

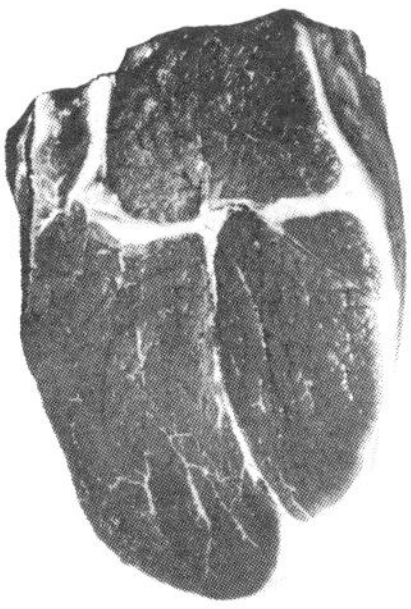

11. Round Rump Roast

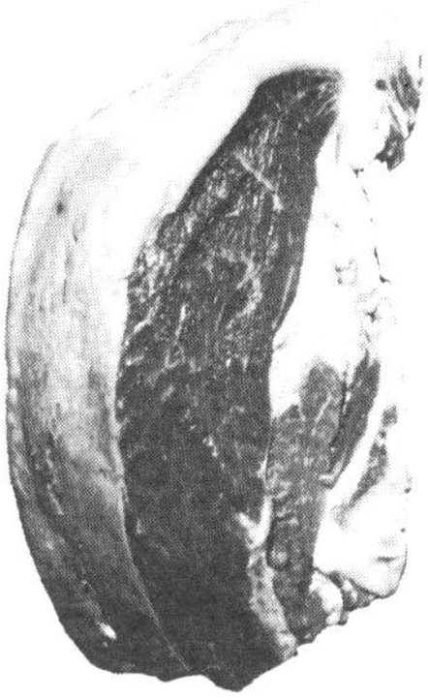

12. Square Rump Roast

13. Blade Roast

14. Short Rib Roast
(may be cut
differently to give
Cross Rib Roast)

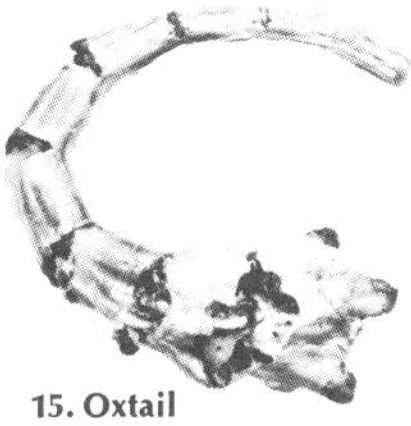

15. Oxtail

16. Flank Steak

17. Brisket Plate
or **Plate**

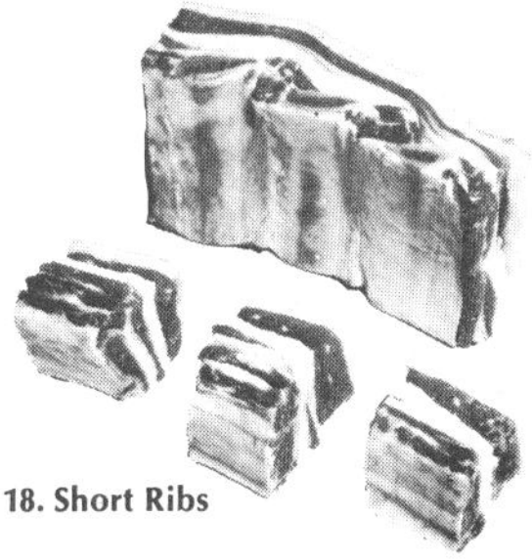

18. Short Ribs

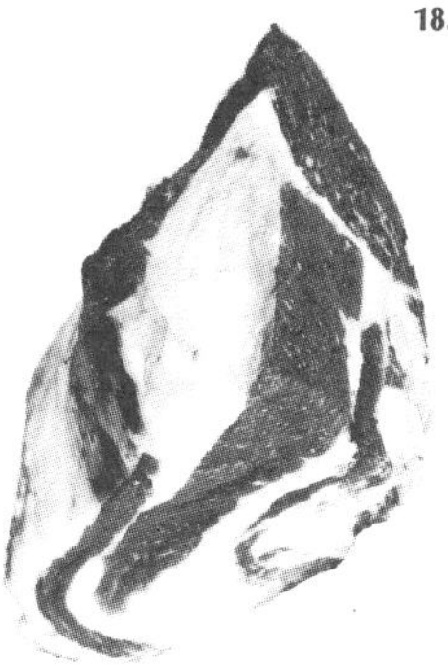

19. Brisket Point
or **Brisket**

**20. Round Bone
Shoulder Roast**

Stewing Beef
from **Chuck (21)**
Neck (22) or
Flank (23)

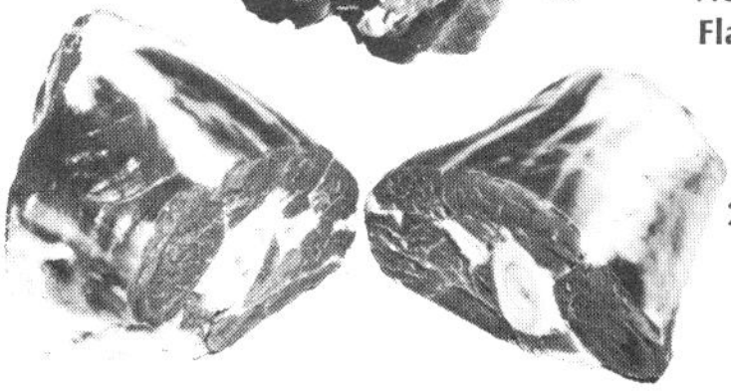

24. Shank
(may be
from
Hind or
Fore Leg)

Cured And Smoked Meats Cooking Chart

Style	Weight — Pounds
REGULAR HAMS	
Bone-in	14 to 16
Dinner Style	
Bone-in sweet pickled	
Boneless	10 to 12
	5 to 6
	2 to 3
Boneless sweet pickled	2 to 3
READY-TO-SERVE HAMS	
Bone-in	13 to 15
Bone-in half ham	4 to 6
Boneless	9 to 11
Boneless half ham	4 to 5
Boneless piece	2 to 3
PICNICS BONE-IN	
Regular	5 to 7
Ready-to-Serve	5 to 7
Regular half size	$2^1/_2$ to $3^1/_2$
Ready-to-Serve half size	$2^1/_2$ to $3^1/_2$
PICNICS BONELESS	
Regular	4 to 6
Ready-to-Serve	4 to 6
Regular half size	2 to 3
Ready-to-Serve half size	2 to 3
COTTAGE ROLLS	
Regular	4 to 6
Regular half size	2 to 3
Ready-to-Serve	4 to 6
Ready-to-Serve half size	2 to 3
MIDGET LOIN ROLLS	
Regular	2 to 3
Ready-to-Serve	2 to $2^1/_2$
BACK BACON PIECE	
Smoked	$1^1/_2$ to $2^1/_2$
Sweet pickled	$1^1/_2$ to $2^1/_2$

Cooking Time Min. per Pound	Directions
15 to 18 min. whole ham 22 min. half ham 18 min. 25 min. 30 to 35 min. 35 to 40 min. To Heat: 10 min. 17 to 22 min. 12 min. 16 to 18 min. 20 to 25 min.	**BAKE** — Oven temperature 325°F. Place in open roast pan. Do not add water. Do not cover. If meat thermometer is used internal temperature should register 130°F. for ready-to-serve products; 160°F. for hams; 170°F for other cuts. **SIMMER** — Cover with water. Bring to boil. Reduce heat and simmer specified time. For boneless hams remove overwrap if present, and loosen casing ends. To bake or simmer follow directions above. New easy-peel casing does not need to be removed prior to cooking. **BROIL OR PANFRY** — Ham slices ³/₄ - 1″ thick, 3 - 4 minutes per side.
25 to 30 min. 15 to 20 min.	Unwrap. Bake or simmer as above.
30 to 35 min. 20 to 25 min.	Remove plastic bag and bake, or prick bag once and simmer as above.
30 to 35 min. 15 to 20 min.	Unwrap. Leave casing on and simmer as above.
35 to 40 min. 15 to 20 min.	Prick plastic bag once and simmer as above.
30 to 35 min. 35 to 40 min. 25 to 30 min. 30 to 35 min.	Prick plastic bag once and simmer as above.
35 to 40 min. 25 to 30 min.	Unwrap and loosen casing. Bake as above.
25 to 30 min. 25 to 30 min.	Unwrap and bake or simmer as above.

Lamb - Pork - Veal Cooking Chart

Tender Cuts			Weight — Pounds
LAMB	**PORK**	**VEAL**	
Leg Loin Roast Crown Roast Rolled Front Front (bone in) Shoulder Roast	Loin Roast Crown Roast Fresh Ham Fresh Pork Butt Tenderloin (Stuffed) Rolled Shoulder	Leg Roast (Fillet) Loin Roast Rump Roast	4 to 7
Rib Chops Loin Chops Shoulder Chops	Loin Chops Rib Chops Tenderloin (Frenched) Butt Chops Spareribs (Braise)	Sirloin Steak Loin Chops Veal Cutlet	**Lamb** — $1/2''$ - $3/4''$ thick **Pork** — $1/2''$ - $3/4''$ thick **Veal** — $1/2''$ - $3/4''$ thick
Less Tender Cuts			**Weight — Pounds**
Lamb	**Pork**	**Veal**	
		Front (Rolled)	3 to 6
Neck Flank Breast Shoulder Shank		Neck Shank Flank Breast	

Cooking Time min. per lb.	Directions
Lamb — 30-35 min. 45 min. (rolled cuts)	**ROAST**—Place meat, fat side up, on a rack in an open pan and insert meat thermometer in centre of largest muscle. Cook, uncovered, in an oven preheated to 325°F. Do not sear the meat or add water.
Pork — 40-45 min.	Cook till meat thermometer registers internal temperature of: **LAMB** — 180°F.
Veal — 35-40 min. 45 min. (rolled cuts)	**PORK** — 185°F. **VEAL** — 180°F.
10 to 12 mins. (total) 20 to 25 mins. (total) 15 to 20 mins. (total)	**BROIL** — See Beef Chart. **PANBROIL** — Slash fat edge of meat to prevent curling. Place meat in a lightly greased frypan over medium heat. Turn frequently to ensure even cooking. Pour off fat as it accumulates. **BRAISE** — Brown meat quickly in hot fat. Lower heat and cook slowly, covered, until tender. A small amount of water or vegetable juice may be added to keep the meat moist.
Cooking Time min. per lb.	Directions
40 to 45 mins.	**ROAST** — As for tender cuts. **BRAISE** — Brown meat on both sides in a heavy baking pan or frypan with a small amount of fat. Add 1/2 cup water. Cover pan tightly and cook slowly to a 325°F. oven or on top of stove, until tender. More liquid should be added as required.
2 1/2 to 3 1/2 hours (total)	**STEW** — Cut meat in small pieces. Dip in seasoned flour and brown in hot fat. Cover with warm water and simmer gently until tender. Do not boil. Add vegetables and seasoning about 30 minutes before meat is done. The gravy may be thickened with flour if desired. **SOUP** — Cook meat with bones in gently simmering water. Celery leaves, onion slices and parsley may be added 30 minutes before meat is done. Season well before serving.

Beef and Kidney Pie

A spiced variation of the traditional English specialty came to us from Calgary, Alberta, the heart of the beef cattle ranch country.

Soak for 1 hour
1 to 1¼ pounds beef kidney
in
4 cups cold water
1 tablespoon salt

Split kidney in half. Remove white membrane, cut away fat, lobes and tubes, and cut into ¼- or ½-inch slices.

Cut into ½- to 1-inch squares
1 to 1¼ pounds boneless stewing beef or flank or chuck

Brown beef in
3 to 4 tablespoons fat

Add kidney and
⅓ cup chopped onion

Brown.

Sprinkle with
2 teaspoons salt
¼ teaspoon pepper

Wrap in cheesecloth and add
3 whole cloves
½ teaspoon pickling spice

Stir in
½ cup flour

Gradually add, stirring to blend in
3½ to 4 cups hot water

Cover. Simmer gently for 1½ to 2 hours. Remove spice bag.

Place meat in greased 2-quart casserole. Cover with pastry or Biscuit Topping (see page 29), slash, and brush with beaten egg, if desired. Bake in preheated 425° F. oven for 35 to 40 minutes, or until filling is bubbling and pastry golden.

Makes 6 servings.

Winnipeg Beef Stroganoff

So thoroughly adopted by Canadian restaurants, beef stroganoff has become a native dish and we have forgotten all about its Russian origin. This modern version does not pound the meat to make it tender, but relies on the tenderness of our high-quality sirloin steak.

Cut into 1- x ¼-inch strips
1½ pounds sirloin steak

Dredge in
1½ tablespoons all-purpose flour

In a heavy frypan melt
¼ cup butter

Add floured meat and sauté, turning to brown on all sides.

Stir in and cook until just tender
1 medium onion, thinly sliced

Remove meat and onions from pan and set aside.

Blend into drippings in pan
2 tablespoons all-purpose flour
1 can (10 ounces) condensed beef bouillon
2 tablespoons tomato paste
1 tablespoon Worcestershire sauce
1 teaspoon salt
½ teaspoon dry mustard

Cook, stirring constantly, until thickened.

Blend in meat, onions and
1 cup thick dairy sour cream
1 can (5½-ounces) sliced mushrooms, drained
3 tablespoons sherry

Heat thoroughly, but do not allow to boil.

Serve on hot, fluffy rice.

Makes 4 to 5 servings.

Corned Beef and Cabbage

On days when a heavy snowfall meant that the family was confined to the house, the boiled dinner proved to be a reliable standby. The pickled beef (which was stored in barrels) bubbled away in a heavy pot on the open fire and a suet pudding simmered in the same pot. In this recipe for corned beef and cabbage, the celery seeds impart a delicate, fresh flavour.

In a large saucepan combine
- **1 (3- to 4-pound) corned beef brisket**
- **1 medium-sized onion, sliced**
- **1 bay leaf**
- **2 garlic cloves**
- **1 teaspoon celery seeds**
- **6 peppercorns**

Bring to a boil and simmer for 3 hours, or until tender.

Cut in wedges
- **1 head cabbage**

Add to meat, and simmer 12 to 14 minutes longer.

Makes 6 to 8 servings.

Flank Steak Roll

From Ontario and the West we received a variety of recipes for stuffing flank steak. This one from Ottawa has a most pleasant flavour attributed to cooking the stuffed steak in beef broth.

Preheat oven to 325° F.

Trim fat and connective tissue from
- **2 flank steaks**

Score on both sides to tenderize and sprinkle with
- **salt and pepper**

Panfry until almost tender
- **½ cup chopped onion**

in
- **3 tablespoons butter**

Stir in and cook 3 to 4 minutes longer
- **½ pound mushrooms, chopped**

Combine with
- **½ pound sausage meat**
- **¾ cup fine dry bread crumbs**
- **½ teaspoon salt**
- **pinch of thyme**
- **pinch of pepper**

Spread stuffing over one steak and cover with second steak. Tie together tightly with string.

In a roasting pan on top of the stove brown stuffed steak on all sides in
- **2 tablespoons shortening**

Dissolve
- **1 beef bouillon cube**

in
- **1 cup boiling water**

Pour over steak, cover, and cook in 325° oven for 2½ hours, or until tender. Remove from pan and keep warm.

Thicken liquid in pan with a paste of flour and cold water. Cook, stirring constantly, until thickened. Add salt and pepper to taste.

Makes 4 to 6 servings.

Hungarian Goulash

Quite naturally, this recipe for Hungarian goulash came from Saskatchewan as, prior to the October, 1956 rebellion in Hungary, the largest concentration of citizens of Hungarian descent could be found in the Qu'Appelle Valley in that province.

Cut into 1-inch cubes
- **2 pounds boneless stewing beef**
  OR
- **1 pound boneless stewing beef and**
- **1 pound boneless stewing veal**

Brown well on all sides in hot fat. Sprinkle with
- **5 to 6 tablespoons all-purpose flour**

and brown again slightly.

Stir in
- **2 teaspoons salt**
- **1 teaspoon paprika**
- **1 teaspoon caraway seeds**
- **pinch of pepper**
- **1 tablespoon Worcestershire sauce**
- **1 medium onion, sliced**
- **3½ cups water**

Cover, and simmer for 2 hours, or until meat is tender.

Just before serving, stir in
- **½ cup thick dairy sour cream**

Serve over cooked noodles, or with Hungarian Dumplings (see page 78), and garnish with parsley.

Makes 4 to 6 servings.

44

Western Hamburgers

Submitted by a Vancouverite with a flair for cooking that becomes obvious when you taste these hamburgers.

In a large bowl beat
1 egg

Mix in
**1 teaspoon savory
½ teaspoon monosodium
glutamate
½ teaspoon sugar
salt and pepper
garlic powder
¼ cup sherry
2 green onions, chopped
1 tablespoon chopped parsley
1 pound lean ground beef
½ cup bread crumbs**

Shape into 4 large patties.

Panfry in small amount of fat, or broil on barbecue.

Makes 4 servings.

Meat and Potato Oven Stew

From Belleville, Ontario, where, at a sectional meeting of the Canadian Home Economics Association, it was decided to write this cookbook. It seems most fitting that this recipe almost looks after itself in the oven.

Preheat oven to 325° F.

Grease a 1½-quart casserole.

Cut into 1-inch cubes
**1 pound shank beef or stewing
beef**

Roll meat cubes in a mixture of
**2 tablespoons flour
½ teaspoon mixed herb seasoning
½ teaspoon salt
pinch of pepper**

In a small frypan melt
2 tablespoons butter

Add and cook until limp
**½ Spanish onion, sliced
OR
2 medium cooking onions, sliced**

Peel and slice
3 medium potatoes

Arrange in prepared casserole alternate layers of potato, meat and onion.

Mix together and pour into casserole
**¾ cup bouillon
2 tablespoons sherry or white wine
½ teaspoon Worcestershire sauce**

Cover casserole.

Bake in 325° oven for 2½ hours, or until meat is tender.

Makes 4 servings.

Planked Steak

A showy dinner dish that relies on our good Canadian beef and long slow cooking to make it deliciously tender.

Preheat broiler.

Place on oiled seasoned wooden board
1 sirloin steak, 2 inches thick

Dust top lightly with
flour

Broil 5 minutes or until lightly browned.

Remove from oven and turn browned side down on board.

Preheat oven to 250° F.

With a pastry tube or spoon, spread around edge of steak a thick layer of
**mashed cooked potatoes (about
3 cups)**

Bake in 250° oven until tender, about 2 hours.

Garnish with cooked fresh vegetables.

Serve immediately, carving into vertical slices.

Makes 8 servings.

Salt-Broiled Steaks

Much of our beef is raised in the West, and the thought of cattle ranches, cowboys and rodeos seems to add to the flavour. Appropriately, this recipe for cooking steak on an outdoor barbecue came from the home of the largest rodeo in Western Canada — the Calgary Stampede.

On a large broiler-grill or toaster with long handles that loop together place
1 (2- to 3-inch thick) lean boneless steak

Cover the top with ½ inch of thoroughly dampened

coarse salt

Place a paper napkin over it.

Turn the grill over and cover the other side of the steak in exactly the same way.

Close the grill and place over a very hot charcoal or wood fire, allowing from 15 to 20 minutes for each side.

To serve, chop salt crust off steak and slice meat across the grain.

Makes 4 servings.

Shepherd's Pie

The name shepherd's pie undoubtedly comes from the original English version which called for lamb, but today beef is commonly used in Canada.

Preheat oven to 350° F.

Grease a 1-quart casserole.

Combine
3 cups minced cooked beef
1 tablespoon instant minced onion
1 teaspoon steak sauce
⅔ cup gravy
salt and pepper

Prepare
2 cups mashed potatoes

Place meat mixture in prepared casserole. Spread mashed potatoes over top.

Bake in 350° oven for 25 to 30 minutes, or until mixture is bubbling and potatoes lightly browned.

Makes 4 servings.

Ontario Spiced Beef

For the uninitiated, one of the finest gastronomical experiences is to be served spiced beef at Christmas. This is definitely not a quick-to-fix dish, in fact it requires three weeks to "cure" the beef. Use a crock or non-metallic container and plastic wrap and lid to cover beef while curing. Keep in a cool place — the fruit cellar or refrigerator. The colour of the meat as it cures is much like old leather, but do not be discouraged.

Don't forget to order the juniper berries from the druggist in advance.

Order from butcher
1 round steak roast of beef (8 to 10 pounds)

Have fat completely removed and the roast tied for spicing.

Rub cut surfaces of beef with about
¾ cup lightly packed brown sugar

Cover, and let stand 1 day in a cool place.

Grind in a food grinder
1 ounce juniper berries

Combine with
½ ounce saltpetre
½ cup salt
2 tablespoons pepper
3 tablespoons ground allspice

On the second day rub some of the spice mixture completely over the roast, making sure the spices get into all the cracks of the meat.

Store remaining spice mixture in a covered jar. Repeat daily for 3 weeks, turning roast each time. Some of the juices come out of the beef but are gradually absorbed into it again as time progresses.

Make a paste of
3 cups all-purpose flour
1 cup water

Completely cover beef with paste.

Bake in preheated 325° F. oven for about 3½ hours, or until tender.

Cool, and remove paste covering.

When slicing, save outside slice and replace to protect meat from drying out. Serve cold.

Curried Lamb

This curry replaces the traditional mango chutney with applesauce, the fruit of our own orchards.

In a frypan or chafing dish fry until crisp
- **3 slices rindless side bacon, cut in small pieces**

Add
- **½ cup sliced celery**
- **1 medium onion, finely chopped**

Stir and cook over medium heat for 5 minutes. Remove from heat.

Blend in
- **2 tablespoons flour**
- **1 tablespoon curry powder**
- **¾ teaspoon salt**
- **½ teaspoon turmeric**

Stir in
- **½ cup water**
- **1 cup milk**

Add
- **2 chicken bouillon cubes**

Cook, stirring constantly, until thickened.

Stir in
- **⅓ cup sweetened applesauce**
- **2 teaspoons sugar**
- **2 teaspoons lemon juice**
- **2 cups cubed cooked lamb·**

Cover, and simmer for 10 minutes, stirring occasionally.

Serve over hot, fluffy rice.

Serve condiments in separate dishes, to be sprinkled on the curry. Suggestions — chopped peanuts, banana slices, chopped hard-cooked egg, crumbled crisp bacon, chopped green onion or chives, chutney, raisins and shredded coconut.

Makes 4 servings.

Rideau Irish Stew

Frozen peas modernize this old-fashioned favourite and the use of bouillon cubes eliminates the need for browning the meat. Both contribute to the delicious colour and flavour of this adaptation.

Trim excess fat from
- **2 pounds stewing lamb**

In a large saucepan combine with
- **2½ cups water**
- **2 beef bouillon cubes**
- **1¼ teaspoons salt**
- **¼ teaspoon pepper**
- **¼ teaspoon thyme**
- **½ cup sliced celery and leaves**

Cover tightly, and simmer 1½ hours, stirring occasionally.

Add
- **3 carrots, quartered**
- **⅓ cup sliced green pepper**
- **6 medium onions, sliced**
- **6 medium potatoes, cubed**

Simmer, covered, 1 hour longer; during last 15 minutes of cooking add
- **1 package (12 ounces) frozen peas**
- **3 tablespoons chopped parsley**

Drain broth into a small saucepan.

Mix to a smooth paste
- **3 tablespoons flour**
- **⅓ cup water**

Stir into broth. Cook over medium heat until flour is cooked and sauce smoothly thickened. Pour over meat and vegetables. Serve very hot.

Makes 6 servings.

Kjaefa — Sandwich Filling

Iceland Day, which is celebrated each August by Icelanders in Canada, marks the occasion when Icelandic immigrants first established a colony at Gimli, Manitoba, in 1875. This Icelandic recipe makes an unusually flavoured meat loaf for slicing thinly.

Wipe with damp cloth and place in large kettle
- **1 (3-pound) shoulder of lamb**
- **1 pound veal (cut from shank)**

Add sufficient hot water to cover meat.

Bring to a boil, reduce heat and simmer for 3½ to 4 hours, or until meat can easily be removed from bones. Remove meat from liquid. Cook liquid until reduced by half.

Cut meat from bones. Put twice through finest blade of food grinder.

46

Strain liquid. In a large heavy saucepan combine 2 cups liquid, ground meat and

2 medium onions, chopped
2 tablespoons salt
1 teaspoon allspice
1 teaspoon pepper
½ teaspoon ground cloves

Bring to a boil, stirring constantly, and simmer for 2 minutes. Remove from heat.

Rinse with cold water or lightly oil a 9 x 5-inch loaf pan.

Turn cooked meat into pan. Cover.

Refrigerate for 24 hours.

Slice thinly to serve for sandwiches.

Glazed Ham

In Canada hams may be purchased pre-cooked or ready-to-cook. We've included both types in this recipe, and by "cooked ham" we mean one you have baked yourself according to package directions.

Remove rind (if necessary) from
1 cooked ham

and score in diamond pattern with a sharp knife

OR

Score
1 precooked ham

Insert in diamonds in ham
whole cloves

Bake in preheated 325° F. oven for 1 hour.

Remove ham from oven and increase temperature to 450°.

HAM GLAZE

Mix together
3 cups lightly packed brown sugar
3 teaspoons dry mustard
2 tablespoons corn syrup
3 tablespoons flour
¼ cup vinegar (to moisten)

Spread over top of ham.

Bake in 450° oven for 30 minutes, or until glaze threads from a spoon. Remove from oven. Keep basting as glaze cools until it hardens.

Kelowna Ham in Cider Sauce

Our fondness for smoked and cured pork dates back to the early settlers, when this was the meat of the winter menu. Through the years the quality of pork has improved greatly until now we have as fine hams and bacon as anywhere else in the world.

Preheat oven to 400° F.

Rub
2 tablespoons brown sugar

into both sides of
2 ham steaks (1 inch thick, about 1 pound each)
Stud the fat on the side with

whole cloves

Bake in a greased baking dish for 20 minutes.

Meanwhile, in a saucepan melt
¼ cup butter

Stir in
¼ cup flour

Blend in
2½ cups cider

Cook over medium heat, stirring constantly, until thickened.

Stir in
⅓ cup raisins

Continue cooking until raisins plump.

Pour sauce over ham steak and continue baking for 30 minutes longer.

Makes 6 servings.

Wiener Schnitzel

To the many German settlers, Canadians owe their love of wiener schnitzel, and through the years the recipe has remained essentially unchanged. Occasionally it is served with a poached or fried egg on top instead of hard-cooked egg slices.

Cut into serving portions
2 pounds veal cutlet

Pound to flatten slightly. Chill thoroughly.

Dip in a mixture of
1 egg, slightly beaten
1 tablespoon milk

Then in a mixture of
½ cup flour
¼ teaspoon salt
pinch of pepper
1½ cups bread crumbs

Let dry for 30 minutes.

Fry until golden brown in
butter

Serve with sliced lemon and sliced hard-cooked egg.

Makes 6 to 8 servings.

Glazed Back Bacon

This Canadian specialty merited the place of honour at a gourmet dinner in New York City a few years ago. The superior quality of our back bacon is renowned outside the country, where it is called Canadian bacon.

Place in large pan
1 (1½ to 2½-pound) sweet pickled back bacon piece

Pour over top
1½ cups apple juice

Cover. Bring to boil. Reduce heat, and simmer for 25 to 30 minutes per pound, or until tender.

Preheat oven to 400° F.

Remove bacon from liquid. Glaze with Ham Glaze (⅓ of recipe on page 47).

Bake in 400° oven for 30 minutes, or until glaze threads from a spoon. Remove from oven. Keep basting as glaze cools until it hardens.

Slice, and serve either hot or cold.

Cottage Roll

If you're looking for a new way to prepare a sweet pickled cottage roll, try this. It has a delicious flavour.

Preheat oven to 325° F.

In a roasting pan with a cover, place
1 cottage roll (about 5 pounds)

Pour over top
2 small bottles of beer or ginger ale

Cover, and bake in 325° oven for about 3 hours, or until tender.

Serve hot or cold.

Ham Slice Baked in Milk

An old-fashioned way of cooking ham that reduced the saltiness of home-cured hams.

Because of fond memories and because of the tenderness that results, many home-makers prefer even the modern sugar-cured ham steaks baked in milk, as in this recipe from Prince Edward Island.

Preheat oven to 300° F.

Trim off excess fat and place in shallow casserole
2 (1 inch-thick) slices cooked ham

Combine and spread over ham
1 teaspoon dry mustard
3 tablespoons brown sugar

Add about
2 cups milk
or enough to barely cover ham.

Add
6 whole cloves
2 bay leaves

Cover, and bake in 300° oven for 30 minutes. Uncover, and bake for 30 minutes longer. Remove from liquid and cut in serving portions.

Makes 6 servings.

Les Côtes de Porc Charlevoix

The pork chops of Charlevoix County, Quebec, are, and would naturally be, cooked with apples and a little maple sugar for good measure.

Sear in a little melted fat
6 pork chops (¾ inch thick)

Sprinkle with
salt and pepper

Sprinkle with a mixture of
6 tablespoons maple sugar
2 tablespoons all-purpose flour

Add
1 cup apple juice

Cover. Simmer over medium heat for 20 minutes.

Core, cut in half, but do not peel
3 apples

Place one apple half on each chop.

Cover and let cook for an additional 20 minutes or until apples are soft and sauce is thick and smooth.

Makes 6 servings.

Jambon de la Cabane à Sucre

In English — Ham in Maple Sap. This Quebec specialty has a flavour all its own, which is almost equally delicious when prepared with the more readily available apple juice.

Place in a large saucepan
1 (8- to 10-pound) ham

Pour over top
3 quarts (15 cups) maple sap or apple juice

Cover, and simmer over low heat for 2½ to 3 hours, or until ham is tender.

Remove from pan, saving juice.

In a small bowl, cover
2 cups raisins
with 2 cups hot juice.

If necessary, remove rind from ham.

Cover fat with a mixture of
2 cups maple sugar

2 teaspoons dry mustard
1 teaspoon ground cloves
¼ cup water

Place ham in a roasting pan, surround with drained raisins and about 1 cup juice drained from raisins.

Bake in preheated 300° F. oven for 30 minutes. Remove ham and keep warm.

Mix to a smooth paste
2 tablespoons flour
¼ cup cold water

Stir into roasting pan and simmer, stirring constantly, until thickened. Serve sauce on warm ham.

Makes 14 to 16 servings.

Pigs' Feet with Meat Balls

The traditional *ragoût aux pattes* of French Canada stands in a class by itself in our cuisine.

Skin
3 pork hocks, halved

Place in a saucepan and cover with water. Bring to a boil. Skim.

Add
1 onion, stuck with 2 whole cloves
1 carrot
1 celery stalk
1 bay leaf
1 tablespoon salt
¼ teaspoon pepper

Simmer for 3 hours.

Meanwhile, combine
1½ pounds ground pork
1 onion, finely chopped
1 teaspoon salt
pinch of pepper
pinch of nutmeg
½ cup soda cracker crumbs

Mix in
1 egg, beaten

Form into small balls. Roll in browned flour (see page 184).

Thicken pork hocks with a mixture of
browned flour (about 1¼ cups)
cold water

Cook, stirring constantly, until thickened. Drop in meat balls and cook for 30 minutes longer. Season to taste.

Serve with mashed potatoes.

Makes 6 servings.

Braised Pork Chops

This recipe, from Montreal, is reminiscent of the traditional *ragoût aux pattes*, but pork chops replace the pigs' feet. The touch of cinnamon and cloves makes an interesting flavour.

In a heavy frypan brown
½ cup flour
stirring frequently.

Remove from pan and make into a smooth paste with
⅓ cup cold water

In frypan combine
4 thick pork chops
3 cups boiling water
1 small onion, chopped

Simmer, covered, for 20 minutes.

Remove chops from pan. Blend flour paste into stock and cook, stirring constantly, until thickened.

Return chops to sauce with
½ teaspoon salt
pinch of pepper
pinch of ground cloves
pinch of cinnamon

Cook, covered, about 1½ hours, or until chops are tender.

Makes 4 servings.

Baked Spareribs and Sauerkraut

Throughout the country, custom demands that sauerkraut be served with spareribs or country sausage. This classic version befits the homemade sauerkraut sold at farmers' markets.

Preheat oven to 350° F.

Place in a roasting pan
4 pounds spareribs

Bake in 350° oven for 30 minutes.

Remove pan from oven and lift out spareribs. Place in the pan
3 pounds sauerkraut

Turn spareribs over, and arrange them over the kraut. Bake for another 1½ hours. Serve with mashed potatoes.

Makes 4 servings.

Barbecued Spareribs

Our cooking techniques have completed the full cycle from the early outdoor campfires of the explorers to the modern kitchen range. With outdoor barbecuing in full swing, we seem to be starting over again. However, none can deny that the smoky barbecue flavour does do something special to spareribs.

Preheat oven to 350° F.

Simmer for 10 minutes
1 cup chili sauce
1 cup finely chopped onion
¾ cup vegetable oil
¼ cup lemon juice
¼ cup vinegar
1 tablespoon brown sugar
1 teaspoon salt
1 teaspoon dry mustard
¼ teaspoon chili peppers
2 garlic cloves, chopped
2 dashes of Tabasco sauce
1 bay leaf

Remove bay leaf.

Place on rack in shallow pan
4 pounds spareribs

Brush thoroughly with the sauce and bake in 350° oven for 1 hour, basting frequently, OR place on charcoal grill, baste with sauce and barbecue slowly, turning and brushing with sauce as required. Time for barbecuing will vary between 30 and 45 minutes.

Makes 4 to 5 servings.

Sweet and Sour Spareribs

After completion of the Canadian Pacific Railway in November, 1885, many Chinese opened restaurants, originally in British Columbia, but eventually throughout the country. As a result there are many Chinese foods that have been adapted to Canadian tastes.

Cut apart and panfry in a little fat until well browned
2½ pounds spareribs

Remove ribs from pan and pour off fat.

Drain and measure juice from
1 can (10 ounces) pineapple tidbits

Add water to juice to make 1 cup. Set pineapple aside.

Mix together in frypan
   2 tablespoons cornstarch
   2 tablespoons sugar
   ½ teaspoon salt
   ⅓ cup vinegar
   3 tablespoons soya sauce

Stir in pineapple liquid.

Cook over medium heat, stirring constantly, until sauce thickens. Add browned ribs, cover, and cook gently for 1 hour.

Add pineapple tidbits, turn ribs and continue to cook for 15 minutes, or until meat is tender and begins to pull away from bones.

Makes 4 to 5 servings.

Fricandeau

Generally *fricandeau* denotes a rump or loin of veal, but the name accompanied this jellied veal and pork loaf received from Quebec. When it is attractively glazed and garnished *fricandeau* seems much more appropriate than meat loaf.

Preheat oven to 325° F.

Put through a food grinder
   ¾ pound veal
   ¾ pound fresh pork
   1 pork kidney
   ½ pound very fat salt pork
   1 medium red onion
   16 soda biscuits (single)

Mix together well with
   2 eggs, well beaten

Mould around
   1 pork tenderloin

Shape in an 8½ x 4½-inch loaf pan and dot with
   butter

Arrange on top
   2 bay leaves

Place mould in a pan of water and bake in 325° oven for 2 hours. Baste with water to keep surface moist.

When cold, place meat in a 9 x 5-inch mould which has a thin layer of set aspic and hard-cooked egg slices in bottom. Surround with remaining aspic.

Refrigerate until 30 minutes before serving.

ASPIC

Soak
   3 envelopes unflavoured gelatine
in
   1 cup cold water

Stir in
   1 tablespoon chopped parsley
   3 cups chicken bouillon

Bring to a boil, and then cool until on the point of setting.

Makes 8 servings.

Scotch-Canadian Haggis

The Scots who came to Canada modified their tastes and ways to suit the new land. This New Brunswick recipe reflects the change in the traditional haggis — a change which recent Scottish arrivals consider akin to sacrilege.

Grease a 9 x 5 x 3-inch loaf pan.

Cut in cubes and fry out the fat from
   2½ pounds pork fat or salt pork

Pour off the liquid grease as it accumulates. When the pieces are golden brown and crisp they are called "cracklings" in Ontario or "kips" in the Maritimes. Drain well. Cool.

Wash and place in a large pot
   1 pork liver (about 3 pounds)

Cover with boiling water and boil for about 1 hour, or until a fork can easily be inserted. Remove liver and allow to cool. Reserve liquid. Put cooled liver and 2 cups of kips through food grinder. Mix together.

Stir in
   1½ cups rolled oats
   2 teaspoons salt
   ½ teaspoon pepper

Add sufficient of the cooking liquid to hold mixture together. Press into prepared pan, cover with wax paper and foil. Steam for 1 hour. Cool.

To serve, slice ½ inch thick and panfry until golden brown on both sides.

Serve piping hot.

Makes 8 servings.

Northumberland Meat Loaf

One of the early settled regions of Ontario, Northumberland County, stretching north from the lake, has many fine cooks. A Cobourg resident who owns and operates the Marie Dressler restaurant sent us this recipe.

Preheat oven to 350° F.

Line bottom of 9 x 5-inch loaf pan or a ring mould with
chili sauce

Mix together
1 pound ground beef
½ pound ground pork
½ pound ground veal
1 teaspoon salt
1 teaspoon granulated sugar
½ teaspoon monosodium glutamate
½ teaspoon rosemary
½ teaspoon celery salt
½ teaspoon pepper
½ teaspoon onion juice
¼ teaspoon garlic powder
¼ teaspoon nutmeg
2 eggs
1 cup bread crumbs soaked in beer or burgundy

Place in prepared pan.

Bake in 350° oven for 65 to 75 minutes.

Makes 8 servings.

Peasant's Coulibiac

Coulibiac traditionally refers to a Russian fish or chicken pie, generally wrapped in a yeast dough. This Canadian adaptation, originating in the West, but sent to us from Montreal, consists of a meat loaf tucked inside a flaky biscuit dough.

Preheat oven to 375° F.

In a large bowl combine
1 pound ground beef
½ pound ground pork
½ pound ground veal

Blend in
1 cup fine dry bread crumbs
¾ cup finely chopped onion
1 garlic clove, finely chopped
2 eggs
2 teaspoons salt
¼ teaspoon black pepper

Turn into a 9 x 5-inch loaf pan, smoothing top. Bake in 375° oven for 1 hour.

Remove from oven and increase temperature to 400°.

Prepare Tea Biscuit dough (see page 29).

After kneading, roll into a rectangle and line a well-greased 9 x 5-inch loaf pan with dough. Place cooked meat loaf in pan and cover with dough, sealing edges well.

Bake in 400° oven for 20 to 25 minutes, or until golden brown.

Remove loaf from pan, slice and serve hot with mushroom or tomato sauce.

Delicious, too, served cold.

Makes 8 servings.

Braised Tongue

A scoop! The favourite dish of one of the Fathers of Confederation — Jonathan McCully of New Brunswick. This braised fresh tongue, slowly cooked in a rich brown sauce, is a wonderful casserole to serve to either commoner or baronet.

Cover with boiling water and simmer for 2 hours.
1 fresh tongue

Drain, reserving water. Remove skin and roots and place tongue in deep pan or casserole.

Surround with
⅓ cup diced carrot
⅓ cup diced onion
⅓ cup diced celery
sprig of parsley

Pour over 4 cups sauce. Cover, and bake in preheated 350° F. oven for 2 hours, turning after first hour.

Serve with baked potatoes and Spiced Crabapple Jelly (see page 142).

Makes 6 servings.

SAUCE

Brown well
¼ cup butter
½ cup all-purpose flour

Stir in 4 cups water or liquid in which tongue was cooked. Season with
salt, pepper and Worcestershire sauce

Main Dishes

These range from satisfying stews to more unusual one-dish meals, but undoubtedly baked beans remains one of the standbys and some say the backbone of our food. This was certainly true in the early days.

Baked Beans

Our settlers relied on them, our explorers and fur trappers regarded them as a necessity, our armies consumed large quantities of them, and during the Klondike Gold Rush they sold for $1.50 per pound. Beans could well be called the foundation of our national cuisine. Baked beans call for long baking to develop the flavour fully. This version specifies both molasses and maple syrup to please both sides regarding sweetening ingredient.

Wash
2 cups navy or pea beans

Soak overnight in
12 cups water

Preheat oven to 250° F.

Drain, and cover with fresh water.

Bring to a boil, and simmer, uncovered, until skins split when blown upon.

Drain and place beans in bean crock or large casserole.

Bury in centre of beans
1 small peeled onion

Mix together and pour over beans
⅓ cup lightly packed brown sugar
1 tablespoon salt
1½ teaspoons dry mustard
½ teaspoon black pepper
¼ cup molasses
¼ cup maple syrup

Insert near surface
¼ pound fat salt pork, sliced

Add sufficient boiling water to cover beans.

Bake, covered, in 250° oven for 8 hours, adding a small amount of boiling water from time to time so that beans do not become dry. Uncover during last 30 minutes of baking.

Serve hot, with Oatmeal Brown Bread (see page 18).

Makes 6 servings.

Tomato Baked Beans

Undoubtedly beans rank as our national dish and just so we satisfy the "with tomato" devotees, here's another recipe.

Soak overnight
1 pound navy or pea beans
in
water to cover

Preheat oven to 250° F.

Drain, and cover with fresh water.

Bring to a boil, and simmer, uncovered, until skins burst when blown upon.

Drain and place beans in large bean crock or 1½ quart casserole.

Mix together and pour over beans
1 cup chopped onion
¼ pound salt pork, chopped
⅔ cup molasses
½ cup catsup
2 teaspoons salt
1 teaspoon dry mustard
2 teaspoons Worcestershire sauce
3 cups boiling water

Bake, covered, in 250° oven for 8 hours, adding a small amount of boiling water from time to time so that beans do not become dry. Remove cover during last 30 minutes of baking.

Makes 6 to 8 servings.

53

Barkerville Gold Digger's Special

This recipe from the West is named after the old Gold Rush centre of Barkerville, British Columbia, now a ghost town being restored to look as it did during its heyday, some ninety years ago.

Fry together
1 pound ground round steak
¼ cup chopped onion
2 tablespoons shortening

Mix in
1 teaspoon salt
pinch of pepper
¼ cup drained canned mushrooms
1 package fresh spinach, chopped

Beat together and stir in
4 eggs

Stir until eggs are cooked. Serve hot, as a quick supper dish.

Makes 4 servings.

Holubtse

Holubtse is the Ukrainian name for stuffed cabbage rolls and literally means "little pigeons." Besides being a family favourite, it is an essential dish for festive occasions, especially at the Christmas Eve supper, when holubtse is served with a meatless filling. This recipe comes from Dauphin, Manitoba, and was one of the dishes served to exchange students from Ontario, in August, 1965.

Combine in a saucepan
2 cups boiling water
2 teaspoons salt
2 cups uncooked rice

Bring to boil, cover, turn off heat and let stand until water is absorbed.

In a frypan melt
¼ cup butter

Add
1 medium onion, finely chopped

Sauté until onion is a light golden colour. Combine with rice and season with salt and pepper. Cool.

Remove core from
1 large cabbage

Place in a deep saucepan and add boiling water in hollow of core to cover completely. Let stand until leaves are soft and pliable. Drain and carefully take leaves apart. Cut off hard centre rib from each leaf and divide leaves into two or three sections.

Preheat oven to 350° F.

Grease a large covered casserole. Cover bottom of casserole with extra leaves.

Place a spoonful of filling on the prepared sections of cabbage leaves and roll up tightly. Arrange in layers in casserole, salting each layer.

Combine
1 to 1½ cups tomato juice
2 tablespoons butter, melted
1 teaspoon salt
pinch of pepper

Pour over holubtse. The liquid should barely show between the rolls. To protect the top from scorching, place a large leaf of cabbage over top before covering tightly.
Bake in 350° oven for 1½ to 2 hours, or until both cabbage and filling are cooked. Serve hot, with crisp bacon, sour cream or any favourite sauce.

Makes about 30.

Wolfe Island Cheese Soufflé

Canadians infrequently serve the puffy soufflés of France with one exception—this golden cheese soufflé, using Canadian cheddar, has been adopted as our own and named after one of Ontario's Thousand Islands, where a cheese factory is located.

Preheat oven to 300° F.

In a saucepan melt
3 tablespoons butter

Blend in
3 tablespoons all-purpose flour
½ teaspoon salt
pinch of dry mustard
pinch of pepper

Gradually stir in
1 cup milk

Stir and cook over medium heat until thickened.

Add
1 cup shredded Canadian cheddar cheese

Stir until cheese is melted. Remove from heat.

Beat until light
3 egg yolks

Stir hot cheese mixture into yolks, blending thoroughly. Cool.

Beat until stiff, but not dry
3 egg whites

Carefully fold in cheese mixture.

Turn into ungreased 1½-quart casserole.

Bake in 300° oven for about 60 minutes, or until set and lightly browned.

Makes 4 to 5 servings.

Caulcannon

This Newfoundland version of the Irish colcannon, (complete with local spelling), is served at Halloween parties or suppers with little prizes or favours hidden in the mixture. It can be made with any vegetables, although white ones are preferred.

Wash and cook together
potatoes
turnips
cabbage
parsnip
onion

Put through potato ricer.

Mix well in a saucepan with
butter
salt and pepper to taste

Heat thoroughly.

French Toast

Golden bread would translate *pain doré*, which is what French Canadians call French toast. No matter what the name given to it, both French and English Canadians have been enjoying this delicacy for generations.

Combine
3 beaten eggs
½ cup milk
1 teaspoon sugar
¼ teaspoon salt

Dip bread slices into mixture and brown on both sides on a well-buttered griddle.

Serve with maple syrup.

Hamburger Pancakes

An ingenious homemaker from Saskatchewan shows us how to stretch ½ pound ground beef. Undoubtedly, the recipe is born of necessity, perhaps during the depression years when Saskatchewan suffered the worst drought in history.

Preheat griddle or heavy frypan. If necessary grease with unsalted fat.

Combine
½ pound hamburger
1 tablespoon chopped onion
½ teaspoon salt
¼ teaspoon baking powder

Stir in
3 egg yolks

Fold in
3 egg whites, stiffly beaten

Drop like pancakes onto hot griddle. Turn once.

Serve alone, or with tomato or mushroom sauce.

Makes 4 servings.

Huskies-in-a-Drift

Huskies are the Eskimo dogs that pull the sleds through the snow. This is a western recipe to use when you forget to purchase the hot dog buns.

Preheat oven to 400° F.

Partially cook
1 pound sausages or wieners

Arrange in shallow 8-inch square baking dish.

Beat together
2 eggs
1 cup milk

Thoroughly beat in
½ cup all-purpose flour

Pour over sausages.

Bake in 400° oven for 25 minutes.

Makes 4 to 5 servings.

Muk-Luk Mock Duck

Edmonton promotes its winter "Muk-Luk Mardi Gras" festival well and our resident correspondent submitted this deliciously flavoured meat recipe without any explanation of the name. Accept it, as we did, for its good eating.

Remove arteries from
1 beef heart

Place in pan, add water to cover, and bring to a boil. Simmer for 1½ to 2 hours, or until tender.

Preheat oven to 325° F.

To prepare stuffing, mix together
1 cup bread or cracker crumbs
2 tablespoons grated onion
2 tablespoons tomato paste
1 teaspoon granulated sugar
1 teaspoon salt
1 teaspoon poultry seasoning
¼ teaspoon pepper

To prepare sauce, blend together
1 tablespoon butter
2 slices onion
1 cup canned tomatoes
½ cup chopped celery
pinch of cayenne
salt and pepper
pinch of monosodium glutamate

Slice cooked meat. Place in casserole alternately with stuffing. Pour sauce over top.

Bake in 325° oven for 30 to 45 minutes.

Makes 8 servings.

Nalysnyky

This recipe came from North Eastern Alberta where many Ukrainians settled. There the people still live simply and the women prove to be excellent cooks, spending considerable time in the preparation of traditional dishes. Nalysnyky are served as a main course dish, accompanied by meat, potatoes, cabbage rolls and vegetables or salad.

Prepare batter for French pancakes (see page 30).

Preheat oven to 300° F.

Mix together thoroughly
½ pound dry cottage cheese
2 tablespoons granulated sugar
½ teaspoon vanilla
1 egg

Fry batter, making pancakes 2½ to 3 inches in diameter. Fill with cottage cheese mixture and roll up into a cylinder.

Arrange attractively in a casserole.

Pour over top about
1 pint (2½ cups) thick dairy sour cream

Bake in 300° oven for 30 to 45 minutes, or until bubbling.

Makes about 8 servings.

Italian-Canadian Pizza

With almost 500,000 people of Italian origin in Canada today, it is only natural that this Italian specialty has become popular, especially in Ontario and Quebec cities where the majority of them settled.

Dissolve
1 teaspoon granulated sugar

in

1 cup lukewarm water (100° F.)

Over this, sprinkle
1 envelope active dry yeast

Let stand 10 minutes. Then stir briskly with a fork.

. In a bowl combine with yeast mixture
¼ cup vegetable oil
1 teaspoon salt
1¼ cups all-purpose flour

Beat until smooth.

Add another
1 to 1¼ cups all-purpose flour

Work in last of flour with a rotating motion of the hand. Turn dough out on a lightly floured surface and knead until smooth and elastic, about 8 to 10 minutes. Place in a greased bowl, rotating dough to grease surface. Cover with a damp cloth and let rise in a warm place until doubled (about 45 minutes).

Meantime, mix together
1 can (5½ ounces) tomato paste
½ cup water
1 teaspoon salt
1 teaspoon crushed oregano
pinch of pepper

When dough is doubled, punch down and divide in half. Form each half into a ball, and place on greased baking sheets. Press out with palms of hands into circles about 12 inches in diameter, making edges slightly thicker.

On each circle of dough arrange
¼ pound mozzarella cheese sliced about ⅛ inch thick
OR
¼ pound sliced cooked sausages
½ cup sliced mushrooms, fried
2 tablespoons chopped green pepper

Cover each round with half of the tomato mixture and sprinkle with
2 tablespoons vegetable oil
2 tablespoons grated Parmesan or old cheddar cheese

Bake in preheated 400° F. oven about 25 minutes.

Makes two 12-inch pizzas.

Poached Eggs in Maple Syrup

This old-time breakfast specialty from the province of Quebec has a most pleasant flavour.

Pour into a frypan to a depth of 1½ inches
maple syrup

Heat to just below simmering (bubbles forming in liquid but not breaking on surface).

Break carefully into a saucer, one at a time
1 egg per serving
and slip gently into pan. Cook until eggs are set, 3 to 5 minutes.

Remove eggs from pan and serve on toast, with syrup poured over top.

Quiche Lorraine

This savoury, main course, cheese-and-bacon custard pie is a specialty of the province of Lorraine in France and crossed the Atlantic fairly recently. Now that Swiss-style cheese is made in Canada, and because of the high quality of our side bacon, it seems right and proper to include the recipe.

Preheat oven to 400° F.

Prepare sufficient pastry to line a 9-inch pie plate.

Crumble into pie shell
6 slices crisply cooked bacon

Cover with
3 ounces grated Swiss-style cheese

Beat together
4 eggs
1½ cups milk
½ teaspoon salt
pinch of pepper

Pour into pie shell.

Bake in 400° oven for 25 to 30 minutes, or until set. If desired, garnish with crisply fried bacon strips. Serve immediately.

Makes 6 servings.

Quiche Maritime

This good company dish, developed by the home economists of Canada's Department of Fisheries, differs from the classic French quiche lorraine in that smoked fish fillets replace the bacon, and a rice crust replaces the regular pastry that surrounds the cheese-custard filling.

Preheat oven to 350° F.

Cut in six wedges each
2 medium tomatoes

Coat to marinate with
French dressing

Cut into pieces 2 to 3 inches long
1 pound smoked fish fillets

Place in a shallow baking dish. Add
1 cup milk

Bake in 350° oven for 20 minutes, or until fish will separate into flakes with a fork. Drain, reserving ¾ cup liquid.

Grease a 9-inch pie plate.

Make rice crust by combining
3 cups cooked rice
2 tablespoons butter, melted
1 egg, beaten

Turn into pie plate and press firmly and evenly over bottom, sides and rim to form a pie shell.

Sprinkle over shell
½ cup grated Canadian cheddar cheese

Arrange cooked fish on top and sprinkle with an additional
½ cup grated cheese

Combine reserved poaching liquid with
2 eggs, beaten

Pour into pie plate.

Bake in 350° oven for 30 minutes.

Remove from oven and arrange drained tomato wedges around edge of filling, skin side up. Return pie to oven and bake for 10 minutes longer, or until custard is set. Garnish with finely chopped chives or green onion tops.

Serve piping hot.

Makes 6 servings.

Baddeck Scotch Eggs

This Cape Breton Island version simplifies the preparation by using sausage meat.

Preheat deep fat to 375° F.

Cool and shell
3 hard-cooked eggs

Mash
½ pound skinless sausages or sausage meat

Shape around eggs, covering completely.

Dip in
1 egg, slightly beaten
Roll in
bread crumbs

Fry in deep fat for 3 to 4 minutes, or until golden brown.

Cut in half and sprinkle with
chopped parsley

Serve hot or cold.

Makes 3 servings.

Tourtière (Pork)

Originally this French-Canadian specialty was prepared with passenger pigeons or *tourtes* as they were known in French. Since the disappearance of these birds, fresh pork or a mixture of different kinds of meat is used — each region having its own preference. Tradition demands that *tourtière* be served on Christmas Eve.

In a heavy 3-quart saucepan combine
  1½ pounds ground lean pork
  1 small onion, minced
  ½ cup boiling water
  1 garlic clove, chopped
  1½ teaspoons salt
  ¼ teaspoon celery salt
  ¼ teaspoon black pepper
  ¼ teaspoon sage
  pinch of ground cloves

Cook over low heat, stirring constantly, until meat loses its red colour and about half the liquid has evaporated. Cover, and cook about 45 minutes longer.

Meanwhile, boil and mash
  3 medium-sized potatoes

Mix mashed potatoes into cooked meat mixture. Cool.

Preheat oven to 450° F.

Prepare sufficient pastry for a 2-crust 9-inch pie. Roll out half and line a deep 9-inch pie plate. Fill with cooled meat mixture. Roll out remainder of dough and cover pie. Flute and seal edges and slash top crust.

Bake in 450° oven for 10 minutes. Reduce heat to 350° and bake for 30 to 40 minutes longer.

Makes 6 to 7 servings.

Gaspé Tourtière

Another *tourtière* recipe, to try and give a good idea of the many different versions.

This is a two-pie size.

Cut in 4 to 6 pieces
  1 (4- to 5-pound) boiling fowl

In a saucepan combine chicken with
  1 onion, stuck with 1 whole clove
  1 branch celery leaves
  1 carrot, sliced
  1 sprig parsley
  1 small bay leaf
  pinch of thyme
  pinch of marjoram
  1 tablespoon salt

Add sufficient cold water to just cover chicken. Cover pan, and cook over low heat until chicken is tender. Cool in broth 1 hour.

Meanwhile, lightly brown in lightly greased frypan
  2 pounds ground lean pork

Stir in sufficient broth from chicken to just cover meat. Cover and cook over low heat for 2 hours.

Remove chicken from bones and chop.

Mix well with pork and taste for seasoning. Allow to cool.

Preheat oven to 450° F.

Prepare sufficient pastry for two 2-crust pies. Divide into 4 equal portions and roll out each separately. Use 2 portions to line two deep 9-inch pie plates.

Divide cooled meat mixture between pie plates. Cover with top crusts. Flute and seal edges and slash top crusts.

Bake in 450° oven for 10 minutes. Reduce heat to 350° and bake for 30 to 40 minutes longer.

Makes 6 to 7 servings per pie.

Tuktoyaktuk Tomato Poached Eggs

A similar recipe was found in an 1889 Canadian cook book, and then this one came in from the West. It makes an excellent dish for Sunday brunch.

In a saucepan combine
1 can (19 ounces) tomatoes, chopped
½ teaspoon salt
pinch of black pepper

Bring to a boil. Reduce heat, and simmer for 5 minutes.

Break into a saucer, one at a time, and slide gently into heated tomato
5 eggs

Cover. Cook slowly until eggs have reached desired firmness.

Serve on hot buttered toast.

Top with grated cheese.

Makes 5 servings.

Varenyky

These filled dumplings came to Canada with the Ukrainian and Polish settlers and still are made by their descendants, the majority of whom continue to live on the Prairies.

Boil
4 medium potatoes

Save potato water.

Mash potatoes and mix together with
1 pound cottage cheese
¼ pound grated cheddar cheese
1½ teaspoons salt
½ teaspoon pepper
½ teaspoon dried mint flakes

Mix together
5 cups all-purpose flour
2 teaspoons salt
2 egg yolks
1¾ cups potato water

Turn dough out on floured surface and knead until smooth. Let stand, covered, for 10 minutes.

Divide into 10 or 15 parts and roll out each ¼ inch thick. Cut with round or square 2½- or 3-inch cookie cutter. Roll each piece ⅛ inch thick.

Place 1 teaspoon of filling in each, moisten edges, fold over and pinch together. Drop into boiling water and boil steadily for 4 to 5 minutes, or until dumplings rise to the surface. Drain. Sprinkle with buttered bread crumbs, butter and onions or finely chopped bacon and onions.

As is the Ukrainian custom, this makes plenty. They keep well in the refrigerator and can be reheated in boiling water or sautéed in a little butter until golden brown.

Makes about 20 servings.

Welsh Rarebit

Should one say "rarebit" or "rabbit"? It is simpler just to eat and enjoy this savoury which particularly suits Sunday night supper.

Combine in a saucepan
¼ cup beer or ale
½ pound grated process cheese
1 tablespoon butter
½ teaspoon dry mustard
¼ teaspoon salt
pinch of cayenne pepper

Stir over low heat until cheese is melted and sauce is smooth and well blended.

Gradually add cheese sauce to
1 egg, slightly beaten

Pour over
4 slices hot buttered toast

Brown lightly under broiler. Serve at once.

Makes 4 servings.

White Hatter Stew

During Stampede week each summer in Calgary, the white cowboy hats are everywhere and the restaurants feature the official dish — white hatter stew. The authentic recipe is reduced here to household-size measurements.

Preheat oven to 400° F.

Heat in pan until slightly smoking
2 tablespoons vegetable oil

Place in pan
2½ pound rump of beef, cut in cubes

Cook in 400° oven for 15 minutes, shaking pan occasionally to brown meat on all sides.

Add
2 large onions, chopped
salt and pepper
½ teaspoon monosodium glutamate
¼ teaspoon paprika
and sprinkle with
2 tablespoons flour

Continue cooking for 20 minutes longer, stirring occasionally.

Stir in
⅔ cup canned plum tomatoes
1 quart (5 cups) brown sauce or gravy
½ cup beer (optional)
1 teaspoon Worcestershire sauce

Wrap in cheesecloth and add
2 bay leaves
few peppercorns
thyme
parsley sprigs

Reduce heat to 300° and continue cooking, covered, for about two hours until meat is tender.

Meantime, prepare biscuit crust.

Sift or blend together
3¾ cups all-purpose flour
2½ teaspoons baking powder
pinch of salt

Cut in with pastry blender
½ cup butter

Beat together
1 egg
1 cup milk

Stir into dry ingredients. Mix together slightly until one lump of dough is obtained. Roll out on floured surface to ¼-inch thickness. Cut out pastry covers the same size as casserole dishes.

When stew is cooked, remove spice bag, spoon meat into individual casseroles and top with pastry covers, sealing tightly to keep flavour in.

Brush tops with milk.

Bake in preheated 425° oven for 20 minutes, or until golden brown.

Makes 6 to 8 servings.

61

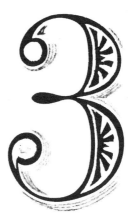

Game

The game birds and wild game, whether big or small, have added much to our diet since the days of the early explorers. We still consider them a special treat, particularly our city dwellers who long for a wild duck, a venison steak or even a good old-fashioned rabbit stew.

For these recipes we have relied on our members living in areas where a day's hunting means a trip of ten or fifteen miles. This ensures that the recipes have been frequently tested by those fortunate enough to have ready access to a plentiful supply of game.

Acadian Chicken

A New Brunswick member sent along this early Acadian recipe with the comment "Poultry was scarce and rabbit was plentiful, so many a fat little rabbit found his way into the early settler's cooking pot. The first time I was served roast rabbit by descendants of the Acadians I thought it was roast duck".

Preheat oven to 350° F.

Wash and wipe dry
   1 rabbit, skinned and drawn

Fill with
   Bread Stuffing (see page 81)

Skewer the opening.

Place in roaster.

Cover rabbit with
   strips bacon or salt pork

Bake in 350° oven for about 1 hour, or until brown and tender.

Makes 2 to 3 servings.

Roast Antelope

The hunting season for antelope depends on the numbers recorded during aerial surveys conducted by wildlife personnel; on occasion, no hunting is permitted. The flavour of antelope is reminiscent of lamb.

Preheat oven to 300° F.

Wipe well
   1 leg roast of antelope

Rub with
   1 garlic clove, cut in half

Spread lightly with
   butter

Sprinkle with
   salt
   few grains of cayenne

Place, skin side down, in roasting pan.

Overlap on top
   slices side bacon

Roast in 300° oven allowing 35 to 40 minutes per pound.

Serve with orange slices, Orange Sauce (see page 80) or currant jelly.

Makes about 6 servings.

Arctic Steak

Arctic steak is frozen whale meat. It is somewhat like beef, but coarse, dark and strong in flavour. To cook follow beef cooking chart.

Rupert's Land Bear Stew

In the early days, until about 1869, the area that is now mainly Alberta, Saskatchewan and Manitoba was known as Rupert's Land. Bears are still hunted in the West as in other parts of Canada, but because they bring to mind the fur trading era, we've named this stew after the land granted to the Hudson Bay Company in 1670.

Wash in cold water
   3 pounds bear meat

Cube meat, discarding fat.

Soak for 15 minutes in
   1 gallon water
   1 cup vinegar

Wipe dry with a cloth.

Fry in deep pan with
   1 small onion, chopped
   1 green pepper, chopped
   3 stalks celery, sliced
   1 garlic clove, chopped
   salt
   pinch of pepper

Cook until meat is browned and onion transparent.

Add and simmer for 2½ hours, or until tender.
   1 can (19 ounces) whole tomatoes
   1 can (5½ ounces) tomato paste
   ½ teaspoon Tabasco sauce

Makes about 6 servings.

Buffalo Birds

From Fort Smith, in the rugged Northwest Territories, we received this recipe for buffaloburgers. Should you not have a ready supply of buffalo meat, use ground round steak.

Preheat oven to 375° F.

Mix together
1 pound ground buffalo meat
1 teaspoon salt
½ teaspoon pepper
1 egg

Pat into four large flat patties on a floured board.

Combine
1 cup fine dry bread crumbs
½ cup chopped celery
1 onion, diced
½ cup grated carrot
½ teaspoon sage
1 egg

Place a mound of stuffing on each patty and form meat around it. Wrap each ball in foil.

Bake in 375° oven for 45 minutes.

Open foil and continue baking for another 15 minutes.

Makes 4 servings.

Buffalo Sukiyaki

Our explorers and fur traders relied on pemmican for their meat on the trail. This was buffalo meat, cut with the grain in thin strips and dried in the sun or over a slow fire. It was then pounded and blended with melted fat. Today strips of fresh buffalo meat may be cooked in the Japanese fashion as in this recipe from the Northwest Territories. Substitute beef sirloin for the buffalo meat when the latter is in short supply. You'll be pleased to see the recipe uses the liquid drained from the canned mushrooms.

Heat in a frypan
2 tablespoons vegetable oil

Add and brown slightly
1½ pounds buffalo sirloin, cut in 2½ x ½-inch diagonal slices

Mix together
¾ cup soya sauce
¼ cup granulated sugar
¼ cup mushroom stock

Add half of this to meat.

Add and simmer for 10 minutes
2 medium onions, thinly sliced
1 green pepper, thinly sliced
1 cup diagonally cut strips of celery

Add remaining soya sauce mixture with
1 can (10 ounces) mushrooms, drained
1 can (10 ounces) bamboo shoots, sliced

Cook for 4 minutes.

Add and cook for 1 minute
1 cup chopped green onion tops

Stir well and serve immediately over hot, fluffy rice.

Makes 6 servings.

Ragoût of Duck

The French word *ragoût*, meaning stew, came from *ragoûtant*, meaning tempting or appetizing, and it applies most fittingly to this duck specialty.

Clean, remove any pinfeathers and cut in pieces
1 duck

In frypan heat
2 tablespoons butter
2 tablespoons vegetable oil

Add meat.

Season with
salt and pepper

Cook until slightly brown.

Remove meat from pan.

Add to pan and cook until brown
1 onion, diced

Stir in
1 garlic clove, finely chopped
sprig parsley
1 cup stock
1 tablespoon vinegar

Return meat to pan, cover and simmer slowly until tender.

Makes about 2 servings.

66

Roast Wild Duck

A Vancouverite, noted for her cooking of wild game, sent this favourite recipe for roasting wild duck. The high temperature cooking for a short time browns the bird and the low temperature cooking for a longer time ensures tenderness. It takes an experienced cook to assess the age of the bird bagged by the hunter, but this recipe takes the guesswork out of cooking a duck of any age.

Preheat oven to 400° F.

Clean ducks, removing any pinfeathers.

To make sufficient stuffing for 1 duck mix together
> **2 cups fine dry bread crumbs**
> **½ cup finely chopped onion**
> **1 tablespoon chopped parsley**
> **2 teaspoons chopped sage leaves**
> **salt and pepper**
> **hot water to moisten**

Stuff ducks and place on rack in roaster. Bake in 400° oven until brown. Reduce heat to 250°. Cover roaster with lid or foil. Bake for 2 to 2½ hours, or until tender.

Pour off all fat before making gravy. Add water to residue in pan.

Thicken with a paste of
> **flour**
> **cold water**

Season to taste with
> **salt and pepper**

Allow 1 duck for every two servings.

Newfoundland Flipper Pie

Flippers are the forepaws of the seal and are considered a great delicacy in our newest province.

Remove all fat from
> **3 seal flippers**

To remove any remaining fat, wash in a mixture of
> **1 cup warm water**
> **1 cup vinegar**

Fry until transparent
> **8 to 10 slices fat salt pork**

Brown flippers in fat.

Add a little water and
> **4 onions, sliced**
> **2 teaspoons Worcestershire sauce**
> **1 teaspoon savory**

Simmer until partly tender.

Add
> **4 carrots, sliced**
> **1 small turnip, diced**
> **2 cups beef stock or consommé**
> **salt**
> **pepper**

Cook for 25 minutes.

Add
> **6 or 7 potatoes, sliced**

Cook until potatoes are tender, about 20 minutes longer. Drain, reserving liquid. Prepare a brown gravy from the liquid, allowing 2 tablespoons flour for each cup of liquid. (If flour is browned in heavy pan first, allow ¼ cup per cup liquid.)

Combine flippers, vegetables and gravy in casserole and season to taste.

Use your favourite pastry recipe to cover pie or see page 170.

Bake in preheated 400° F. oven for about 25 minutes, or until browned and crusty.

Makes 6 servings.

Roast Wild Goose

Wild goose is not as fat as the domestic variety and has a tendency to dry out during cooking. A wise cook bastes with liquid during roasting as in this recipe from Alberta, or you may prefer to protect the bird with a layer of salt pork or bacon strips.

Clean and remove any pinfeathers from
1 goose

Mix together and place in cavity
1 large onion, chopped
1 tart apple, chopped
1 cup chopped celery

Place goose in covered roaster and let stand overnight in a cool place.

Preheat oven to 400° F.

Remove vegetables and apple from goose and fill with Apple-Raisin Stuffing (see page 81). Sew up bird.

Mix together
1 tablespoon flour
1 teaspoon salt
1 teaspoon sage
1 teaspoon paprika
1 teaspoon pepper

Rub well into skin of bird.

Roast, uncovered, in 400° oven until light brown. Reduce heat to 325°. Baste every 15 minutes with a mixture of
1 cup apple juice
1 cup grapefruit juice
½ cup prune juice

Allow 20 minutes per pound cooking time.

Makes about 6 servings.

Klondike Stew

A word of caution about moose meat, indeed meat from all antlered animals. Remove all the fat as this has a gamy flavour that is too strong for many people. Then, either cook in liquid, as with this Klondike Stew, or replace the fat by covering the meat with side bacon. Should you wish, use equal parts of sherry and water to marinate the moose meat.

Brown
3 pounds moose meat, cubed
in
¼ pound butter
Stir in
1 onion, chopped

Cook until onion is soft.

Blend in
2½ cups water
salt
pepper
1 bay leaf
½ teaspoon thyme

Simmer for 2 hours.

Cut up and stir into stew
2 carrots
2 parsnips
1 small turnip
6 potatoes

Cook for 1 hour, or until vegetables are tender.

Mix together to make a paste
½ cup all-purpose flour
½ cup water

Stir into hot stew. Season to taste.

Simmer for 5 minutes longer.

Makes 6 servings.

Braised Partridge

The name partridge causes some confusion in Canada as it is sometimes applied to several kinds of quail as well as ruffed grouse, and the partridge of Newfoundland is the native ptarmigan. The average partridge weighs from 12 to 13 ounces and serves one person. Roast or broil young ones and braise or stew older birds.

Clean and remove any pinfeathers from
4 partridge

Sprinkle inside and out with
salt
pepper

Combine
4 cups shredded cabbage
4 slices cooked bacon, crumbled

Spoon into cavity of each bird.
Wrap each bird in
4 cabbage leaves (total of 16)

Tie with string.

Arrange partridge in large skillet, electric frypan or Dutch oven.

Add
2 tablespoons butter
1 cup chicken broth
4 carrots, sliced
1 teaspoon salt
¼ teaspoon crushed thyme
¼ teaspoon crushed tarragon
¼ teaspoon pepper

Cover, and simmer over low heat for 25 to 30 minutes, or until birds are tender. Remove cabbage leaves.

Serve partridge with sauce from pan.

Makes 4 servings.

Roast Pheasant

Our present-day pheasant is a surprising facsimile of the original Chinese ringneck although it is a composite of species including the English ringneck and the Mongolian pheasant. The cock is a showy, arrogant bird from 2¾ to 5 pounds. The hen is chunky and colourless by comparison, weighing from 2 to 3 pounds. Both are excellent birds for the table, having white-meated breasts and dark-meated legs. Broil or bake young pheasants (they have short, round claws) with a generous covering of bacon and frequent basting. Braise or stew older birds (they have long, sharp claws), or try this recipe from Saskatchewan.

Preheat oven to 350° F.

Clean and remove any pinfeathers from
1 pheasant

Season inside and out with
salt
pepper

Stuff with
4 apples, quartered and cored

Truss for roasting. Place in a roasting pan.

Cover with mixture of
1 cup thick dairy sour cream
salt and pepper

Bake, covered, in 350° oven for 1½ to 2 hours, or until tender.

Makes 2 to 4 servings.

Prairie Chicken Casserole

A most important game bird of Manitoba, the Prairie chicken makes a special-occasion dish of sufficient stature to merit serving with another Manitoba delicacy, wild rice.

Wash thoroughly
breasts and legs of 1 prairie chicken

Soak in salt and water (about ½ tablespoon to 1 cup water) overnight. Rinse well with cold water.

Preheat oven to 350° F.

Place breasts and legs in casserole.

Cover with a layer of
sliced onion (about 1 medium)

Add
1 can (10 ounces) condensed cream of mushroom soup
1 can (5½ ounces) mushroom pieces (including liquid)

Add enough water to cover.

Bake, covered, in 350° oven for 1½ to 2 hours.

Serve with wild rice or fried rice.

Makes 3 to 4 servings.

Rabbit Casserole

As a general rule, wild rabbit should be cooked in liquid unless quite young. These vegetarian animals have been a hunter's salvation on many an occasion when other game seemed to have vanished. We particularly like the tomato flavour with rabbit.

Preheat oven to 350° F.

Wash and cut into serving pieces
1 rabbit

Dredge with a mixture of
1½ cups all-purpose flour
1 teaspoon salt
½ teaspoon pepper
1 tablespoon paprika

Fry
5 or 6 slices chopped side bacon
in
vegetable oil

Add
1 medium onion, chopped

Cook until onion is transparent. Remove bacon and onion. Brown rabbit pieces in bacon fat. Place in casserole. Sprinkle with bacon and onion.

Combine in order given
2 tablespoons all-purpose flour
1 can (19 ounces) tomato juice
1 teaspoon gravy colouring
½ teaspoon salt
pinch of thyme
1 bay leaf

Pour sauce over rabbit. Cover.

Bake in 350° oven for 1½ hours.

Makes about 3 servings.

Baked Seal Meat

From Newfoundland we learn how to prepare seal meat to suit our tastes. The Eskimos do not require all the preliminaries but it certainly does remove the slightly fishy flavour. The seal meat is usually cut in strips or cubes before marinating.

Remove all fat from about
4 pounds seal meat

Mix together and pour over meat
3 cups hot water
1½ teaspoons baking soda
¼ cup vinegar

Soak for 3 hours. Drain. Store meat in refrigerator overnight.

Preheat oven to 300° F.

Roll meat in a mixture of
1 cup flour
1 teaspoon dry mustard
1½ teaspoons salt

Place in roaster with
fat or butter

Pour over meat
juice of 1 lemon
¼ cup rum

Roast, covered, in 300° oven for 3 hours, adding water after first hour of cooking.

Make a paste of
flour
water

Stir into drippings in pan to make a gravy.

Makes about 8 servings.

Baked Turr (Seabird)

Turrs are native migratory salt-water birds that may be hunted only in Newfoundland. To get best results, cook out the fat and discard, then continue cooking with a protective covering of salt pork or bacon slices as in this typical recipe.

Clean and drain well
1 turr or seabird

Prepare dressing of
2 cups bread crumbs
1 small onion, chopped
1½ teaspoons savory
½ teaspoon salt
¼ teaspoon pepper
1 tablespoon shortening, melted

Stuff bird and place in roaster.

Sprinkle with
salt

Bake in 350° F. oven for 1 hour. Prick skin with fork to drain off fat. Remove bird and drain fat from roaster.

Arrange over bird
¼ pound salt pork

Return to oven and bake until pork is brown.

Add
4 to 5 cups hot water
1 large onion
1 teaspoon salt

Bake until brown and tender. Baste or turn occasionally.

Gravy may be made with liquid in roaster, and pastry added to make a pie, if desired.

Venison Barbecue

In Canada venison generally refers to the flesh of the deer. It may be cooked in the same way as beef, but do not over-cook as it has a tendency to dry out in a much more pronounced way than beef. For this reason we particularly like this Alberta recipe that calls for cooking the steaks in a barbecue-type sauce.

Preheat oven to 350° F.

Remove fat from
3 pounds venison (steaks or chops)

Sear in frypan with
sliced salt pork or other fat

In a saucepan combine
1 cup catsup

1 tablespoon salt
3 slices lemon
2 tablespoons tarragon vinegar (if desired)
1 onion, sliced
⅓ cup steak sauce
1 tablespoon chili sauce

Bring to a boil, stirring to prevent sticking. Place venison in a casserole and cover with sauce.

Bake in 350° oven for 1½ to 2 hours, turning occasionally.

Makes 3 servings.

Roast Venison

Many people prefer to marinate or cook venison in wine and there is little doubt that it improves the flavour tremendously. A Toronto resident, who was born in Midland, Ontario, submitted this recipe with the comment "The aroma is so temptingly good we stayed up until 11:00 P.M. to sample it on one occasion."

Preheat oven to 500° F.

Trim, removing any dry pieces of skin and fat from
1 venison roast

Wipe with damp cloth.
Place in roasting pan and sear in 500° oven for 5 to 10 minutes. Reduce heat to 425°.

Arrange over roast
6 to 8 slices bacon

Roast, uncovered, in 425° oven for 30 to 40 minutes. Remove bacon when browned.

Combine
1 cup beef bouillon or consommé
1 cup red or white wine
or fruit juice
¼ cup lemon juice
3 tablespoons chopped onion
1 garlic clove, crushed
1 teaspoon salt
½ teaspoon pepper
¼ teaspoon thyme

Pour over roast.

Cover meat loosely with foil and continue roasting until tender (about 20 minutes per pound for medium rare).

Baste frequently during roasting.

Poultry

Not so very long ago every farmer's wife kept a few hens and sold the eggs for pin money. Spring chickens were available when the flocks were culled in the spring, and young cockerels were the broiler-fryers of the day — rather scrawny, but a change from the roasting or the stewing chicken. Turkeys appeared in limited amounts at Thanksgiving and in more abundant supply at Christmas and New Year's. Large birds were the order of the day and quality was often sketchy.

How things have changed! Canadians are the world's largest per capita turkey consumers, and why not, with excellent quality birds of varying sizes from 4 to 24 pounds available all year round at economical prices. Plump, meaty broiler chickens, whole or cut in portions, appear throughout the year, and the roasting chicken has come into its own again. There has been an increase in the Canadian production of duck and geese, too, and our Brome Lake Duckling particularly is noted for its high quality.

Barbecued Chicken

Some prefer a barbecue sauce for chicken, but we like the crispy golden goodness of this simplified recipe. It is a wise precaution to brush again with vegetable oil if the chicken shows signs of drying out.

Grease grill with
   butter or vegetable oil
Brush
   chicken quarters or halves
with
   butter or vegetable oil
Sprinkle with
   salt, pepper and paprika
Place skin side down on grill, about 3 inches from coals. Brown for about 3 minutes. Turn and brown underside for 3 minutes.

Raise grill to 4 to 6 inches from coals and continue cooking until chicken is tender, about 20 to 45 minutes.

Chicken Breasts in Maple Syrup

From Quebec we received this delectable concoction that shows the influence of French cuisine adapted to Canadian products.

Preheat oven to 350° F.
Bone
   4 chicken breasts
Roll each in
   flour
seasoned with
   salt and pepper
Fry
   3 large mushrooms, finely chopped
   ½ cup finely diced ham
   ½ teaspoon dried chives
in
   2 tablespoons butter
Cook 2 to 3 minutes, or until mushrooms are tender.

Slit thick portion of each chicken breast and insert one spoonful of ham mixture. Pinch edges together to seal.
Brown in frypan in
   ¼ cup butter

Remove meat from pan.

To frypan add
1 cup thinly sliced onion

Fry until slightly browned.

Arrange chicken breasts in small casserole.

Top with onion and sprinkle with
pinch of savory

Spoon over each chicken breast
1 tablespoon maple syrup

Add ½ cup water to frypan to clean the pan and then pour over chicken.

Bake, uncovered, in 350° oven for 30 minutes.

Makes 4 servings.

Chicken Cacciatore

This Italian specialty from Toronto was originally made with olive oil, but has been adapted to the Canadian preference for the milder flavoured vegetable oil.

Cut into serving pieces
1 (3-pound) chicken

Fry until golden in
¼ cup vegetable oil

Add and brown lightly
½ cup finely chopped onion
⅓ cup finely chopped green pepper
1 or 2 garlic cloves, finely chopped

Stir in
1¾ cups canned tomatoes
½ can (7½ ounces) tomato sauce
¼ cup red wine or wine vinegar
1 teaspoon salt
¼ teaspoon pepper
¼ teaspoon dried thyme or oregano
½ bay leaf

Simmer, covered, for 1 hour, or until chicken is tender.

Pour sauce over chicken when serving.

Makes 3 to 4 servings.

Chicken Canuck

"Modern and recent but deliciously flavoured" aptly describes this recipe. The original version was developed and named by the Poultry Products Institute.

Grease a shallow baking dish.

Cook in boiling salted water until tender
4 medium potatoes
8 medium carrots

Meanwhile, in a small saucepan melt
¼ cup butter

Blend in
¼ cup all-purpose flour
¼ teaspoon rosemary
¼ teaspoon marjoram
¼ teaspoon oregano

Gradually stir in
1 cup chicken broth
OR
½ cup chicken broth and
½ cup milk

Cook, stirring constantly, until thickened.

Add
¼ cup cream (18%)

with meat from
2 large chicken breasts, cooked
OR
4 chicken legs, cooked
and
2 tablespoons chopped pimiento, (optional)

Reheat.

Drain vegetables and cut into thick slices. Arrange in prepared baking dish. Top with hot chicken mixture, dot with
butter

Sprinkle with
⅓ cup grated cheddar cheese
pinch of paprika

Broil 4 to 5 inches from heat until cheese is melted.

Serve with cooked shredded cabbage.

Makes 4 servings.

Speedy Method for Roasting Turkey

Wrap the oven-ready bird completely and tightly with aluminum foil. Roast as follows at 450° F. for approximately —

8 to 10 lbs.	3 to 3¼ hrs. total time
10 to 12 lbs.	3½ to 3¾ hrs. total time
14 to 16 lbs.	3¾ to 4 hrs. total time
18 to 20 lbs.	4 to 5¼ hrs. total time
22 to 24 lbs.	5¼ to 6 hrs. total time

Decrease time by 45 minutes
if bird is not stuffed.

Poultry Cooking Chart

Oven-ready Weights in Pounds	Amounts per Person Drawn or Eviscerated
Chicken 2½ to 3½ 3½ to 4¾ 4¾ up	½ to ¾ lb.
Capon 5 to 8	¾ lb.
Turkey 4 to 6 6 to 8 8 to 10 10 to 12 12 to 14 14 to 16 16 to 18 18 to 20 20 to 24	¾ to 1 lb. ½ to ¾ lb.
Chicken Broilers	½ bird or ½ to ¾ lb.
Fryers	½ bird or ½ to ¾ lb.
Duck	½ to ¾ lb.
Goose	½ to ¾ lb.

Undrawn	Cooking Times (hours)	Directions
¾ to 1 lb.	1½ to 2 2¼ to 2½ 2¾ to 3	**ROAST** — Wipe inside with damp cloth and stuff loosely with your favourite dressing. Turn back skin on neck, fold wings across the back with tips touching. Tie legs together. Place bird on rack in open roaster. If desired, cover bird with parchment or foil. Use a 325° F. oven and cook till internal temperature of meat on the inside of the thigh reaches 195°-200° F., or until drumstick twists easily.
1 lb.	3 to 4	
1 to 1¼ lbs. ¾ to 1 lb.	3 to 3¾ 3¾ to 4½ 4 to 4½ 4½ to 5 5 to 5¼ 5¼ to 6 6 to 6½ 6½ to 7½ 7½ to 9	
½ bird or ¾ to 1 lb.	30 to 35 mins.	Place chicken pieces skin side down on cold broiler rack, 5 inches from broiler, in preheated oven. Brush with butter. Broil underside for 18 to 20 minutes. Turn over, coat with butter, broil for 10 to 14 minutes.
½ bird or ¾ to 1 lb.	35 to 40 mins.	Dip pieces in flour or crumbs and seasonings. Brown in hot fat, reduce heat, cover, cook until tender. Remove cover to brown and crisp quickly.
1 lb.	25 to 30 mins. per lb.	Roast, uncovered, at 325° F., with a small amount of water, for 25 to 30 minutes per pound. Pour off excess fat as it accumulates.
1 lb.	25 to 30 mins. per lb.	Roast, covered, at 450° F., for 1 hour. Pour off accumulated fat. Sprinkle with seasoned flour. Add 1 cup water and roast uncovered, at 325° for 25 minutes per pound.

Chicken in Cider

It's best to simmer a boiling fowl in something that gives flavour to the bird. This rural Ontario recipe is ideal when one begins to wonder whether the apple cider will keep much longer.

Preheat oven to 350° F.

Cut into serving portions
   1 (5-pound) boiling fowl

Brown in
   4 to 5 tablespoons butter
Remove from pan.

Pour into pan
   1 cup cider or apple juice
and heat to clean the pan.

Peel, core and slice
   2 pounds tart apples

In a baking dish, place a layer of apple slices, cover with a layer of chicken, sprinkle with
   salt and pepper

Repeat with one more layer of apple and one of chicken. Season and cover with a layer of apple. Pour heated cider over top.

Cover dish.

Bake in 350° oven for 1½ hours.

Makes 6 servings.

Chicken Fricassee

In France *fricassée* applies almost exclusively to a method of preparing poultry in a white sauce. In Canada the word denotes various kinds of stew made with white sauce or a gravy-type sauce. This recipe uses all the delicious browned bits in the pan to make a thickened gravy. If you prefer, you may omit the chicken broth with the 2 tablespoons flour and add to casserole 1½ cups thick dairy sour cream.

Preheat oven to 325° F.

Cut in pieces
   1 (4-pound) fowl

Rub with
   3 tablespoons vinegar

Mix together in a paper bag
   ½ cup all-purpose flour
   1 teaspoon salt
   pinch of pepper
   2 teaspoons paprika

Add chicken, a few pieces at a time, and shake to coat evenly.

Brown chicken on all sides in ¼- to ½-inch-deep hot fat. Remove chicken and drain off all but 2 tablespoons fat. Stir into fat in pan
   2 tablespoons flour

Blend in
   1½ cups chicken stock or broth (chicken bouillon cubes may be used to make broth)

Cook, stirring constantly, until thickened.

Place chicken and gravy in a 2-quart casserole with
   ⅓ cup chopped onion
   ¼ cup chopped celery leaves

Bake, covered, in 325° oven for 1½ to 2 hours, or until chicken is tender.

Makes 4 to 6 servings.

Chicken Pot Pie

The evolution of the pot pie from the recipe the pioneer housewife brought to Canada (and modified to suit conditions here) to the present-day favourite, follows the change in cooking equipment in the home. The bake-kettle variety, heaped on the lid with hot embers, was turned gently and frequently in the open fireplace. The advent of the oven presented baking difficulties that led a not-too-recent Canadian cookbook author to suggest that pot pie belonged to her "grandmother's day" This flaky biscuit crust covering the tenderly simmered bird presents this centuries-old English favourite in a most rewarding way.

In a Dutch oven place
   1 (4½-pound) fowl
   3 cups water
   2 to 3 slices onion
   1 small carrot
   2 teaspoons salt
   1 teaspoon monosodium glutamate
   1 bay leaf

Bring to a boil. Reduce heat and simmer, covered, for about 2 hours, or until meat is tender. Add more water if necessary.

If desired, the following vegetables may be added for the last 20 minutes cooking time

6 small potatoes
3 carrots, sliced
½ cup sliced celery
6 small onions
1 cup cubed turnip
¼ pound mushrooms, sliced

Remove cooked chicken from bones. Place chicken pieces and vegetables in a 2-quart casserole.

Thicken gravy with a paste of
flour
cold water

Pour over chicken.

Prepare Tea Biscuit dough (see page 29). Cut out biscuits and arrange on top of casserole.

Bake in preheated 425° F. oven for 10 to 15 minutes, or until top is golden brown.

Makes 6 servings.

Chicken Sea Pie

The name comes from the French *ci-paille* and it was a favourite in the lumber camps of northern Quebec at the turn of the century. Our up-dated version has a crispy brown crust covering tender chunks of chicken in a thick, flavourful sauce. When cold, the pie jells and may be sliced.

Preheat oven to 450° F.

Grease thoroughly a flat-bottomed 2-quart baking dish (with lid).

Blend or sift together
2 cups all-purpose flour
2 teaspoons baking powder
½ teaspoon salt

With a pastry blender or two knives cut in
⅓ cup shortening
With a fork, stir in
¾ cup water

Add sufficient water to make a soft, slightly sticky dough. Roll out ⅓ of dough and line bottom of casserole.
Bone and cut in serving pieces
1 (3-pound) chicken
Mix together

6 to 8 green onions, sliced
2 tablespoons chopped parsley
2 tablespoons chopped celery
    leaves

Arrange half of chicken pieces on dough. Top with half of onion mixture.

Sprinkle with
½ teaspoon salt
pinch of pepper
pinch of savory
pinch of majoram
pinch of thyme

Cover with another layer of dough.
Repeat layers of chicken, onion mixture and seasonings.

Top with remaining ⅓ of dough and cut a circle out of centre.

Pour boiling water through centre opening until just visible. Cover and bake in 450° oven for 25 minutes. Reduce heat to 350° and bake 1 hour longer. Again pour boiling water through centre opening until just visible. Cover and bake an additional 1½ hours.

Remove lid and pour over crust
1 cup milk

Continue baking in a 350° oven for 30 minutes, removing cover for last 20 minutes.

Makes 6 servings.

78

Hungarian Chicken Paprika

Many of the recent Hungarian arrivals have settled in Ontario thus increasing the popularity of their traditional foods. This specialty, from Courtland, Ontario, is complete with the noodle-type dumplings that custom demands.

In a large skillet fry until tender but not browned
½ cup finely chopped onion
in
¼ cup shortening
Combine and stir into onions
1 teaspoon salt
1 tablespoon paprika
½ teaspoon black pepper
Add
1 (3- to 4-pound) chicken, cut in pieces
Fry until all sides are lightly browned.
Stir in
1½ cups water
Cover. Cook over low heat for about 1½ hours, or until chicken is tender.
Remove chicken from skillet.
Stir into liquid
1 cup thick dairy sour cream
Heat but do not allow to boil.
To serve, pour over chicken and dumplings.
Makes 6 servings.

HUNGARIAN DUMPLINGS
Beat together until dough is not lumpy
3 eggs, well beaten
½ cup water
2 cups all-purpose flour
2 teaspoons salt
In a 3-quart saucepan bring to a boil
6 cups water
1 teaspoon salt
Spoon ¼ teaspoon of batter at a time into boiling water. Use edge of a teaspoon, cutting batter against side of bowl. Boil, uncovered, for 10 minutes. Drain and keep warm.

Piquant Honey Chicken

From Ottawa, our nation's capital, we received this delightful glazed chicken specialty. "Piquant" best describes the flavourful blend of honey, lemon and ginger.

In a heavy frypan melt
2 tablespoons butter
Cut in serving portions and brown quickly on all sides
1 (2½- to 3-pound) chicken
Combine and pour over browned chicken
½ cup honey
½ cup water
¼ cup butter, melted
¼ cup lemon juice
1 teaspoon ground ginger
Cover and cook over low heat, basting occasionally, for 35 to 40 minutes, or until chicken is tender.
Makes 5 to 6 servings.

Coq au Vin

Recipes for *coq au vin* were brought to this country by the early French settlers, and it has retained its popularity to the present. Originally diced salt pork was used, but this more modern version calls for side bacon.

Cut into serving pieces
1 (4-pound) chicken
Season with
salt
white pepper
In a heavy saucepan fry until golden brown
½ cup diced bacon (3 or 4 slices)
Remove and drain on absorbent paper.
Add to bacon fat in pan and melt
2 tablespoons butter
Add chicken pieces and brown on all sides. Remove from pan and drain on absorbent paper. Pour off any excess fat, leaving about 3 tablespoons in pan.
Add
12 small onions
½ pound button mushrooms
Cover pan and cook for 5 minutes, or until onions begin to brown slightly.
Remove cover. Add
¼ cup finely chopped green onion
1 garlic clove, crushed
Cook for 1 minute.
Stir in and cook until browned
3 tablespoons flour
Gradually add
½ cup water
2 cups red wine

Cook, stirring constantly, until smooth. Return chicken to pan.

Tie in a cheesecloth bag and add
2 stalks celery
2 sprigs parsley
½ bay leaf
3 peppercorns
1 whole clove
¼ teaspoon thyme

Sprinkle with cooked bacon. Cover, and bring to a boil. Reduce heat and simmer for 45 to 60 minutes, or until chicken is tender.

Arrange chicken and vegetables in serving dish. Skim any excess fat from sauce and remove cheesecloth bag. If sauce is too thin, boil over high heat to obtain desired consistency. Pour sauce over chicken. Sprinkle with chopped fresh parsley.

Makes 4 servings.

Pimiento Chicken Wings

Canadian recipes for chicken wings, legs or breasts indicate the recent trend towards purchasing chicken parts. Wings are most economically priced and this deliciously flavoured recipe presents them at their best.

Wipe with a damp cloth
2 pounds chicken wings

In medium-sized paper bag combine
1 cup all-purpose flour
2 teaspoons salt
4 teaspoons paprika
1 teaspoon chili powder
½ teaspoon pepper

Shake chicken wings in bag, a few at a time, to coat thoroughly with flour. Brown in hot fat in heavy pan.

Meanwhile, drain and force through a sieve
8 canned pimientos

Mix with
1 cup finely chopped onion
2 garlic cloves, finely chopped
2 cups water

Drain any excess fat from pan. Pour pimiento mixture over browned chicken. Cover pan. Simmer for 45 minutes to 1 hour, or until chicken is tender.

Add more water if necessary.

Remove wings to hot serving dish and keep warm.

Blend to make a smooth paste
¼ cup all-purpose flour
water

Stir into liquid. Boil, stirring constantly, until thick and smooth. Pour over chicken.

Makes 6 to 8 servings.

Poulet Orléans

Poulet Orléans originated with the Ministère du Tourisme de Québec, and the name undoubtedly refers to the Ile d'Orléans in the St. Lawrence River, near Quebec City, where apples are plentiful.

Preheat oven to 350° F.

Clean and prepare for stuffing
2 (2 to 2½-pound) chickens

Rub inside of body cavity with
cognac

and sprinkle with
salt
paprika

Mix together
2 cups diced toasted bread
½ cup sliced celery
½ cup sliced unpeeled apples
¼ cup raisins
3 tablespoons melted butter
pinch of thyme
pinch of parsley

Stuff chickens and truss.

In a pan brown stuffed chicken in
butter

Slice thickly and brown lightly in pan
6 unpeeled apples

Cover bottom of casserole dish with browned apple slices. Place chickens in casserole. Cut in half and arrange on breasts.
2 slices bacon

Surround with remaining apple slices.

Bake, covered, in 350° oven for about 1¾ hours, or until tender. Remove cover to brown.

Serve in casserole.

When ready to serve, baste with
½ pint cream (18%)
1½ ounces cognac

Makes 6 servings.

Sweet and Sour Pineapple Chicken

Small wonder that this Chinese specialty is exceedingly popular in Quebec, Ontario and British Columbia. The colour and flavour are exactly right and we thank the Vancouverite who shares it with us. The sauce is equally good with spareribs.

Blend together only until combined
1 cup prepared pancake mix
1 cup water
pinch of garlic powder

Let stand, covered, in refrigerator for 1 hour.

Dip 1-inch cubes of **cooked chicken** *into batter. Drain a few seconds and fry in shallow hot fat until golden brown, about 5 minutes. Serve with Sweet and Sour Sauce and cooked rice.*

Makes 5 to 6 servings.

NOTE: Pieces of uncooked chicken may be used. Prepare as directed above but deep fat fry at 325° F. until tender, about 10 minutes.

SWEET AND SOUR SAUCE
Drain
1 can (19 ounces) pineapple cubes or tidbits

Measure (adding water if necessary)
1 cup drained juice

In a saucepan bring to a boil together with the pineapple juice
1½ cups tomato juice
1 cup water
1 cup vinegar

Mix well together
⅓ cup granulated sugar
¼ cup cornstarch
pinch of garlic powder

Gradually blend dry ingredients into liquid, stirring constantly until thickened.

Stir in drained pineapple and
1 green pepper, thinly sliced
½ cup finely shredded cabbage

Cook until cabbage becomes slightly transparent, but not long enough for green pepper to become soft.

Season to taste with
salt and pepper

If sauce becomes too thick, thin with a little water.

Rice Lake Duckling with Orange Sauce

The name implies that the duckling has been deliciously fattened on the wild rice growing on the shores of this Ontario lake. We hope so, but at any rate, the orange sauce and pickled orange slices make this Cobourg recipe fit for gourmets the world over.

Preheat oven to 300° F.
Clean
1 (5-pound) duckling
Rub inside and out with
powdered ginger
Sprinkle with
salt
pepper
Place in cavity
1 medium onion
1 tart apple
Roast in 300° oven for 2½ hours.

Makes 5 servings.

ORANGE SAUCE
Remove grease from roasting pan.
Stir in
½ cup orange juice
½ cup white wine
Simmer to remove bits from pan.
Mix to a smooth paste
3 tablespoons flour
⅓ cup cold water
Stir into hot liquid and cook, stirring constantly, until thickened. Strain. Garnish duck with Pickled Orange Slices. (see page 138).

Serve sauce separately.

Curried Turkey

Designed for those who long for a *real* curry with lots of zip, this recipe follows the best practice for developing the flavour by cooking the curry with the onion.

In large saucepan melt
¼ cup butter
Blend in
¾ cup all-purpose flour
Stir in
3½ cups turkey or chicken stock

Cook over medium heat, stirring constantly, until thickened.

Simmer for 20 minutes or until desired consistency. Season with

salt
1 teaspoon lemon juice
¼ teaspoon nutmeg

In small saucepan melt

2 tablespoons butter

Add and cook until soft but not browned

1 cup finely chopped onion

Stir in

2 bay leaves
¼ teaspoon thyme
1 tablespoon curry powder
½ cup chicken stock

Bring to boil and stir into first mixture.

Simmer for 15 minutes. Strain.

Just before serving add and heat

3 cups cubed cooked turkey
½ cup cream (18%)

Makes 4 to 5 servings.

Apple Raisin Stuffing

Mix together

4 cups soft stale bread crumbs
2 cups chopped apple
1 cup raisins
⅓ cup finely chopped onion
2 teaspoons salt
1 teaspoon poultry seasoning

Stir in

½ cup butter, melted

Delicious for stuffing roast goose.

Makes about 6 cups.

Bread Stuffing

Fry until onion is transparent

½ cup finely chopped onion
½ cup chopped celery
⅓ to ½ cup butter, melted

Mix thoroughly

7 cups soft stale bread crumbs
(one 24-ounce loaf)
1 teaspoon salt
¼ teaspoon pepper
2 teaspoons poultry seasoning or combination of sage and savory

Combine all ingredients and mix lightly but thoroughly.

Makes about 6 cups, or sufficient for an 8- to 10-pound bird.

Old-Fashioned Stuffing

Omit butter and celery. Reduce onion to ¼ cup. Add ¼ pound cooked sausage meat.

Giblet Stuffing

Simmer giblets in water until tender. Drain. Chop and add to stuffing. If desired, a little of the broth may be added.

Oyster Stuffing

Use ¼ cup butter and add 1 pint oysters, chopped, ¼ cup oyster liquor and 1 tablespoon lemon juice.

Wild Rice Stuffing

Wild rice was a staple food of the Manitoba Indians who collected it in the marshy areas around the reedy lakes; now they harvest it for sale to a commercial firm. To show it off, the stuffing may be baked separately and then used as a bed on which to serve the wild duck or other game.

Wash and drain

1 cup wild rice

In a frypan melt

¼ cup butter

Add rice with

½ pound sliced fresh mushrooms
¼ cup chopped onion

Cook until rice begins to turn yellow.

Remove from heat and stir in

1 can (10 ounces) consommé
1½ cups water
½ teaspoon savory
¼ teaspoon salt
¼ teaspoon sweet basil
½ cup fine dry bread crumbs

Makes about 4 cups.

Fish

The bounty of the Grand Banks off Newfoundland led to the first settlement in Canada. Subsequently our innumerable inland lakes and both the Atlantic and Pacific Oceans have yielded a tremendous harvest of fish to grace our tables. These recipes represent the best from coast to coast.

Cod Tongues

From Newfoundland, where fish means cod unless otherwise specified, we received this recipe for cooking cod tongues, a specialty of the island. More than any other fish, cod has helped to make history: it was cod that first attracted white settlers to this continent.

Wash in salted water
   cod tongues
Scrape lightly to clean.
Roll in
   flour, cornmeal or fine oatmeal
Fry in pork fat until brown on both sides.
Cod heads, sounds, jowls or "fishes faces" are prepared in the same way.

Cod au Gratin

Even in the Newfoundland courts of law "fish" means "cod". A husky fish with a market weight of from two-and-a-half to twenty-five pounds, the cod has been referred to as the "beef of the sea."

Preheat oven to 350° F.
Grease 3 individual casseroles.
Simmer until it flakes easily
   1 pound cod fillets
in
   1½ cups milk
taking care not to let the milk boil.
Drain, reserving liquid. (If necessary, add cold milk to make 1½ cups.) Flake cod into prepared casseroles.
Combine in saucepan and cook over medium heat
   3 tablespoons butter, melted
   4 tablespoons flour
   ½ teaspoon salt
   pinch of pepper
Gradually stir in the reserved liquid. Cook, stirring constantly, until thickened. Add ½ cup sauce to each casserole.
Top each with
   2 tablespoons grated cheese
Place casseroles in shallow pan containing about ¼ inch of water.
Bake in 350° oven for 15 to 20 minutes, or until piping hot and cheese is melted.
Makes 3 servings.

Fish and Brewis

As quoted from *The Treasury of Newfoundland Dishes:*

"Newfoundland families in all income brackets, and in all geographical locations, serve fish and brewis with varying frequency, especially for Sunday morning breakfast. Sometimes the brewis is served with bacon or ham instead of fish. The fish, of course, is the salt cod and the brewis is made from the hard bread which can now be bought in grocery stores."

Soak in cold water for 12 hours
2 pounds salt cod

Soak in cold water for 12 hours
1 pound hard bread

Drain fish and cover with fresh cold water. Bring to a boil and cook for 30 minutes, or until fish is tender. Remove from heat and drain.

Cook hard bread in water, uncovered, for 5 minutes. Strain.

Serve on breakfast plate — one square of salt fish and serving of brewis topped with scrunchions.

SCRUNCHIONS
Cut into ¼-inch squares
¼ pound fat salt pork
Fry until crisp.

Hugger-in-Buff

Traditional recipes on Canada's East Coast evolved mainly from the use of foods that could be stored for the long cold winter. In every house there was a supply of dried, salt codfish, potatoes and fat salt pork. A favourite combination of these ingredients was known in different areas as fish and scrunchions, Dutch mess and house bankin as well as hugger-in-buff. Although the origin of the names is lost in history, the dish still retains its popularity in the fishing villages.

Freshen by soaking overnight in sufficient water to cover
1 pound salt cod

Cut in serving portions.
Peel and cut into eighths
4 medium potatoes

Place cod and potatoes in a saucepan, cover with boiling water and simmer for about 20 minutes, or until potatoes are tender. Drain and place on a warm platter.

While fish and potatoes are cooking, fry until crisp
¼ pound fat salt pork, diced

Remove pork scraps from pan.
Place in pan and cook until tender
2 medium onions, sliced

Return pork scraps to pan with
2 tablespoons vinegar
¼ cup milk

Bring liquid to a boil and pour over potatoes and cod.

Makes 4 servings.

St. Andrews Clam Pie

Summer is clam digging season down East. Each year, millions of Atlantic coast clams are raked, scooped, hoed or dredged from their sandy moorings, to end up fresh or canned on someone's dining room table. Maritime homemakers know dozens of appetizing ways of preparing these bivalves. This recipe for clam pie was originally developed by a homemaker living in St. Andrews, New Brunswick, for her husband to take on weekend hunting trips.

Preheat oven to 325° F.
Grease a 13 x 9-inch baking pan.
Strain, reserving liquor
2 cans (5 ounces each) clams
Wash clams well.
Panfry until crisp
¼ pound side bacon, diced
Peel and thinly slice
5 medium potatoes
Arrange half of potatoes in prepared pan with half of
2 medium onions, thinly sliced
Arrange half of clams on top.
Sprinkle with
½ teaspoon salt
¼ teaspoon pepper
Repeat with remaining potatoes, onion and clams. Season again. Sprinkle with bacon scraps and rendered fat.
Pour over all
2 cups liquid (clam liquor plus water)
Bake in 325° oven for 1 hour.
Prepare sufficient pastry for a 2-crust pie.
Remove pan from oven and cover with pastry. Prick pastry to allow steam to escape.
Return to a 450° oven for 20 minutes, or until pastry is lightly browned.
Makes 8 servings.

85

Maddock Finnan Haddie

Scotland's national dish shows off our own smoked haddock so well that we have adopted it as our own, but we serve it at dinner rather than at breakfast.

Skin and cut in pieces
1 smoked haddock

Lay pieces in heavy pan and dot with
1 tablespoon butter

Cover pan and steam for 5 minutes.
Thicken
¾ cup milk

with
1 tablespoon cornstarch

Pour over fish, bring to a boil and boil for 1 minute.
Serve with sauce poured over fish.

Fish Cakes

In the Atlantic Provinces there are many recipes for fish cakes, all with regional variations, but basically the cakes are a combination of salt fish and mashed potatoes. Raw onions, cooked onions, eggs, butter and seasonings are added in varying amounts according to custom and area. Sir James Dunn, industrialist and financier, preferred these fish cakes nearly green with parsley.

Cover with cold water and let stand overnight
1 pound boneless salt cod

Drain.

Cover with fresh cold water and bring slowly to simmering point. Drain and flake fish.

OR

Simmer
1 pound fresh cod or haddock

Combine drained, flaked fish with
2 cups mashed cooked potatoes
1 small onion, chopped
2 tablespoons butter, melted
1 egg, beaten
3 to 4 tablespoons chopped parsley
salt and pepper

Shape into cakes (if necessary use a little flour to hold them together). If desired, cakes may be coated with
¼ cup fine dry bread crumbs

Panfry in hot fat until crisp and brown. Turn and brown on other side.

May be served with Tomato Sauce (see page 90) or heated chili sauce.

Makes 4 to 6 servings.

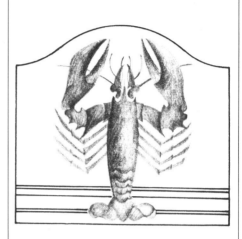

Stuffed Halibut Steaks

Generally, halibut steaks should be at least one inch thick, since they have a tendency to dry out if much thinner. Should the steaks not measure up to the ruler test, then try stuffing two of them as in this Nova Scotia recipe.

Preheat oven to 450° F.

Grease a baking dish.

In frypan melt
¼ cup butter

Add and cook for about 15 minutes, or until tender
¼ cup chopped onion
¼ cup diced celery

Add
½ teaspoon salt
¼ teaspoon seasoning (savory, thyme, tarragon, sage, mint, poultry seasoning, etc.)

Stir in, tossing lightly
2 cups soft bread crumbs

Add
1 tomato, chopped

Spread stuffing between
2 halibut steaks ½ to ¾ inch thick (about 1 pound each)

Place in prepared baking dish.

Brush with

melted butter

Measure total thickness of steaks and stuffing.

Bake in 450° oven, allowing 10 minutes per inch thickness for fresh fish, 20 minutes per inch thickness for frozen fish.

Makes 4 to 6 servings.

Boiled Lobster

Years ago on our Atlantic seaboard lobsters could be purchased for a penny apiece. Today the demand is so great you would pay more than a hundred times that much, as in most years the lobster fishery is the most valuable of all the east coast fisheries. Atlantic lobsters range in weight from three-quarters of a pound to over three pounds.

Fill a deep kettle with enough water to cover lobsters.

For each quart of water add

1 tablespoon salt

Bring water to a rapid boil.

Grasp live lobster across middle of back and plunge head first into water. With a wooden spoon, push lobster under water. When water has returned to a boil, reduce heat and simmer 15 minutes for first pound, 5 minutes for each additional pound. Remove from water and cool.

Set lobster on its back, and with a sharp knife or scissors, slit open on underside from head to tail. Remove dark intestinal vein that runs through body at the centre. Cut off membrane. Discard sac or "lady" behind the head. Serve hot or cold with lemon and drawn butter.

Broiled Lobster

The lobster that most Canadians are familiar with is characteristic to the shores of North America and Europe, in the cold waters of the North Atlantic Ocean. It is easily identified by its large heavy claws.

Plunge into boiling water for about 5 minutes

4 (1-pound) live lobsters

Remove from water.

Split lengthwise and clean: remove dark vein that runs through the body at the centre. Cut off membrane. Discard sac or "lady" behind the head.

Open as flat as possible.

Lay shell side down on grill, or shell side up on broiler pan.

Broil or barbecue using medium heat, for 15 minutes, brushing with

melted butter

Turn lobsters and grill for 5 minutes longer.

Serve with melted butter, vinegar, and salt and pepper.

Makes 4 servings.

Deer Island Lobster Stew

This is the way lobster fishermen along the New Brunswick Bay of Fundy coast make stew. We've named it after the island, near St. Andrews, where one of the world's largest lobster pounds is located.

Boil and allow to cool (see above)

2 (1¼-pound) live lobsters

Remove meat from shells and cut into chunks.

OR

Thaw

1 can (14 ounces) frozen lobster meat

In a saucepan melt

¼ cup butter

Add lobster meat and cook until pink.

Season with

½ teaspoon salt
pinch of pepper

In a large saucepan melt

2 tablespoons butter

Add and fry until transparent

1 medium onion, finely chopped

Stir in

2 cups diced raw potatoes
1 teaspoon salt
2 cups boiling water

Simmer over medium heat for about 5 minutes, or until potatoes are cooked. Stir in cooked lobster and

2 cups whole milk, heated

Heat thoroughly, but do not boil. Pour into serving bowls that contain

broken soda crackers

Makes 4 to 5 servings.

French Fried Scallops

Nine out of ten of Canada's scallops come from the Digby area of Nova Scotia, home of the dragger fleet that fishes off St. George's Bank. Scallops have been referred to as the "filet mignon of the sea."

Preheat deep fat to 375° F.

Wipe with a damp cloth and cut if necessary
  1 pound scallops
Roll in a mixture of
  ¼ cup all-purpose flour
  salt
  pepper
Dip in a mixture of
  1 egg
  2 tablespoons cold water
Then roll in
  ¾ cup fine dry bread crumbs
Fry in preheated deep fat for about 3 to 4 minutes, or until golden brown.

Serve with Tartar Sauce (see page 93).

Makes 3 to 4 servings.

Malpeque Oyster Stew

One of the indications of the richness of the new land that impressed the earliest arrivals to our country, was the great abundance, large size and excellence of the oysters they found along the coastline. We have named this delectable stew after Malpeque Bay, Prince Edward Island, where the oysters are noted for their quality.

In a frypan melt
  ¼ cup butter
Add
  1 pint shucked (shelled) oysters and their liquor
Simmer for about 3 minutes, or until edges begin to curl.
Scald
  1 quart (5 cups) milk
Stir oysters into milk and add
  1½ teaspoons salt
  pinch of pepper
  pinch of nutmeg
Serve immediately.

Makes 6 servings.

Scalloped Oysters

The oyster beds of Maritime Canada produce fine-quality oysters, but these are not named according to the producing region as frequently as in the United States. Malpeque Bay (P.E.I.) and Cara-quettes (New Brunswick) are to a limited extent exceptions. Be sure not to over-cook oysters as they lose their tenderness — for small-sized oysters you may find it necessary to reduce the cooking time in this recipe.

Preheat oven to 350° F.
Grease a small casserole thoroughly.
Place in prepared casserole
  ½ pint shucked (shelled) oysters
alternately with
  1¼ cups coarse cracker crumbs
Combine and pour over oysters
  ½ cup butter, melted
  ½ teaspoon Worcestershire sauce
  ¼ teaspoon salt
  pinch of pepper
Cover with a layer of crumbs.
Pour over top
  ¼ cup milk
Bake in 350° oven for 30 minutes.

Makes 2 to 3 servings.

Soused Herring or Mackerel

Originally pickling was a means of preserving the fish, but now it is considered a great delicacy, particularly in Nova Scotia and Prince Edward Island. This recipe captures the flavour, but no attempt has been made to preserve the herring or mackerel.

Preheat oven to 350° F.
Fillet and skin
  2 pounds fresh herring or mackerel
Cut into serving pieces.
Place fish in baking dish and add
  1 cup vinegar
  ½ cup water
  1 teaspoon salt
  1 tablespoon mixed pickling spices
  2 thin slices onion
Cover, and bake in 350° oven for 15 minutes.

Allow to cool in liquid. Drain before serving.

Makes 3 to 4 servings.

Gibelotte Sorelaise

A French-Canadian dish eaten in many homes around Sorel, Quebec, where *barbotte* (catfish) are plentiful in the early spring.

Skin and clean
2 pounds barbotte (catfish)

Cover fish with boiling water and simmer gently for 5 minutes. Drain and cool. Remove bones.

Panfry until crisp and brown
1 pound salt pork, diced

Remove pork scraps from pan.

In the same pan fry until tender
1 onion, chopped
1 pound fresh mushrooms, sliced

In a deep kettle combine fried vegetables with
4 cups sliced raw potatoes
2 cups sliced raw carrots
1 can (10 ounces) green peas
1 can (10 ounces) niblet corn
1 can (28 ounces) tomatoes
1½ teaspoons salt

Cover, and simmer about 1 hour. Add fish and pork scraps. If stew is too thick, add boiling water or fish stock to obtain desired consistency.

Cover, and simmer gently 10 minutes longer.

Makes 12 servings.

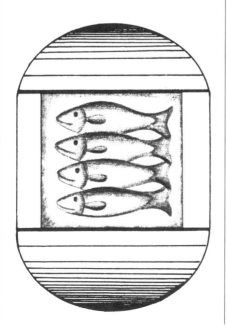

Quebec Salmon Pie

In rural Quebec this version of shepherd's pie is a family favourite. Some recipes do not call for the addition of a pastry top.

Preheat oven to 400° F.

Grease individual casseroles or a 9-inch pie plate.

Drain, flake and crush bones from
1 can (15½ ounces) salmon
OR
Flake sufficient cooked fresh salmon to give
2 cups flaked salmon

Combine
2½ to 3 cups mashed potatoes
½ cup finely chopped onion
3 tablespoons butter
½ teaspoon salt
¼ teaspoon savory
pinch of pepper

Place half the potato mixture in bottom of prepared casseroles. Cover with salmon. Top with remaining potato.

Prepare sufficient pastry and cover casseroles or pie plate.

Bake in 400° oven for 25 to 30 minutes, or until golden brown.

Makes 6 servings.

Fried Bass

Staple ingredients in a Canadian fisherman's knapsack are cornmeal and lemon; sometimes a plastic lemon filled with juice replaces the fresh fruit. The following recipe, the most commonly used for freshly caught fish, explains why.

Combine
1 cup cornmeal
1 teaspoon salt
pinch of pepper

Heat
¼ cup bacon fat (or butter)
in a heavy skillet.

Roll
2 to 3 pounds cleaned whole bass
in cornmeal and brown in fat about 6 minutes on each side, or until fish flakes easily with a fork.

Mix together
1 tablespoon lemon juice
1 teaspoon Worcestershire sauce

Pour over fish when serving.

Makes 4 to 6 servings.

Fish Rolls

Maritimers prefer their fish plainly cooked without embellishments but we hasten to add that cod, haddock and sole, being mild-flavoured, suit a little dressing-up and saucing as in this inlander's recipe.

Preheat oven to 350° F.

Spread flat (if very thick, split into thin, lengthwise slices)
   1 pound fresh fillets (cod, haddock or sole)

Combine
   1½ cups coarse soft bread crumbs
   2 tablespoons soft butter
   1 tablespoon finely chopped onion
   1 tablespoon chopped parsley
   1 teaspoon salt
   pinch of pepper
   1 egg, slightly beaten

Spread stuffing on fillets. Roll up like a jelly roll and secure with toothpicks.

Coat rolls with a mixture of
   2 tablespoons flour
   salt and pepper

In a frypan brown in
   2 tablespoons shortening

Arrange rolls in shallow baking dish and spread with
   1 can (10 ounces) condensed cream of mushroom soup

Sprinkle with a mixture of
   1 tablespoon butter
   1 cup soft bread crumbs
   pinch of salt

Bake in 350° oven for 40 minutes, or until fish flakes easily with a fork.

Makes 4 servings.

Broiled Perch

The tender, delicate flavour of perch from our inland lakes responds best to the simplest cooking method as in this Ontario recipe.

Place, if unskinned, skin side down on greased broiler rack
   2 pounds large perch fillets

Sprinkle with
   ½ teaspoon salt

Brush with a mixture of
   2 tablespoons melted butter
   1 teaspoon lemon juice
   pinch of marjoram

Broil 2 to 3 inches below heat for about 5 minutes.

Makes 4 servings.

Fried Pickerel Fillets with Tomato Sauce

Pickerel is the fish of many names—walleye, or wall-eyed pike, pike-perch, and in French Canada *doré*. This Ontario recipe serves it with a simple-to-make sauce.

Cut in serving portions
   2 to 3 pounds pickerel fillets

Combine
   1 egg
   2 tablespoons milk

Dip fish in egg mixture and then in
   flour

Fry until brown on both sides in
   melted butter

TOMATO SAUCE

Meanwhile, fry
   ¾ cup chopped onion
in
   ¼ cup butter

Blend in
   2 tablespoons flour

Stir in
   1 can (10 ounces) condensed cream of tomato soup
   1 soup can of water

Bring to a boil and simmer for a minute or two.

Pour over cooked fillets to serve.

Makes 4 to 6 servings.

Pike with Orange Rice Stuffing

The pike, or jackfish, can be bought dressed or filleted, fresh or frozen. When cooked the flesh becomes white, firm and flaky.

Preheat oven to 450° F.

Grease a baking pan.

Clean, removing scales and fins,
   1 (3- to 4-pound) pike

If desired, remove head and tail.

Wash and dry fish and sprinkle inside with
   salt

Stuff fish loosely with Orange Rice Stuffing. Fasten the opening with small skewers or toothpicks and lace with string. Place fish on prepared pan and brush with

melted butter

Measure stuffed fish at thickest part.

Bake in 450° oven allowing 10 minutes cooking time per inch of stuffed thickness.

ORANGE RICE STUFFING

Melt in a saucepan

¼ **cup butter**

Stir in

1 **cup chopped celery with leaves**
3 **tablespoons chopped onion**
2 **tablespoons grated orange rind**

Cook about 5 minutes, or until tender.

Blend in

¾ **cup water**
½ **cup orange juice**
2 **tablespoons lemon juice**
½ **teaspoon salt**

Bring to a rolling boil and stir in

1 **cup packaged precooked rice**

Cover, remove from heat and let stand for 5 minutes. (The excess moisture in the stuffing will be absorbed during baking of fish.)

Makes 4 to 5 servings.

Fisherman's Trout

This campfire way of cooking freshly caught trout uses materials at hand and no frypan. Merely reading the recipe brings back memories of an outdoor campfire on the shores of one of Canada's innumerable inland lakes.

Prepare a bed of glowing coals.

Clean

trout

Wrap in fern leaves.

Pack each in mud, ½ to 1 inch thick.

Make a pit in the centre of the coals. Lay mud-wrapped fish in pit and cover with coals.

Requires 45 minutes to 1 hour to cook, when the dried mud will crack off.

If desired, sprinkle with

salt
pepper
lemon juice

Salmon Loaf

For party occasions this salmon loaf is pressed into a fish-shaped mould, but for everyday eating an oven-proof bowl or loaf pan is used. Steaming keeps the mixture from drying out during cooking. For economy, use the lighter coloured varieties of salmon.

Blend together

1 **can (15½ ounces) salmon**
1 **cup mashed cooked potatoes**
½ **cup milk**
1½ **cups crushed cracker crumbs**
2 **eggs**
2 **tablespoons lemon juice**
1 **tablespoon butter**
½ **teaspoon salt**
¼ **teaspoon pepper**

Pack into greased bowl or mould. Cover with wax paper and foil. Tie tightly.

Steam for 1½ hours.

Serve hot, with lemon or egg sauce, or serve cold, with mayonnaise.

Makes 8 servings.

Lake Erie Smelt

Parmesan cheese highlights the flavour of this delicate fish, which abounds in Canada's inland lakes. It is a true sign of spring when one reads in the newspaper where the smelts are running, or sees the night-time fishermen with their nets. Smelting is a family activity with members of all ages participating.

Clean and bone

2 **pounds smelts**

Coat with a mixture of

½ **cup flour**
½ **teaspoon salt**
pinch of pepper

Dip in a mixture of

1 **egg, beaten**
1 **tablespoon lemon juice**

Roll in a mixture of

½ **cup cracker crumbs**
⅓ **cup grated Parmesan cheese**

Panfry in about ¼ inch hot fat. When golden brown on one side, turn and brown the other side.

Makes 6 servings.

Whitefish Filet Piquant

The whitefish is an inland lake fish that is sold either whole or filleted. This Ontario recipe provides a tangy way of cooking the fillets, which may be either fresh or frozen.

Preheat oven to 450° F.

Grease a shallow baking dish.

Cover bottom of prepared dish with
½ cup bread crumbs

Arrange in dish
2 pounds whitefish fillets

Mix together until smooth
½ cup butter, melted
1 tablespoon vinegar
1 tablespoon Worcestershire sauce
1 tablespoon lemon juice
1 teaspoon salt
1 teaspoon prepared mustard
pinch of pepper

Pour over fish, allowing mixture to cover each fillet.

Sprinkle with
paprika

Bake in 450° oven, allowing 10 minutes per inch thickness for fresh fish, 20 minutes per inch thickness for frozen fish.

If necessary, baste once or twice during cooking.

Makes 6 servings.

Cook over medium heat, stirring constantly, until thickened.

Stir in
½ cup chopped onion
OR
2 tablespoons instant minced onion
1 teaspoon dry mustard
2 teaspoons parsley flakes
2 tablespoons lemon juice
½ cup sherry (optional)
2 teaspoons Worcestershire sauce

Add and mix together lightly
½ cup chopped pimiento
2 cans (7 ounces each) tuna chunks with oil
2 cans (4¼ ounces each) shrimps, drained
2 cans (6 ounces each) crabmeat, drained

Turn into prepared casserole.

Mix together and sprinkle over top
6 tablespoons butter, melted
1⅓ cups corn flake crumbs

Bake in 400° oven for 20 minutes, or until bubbling.

Garnish with sliced tomatoes.

Makes 12 servings.

Brandon Seafood Newburg

Traditionally Newburg is made with lobster, but for inlanders, this version suggests a more economical assortment of seafood, blended with pimiento to give the reddish colour. We've named it after a city on the banks of the Assiniboine River, in our most central province, Manitoba.

Preheat oven to 400° F.

Grease a 2-quart casserole lightly.

In a saucepan melt
¼ cup butter

Blend in until smooth
¼ cup flour

Gradually blend in
2 cups milk

Baked Whitefish with Tartar Sauce

Whether the whitefish comes from Lake Wabamum, in Alberta, or Great Slave Lake, in the Northwest Territories, this stuffing enhances the delicate flavour. For easier serving, the fish may be boned and the two fillets stuffed.

Preheat oven to 450° F.

Line a shallow pan with parchment or foil. Arrange cheesecloth on top of this (fish can then be lifted out easily to platter).

Clean, wash and dry thoroughly
1 (6-pound) whitefish

Stuff loosely with Lemon Rice Stuffing, allowing about ¾ cup for each pound of dressed fish.

Brush with
vegetable oil

Sprinkle with
flour
paprika
salt

Wrap with
4 or 5 strips bacon

Place on prepared pan. Bake in 450° oven allowing 10 minutes per inch thickness.

To serve, garnish with tomato or lemon slices and crisp cornmeal scrunchions (cornmeal-covered salt pork that has been diced and panfried until crisp). Serve with Tartar Sauce.

Makes 10 servings.

LEMON RICE STUFFING

Cook about 5 minutes or until tender
1 cup finely diced celery
⅓ cup finely chopped onion
in
⅓ cup butter

Add and bring to a boil
1½ cups water
¼ cup lemon juice
1 tablespoon grated lemon rind
1 teaspoon salt
¼ teaspoon thyme
pinch of black pepper

Add and mix just sufficiently to moisten
1½ cups packaged precooked rice

Cover. Remove from heat and let stand 5 minutes.

TARTAR SAUCE

Combine in a small bowl
1 teaspoon icing sugar
1 teaspoon dry mustard
¼ teaspoon salt
pinch of pepper
pinch of onion powder
2 egg yolks

Beat at high speed of electric mixer.

Slowly add
½ cup vegetable oil
Alternately with
3 tablespoons vinegar

When sauce is thickened, stir in
1 tablespoon chopped olives
1 tablespoon capers
1 tablespoon chopped pickle
1 tablespoon chopped parsley

Winnipeg Goldeye

The goldeye was first smoked by a Scotsman living in Winnipeg who became lonely for his homeland and for the taste of his favourite fish, a kipper. The fish that he smoked to a rosy hue, hoping to get the taste and colour of a kipper is known today as the Winnipeg Goldeye.

Goldeye may be cooked with head and tail on or off.

Place
1 goldeye per serving

on greased foil. Fold foil over fish, securing open edges with double folds to make package watertight.

Place package in rapidly boiling water. When water returns to a boil, cover, and cook for 10 minutes (20 minutes if frozen).

Unwrapped goldeye may be cooked for 15 to 20 minutes in a steamer or simmered in water for 10 minutes, or until the fish flakes readily. Serve hot, with lemon wedges.

NOTE: This is the recommended method for poaching salmon or other fish to retain all the delicate flavour.

Poached Alaska Black Cod

The Alaska black cod is not even a close relative of the Atlantic cod, but when smoked is considered a delicacy by Canadians living along our Western coast.

Place in a frypan or saucepan
2 pounds Alaska black cod

Cover fish with cold water.

Cover pan, set over low heat and simmer for 1 minute. Drain.

Repeat simmering process once or twice, depending on saltiness of fish.

Simmer in last water until fish flakes readily when tested with a fork, about 10 minutes per inch thickness. Drain.

Serve plain, with lemon or butter sauce.

If desired, place cooked fish in a greased casserole, add milk and bake in preheated 350° F. oven for 10 minutes, or until milk is hot.

Makes 6 servings.

Golden Broiled Arctic Char Steaks

94

Arctic char, or *ilkalupik* as the Eskimos call this pink-fleshed fish of the northern ocean, has become a gourmet item of restaurants and hotels in southern Canada. Catching the fish is an Eskimo family affair; the fish are trapped in stone weirs and all help to spear them.

On a greased broiler pan place
2 pounds char steaks

Mix together
1 tablespoon chopped onion
2 tablespoons lemon juice
1 teaspoon salt
pinch of pepper
¼ teaspoon tarragon
¼ cup butter, melted

Baste steaks with half of sauce and broil 2 to 4 inches from heat for fresh fish, (6 to 8 inches for frozen). When browned, turn over and baste with remaining sauce. Broil 10 minutes per inch thickness for fresh char, 20 minutes per inch thickness for frozen. Sprinkle with paprika and garnish with parsley.

Makes 4 servings.

Oyster Bay Fried Oysters

Oysters harvested off the Gulf Islands and the east coast of Vancouver Island attain a great size yet remain tender and delectable. Tourists visiting Campbell River's famous fishing grounds are amazed at the large piles of oyster shells lying between the road and seashore. In season, roadside cafés specialize in fried oysters and oyster stew.

Beat together slightly
1 egg
1 tablespoon water or oyster liquor

Heat frypan over medium heat or preheat skillet to 375° F. Add
⅓ cup vegetable oil

Roll
1 dozen (½ pint) shucked (shelled) oysters

in a mixture of
1 cup bread crumbs
salt
pepper

Dip into beaten egg and again roll in crumbs. Cook in frypan until delicately browned. Drain on absorbent paper.

Serve with
fried and drained slices bacon

Garnish with
lemon slices
parsley sprigs

Makes 2 servings.

Stuffed Fraser River Salmon

Many may prefer to stuff salmon fillets as suggested in this recipe from Vancouver — it does make for easier serving at the table.

Clean and fillet
1 (6- to 7-pound) salmon or halibut

Preheat oven to 450° F.

Drain and chop coarsely
1 small can shrimps or lobster

Mix in
5 cups soft bread crumbs
1 cup finely chopped celery
3 tablespoons finely chopped onion
2 tablespoons finely chopped green pepper
1 tablespoon grated lemon rind
1 tablespoon lemon juice
1½ teaspoons chopped parsley
1 teaspoon salt
¼ teaspoon pepper
⅓ cup butter, melted
½ cup water

Butter a sheet of foil large enough to wrap around the salmon. Place 1 salmon fillet on foil. Press stuffing onto fillet and cover with other fillet. Fold foil over fish and seal in a packet.

Place on a baking sheet and bake in 450° oven, allowing 10 minutes per inch thickness.

Makes 10 servings.

Campbell River Baked Salmon

British Columbia salmon in season may be purchased in most cities and towns across the country, but many an ardent fisherman has travelled to such famous spots as Campbell River on northern Vancouver Island to try his luck. Naturally it should be prepared as in this recipe from Vancouver.

Preheat oven to 450° F.

Clean, wash and dry thoroughly a
  6 pound whole salmon

Place on a piece of foil sufficiently large enough to enclose fish, and transfer to baking sheet.

Sprinkle inside of fish with
  salt

Stuff loosely with Bread and Onion Stuffing, allowing about ¾ cup for each pound of dressed fish.

Fasten opening with skewers and lace with string or sew with coarse thread.

Rub outside of fish with
  ¼ cup soft butter

Combine
  ¼ cup white wine
  ¼ cup white vinegar
  1 tablespoon tarragon vinegar

Spoon a small amount over fish. Fasten ends and seam of foil, leaving loose at centre. Bake in 450° oven, allowing 10 minutes per inch thickness. During baking period, baste occasionally with remaining liquid.

Makes 10 servings.

BREAD AND ONION STUFFING
Cook about 5 minutes or until tender
  ⅓ cup chopped onion
  ⅓ cup diced celery
in
  3 tablespoons butter
Add and toss lightly
  1 teaspoon salt
  ½ teaspoon seasoning, (poultry seasoning, savory, thyme, sage, etc.)
  pinch of pepper
  3 cups soft bread crumbs
Makes sufficient to stuff a 6-pound fish.

Spicy Broiled Salmon Steaks

The Atlantic and Pacific salmon are different species, and far be it from us to enter into a discussion of the relative merits of each. Both are frequently called after the river where they are caught — Miramichi, Restigouche, and, in the West, Fraser River and Campbell River to name a few examples.

Place in a greased broiler pan
  2 pounds salmon steaks, cut 1 inch thick
Combine
  ¼ cup vegetable oil
  3 tablespoons lemon juice
  1 tablespoon finely chopped onion
  1 teaspoon grated lemon rind
  ½ teaspoon salt
  ¼ teaspoon dried marjoram
  pinch of pepper
Pour over salmon steaks and marinate for 15 to 20 minutes, turning once.

Broil 2 to 4 inches below heat. Allow a total of 10 minutes broiling per inch thickness for fresh salmon steaks. Turn once after 5 minutes and brush with marinade.

Makes 4 to 6 servings.

Smoked Salmon Scramble

Salmon is a fish of international fame and the pride of our Pacific northwest. About three-quarters of the large West Coast catch finds its way to the canneries, but when salted and smoked, salmon is a gourmet's delight.

Cut or break into small pieces
  ¼ pound smoked salmon
    OR
  1 can (3½ ounces) smoked salmon
Beat slightly
  6 eggs
Stir in salmon with
  ¼ cup milk
Pour into hot frypan containing
  1 tablespoon butter
Stir slowly over medium heat until cooked.

Garnish with chopped parsley.

Makes 3 to 4 servings.

Cakes, Fillings, and Icings

Cakes

Many years ago cakes were leavened with eggs or, sometimes, yeast. The use of baking powder is a more recent innovation. Recipes for baking powder, in fact, appeared in cook books at one time, as it was made in the home.

Some of these cakes originated years ago; some like the chiffon cakes are completely modern, but all of them are moist, tender and flavourful, and all of the recipes have been completely updated. We've included an assortment of fillings and icings which show them off at their prettiest.

Penticton Apple Chiffon Cake

This recent addition to the innumerable applesauce cake recipes available has a lightness and flavour all its own. Nova Scotia, New Brunswick, Southern Quebec, Ontario and British Columbia are renowned for the high quality of the apples they produce both for domestic markets and for export; the best-known varieties grown are McIntosh, Northern Spy and Delicious.

Preheat oven to 350° F.

Beat to form stiff but moist peaks
  6 egg whites
  ½ teaspoon cream of tartar
Gradually add
  ¾ cup granulated sugar
beating until very stiff and shiny.

Sift together into small mixer bowl
  1¾ cups pastry (soft wheat) flour
  3 teaspoons baking powder
  1 teaspoon salt
  1 teaspoon cinnamon
Blend in
  ½ cup lightly packed brown sugar
Add and beat until smooth (30 seconds with mixer)
  ½ cup vegetable oil
  6 egg yolks
  1 cup sweetened applesauce
Fold egg yolk mixture thoroughly into meringue.

Turn into ungreased 10-inch tube pan. Bake in 350° oven for 55 to 65 minutes, or until cake springs back when lightly touched.
Invert and cool in pan. When cool, loosen edges and remove cake.

Rougemont Applesauce Cake

An applesauce cake, by its very nature, is moist, and this one from Rougemont, east of Montreal, has a delightful spicy flavour and aroma.

Preheat oven to 350° F.

Grease a 9-inch square cake pan.

Line bottom with wax paper or dust lightly with flour.
Sift together
  1¾ cups pastry (soft wheat) flour
  2 teaspoons baking powder
  ½ teaspoon salt
  1½ teaspoons cinnamon
  ½ teaspoon nutmeg
Cream
  ½ cup shortening
Blend in, beating until light and fluffy
  1 cup lightly packed brown sugar
Beat in
  2 eggs
  ½ teaspoon vanilla

Stir dry ingredients into creamed mixture alternately with
  1 cup sweetened applesauce
Make 3 dry and 2 liquid additions, combining lightly after each.
Turn into prepared pan.

Bake in 350° oven for 40 to 45 minutes, or until cake springs back when lightly touched.

Bûche de Noël—Yule Log

Yule log for serving between Christmas and New Year's.

Prepare Jelly Roll (see page 103).
Dissolve
  1 teaspoon instant coffee
in
  1 tablespoon boiling water
Allow to cool.

Melt, then set to one side
  4 squares unsweetened chocolate
Beat together until fluffy
  ¼ cup butter
  1¼ cups sifted icing sugar
  2 egg yolks
  cooled coffee
  1 teaspoon vanilla

Blend in 1 tablespoon of the melted chocolate.

Use ¾ cup as filling for jelly roll.

Blend the rest of the melted chocolate into remaining filling and spread on outside, marking to resemble a log.

Butter Cake

Many Canadian homemakers know the classic butter cake by heart to whip up at a moment's notice. The easy variation shows off the fantastic wild blueberry crop of Cumberland County, Nova Scotia, and is delicious served warm.

Preheat oven to 350° F.

Grease an 8-inch square cake pan. Line bottom with wax paper or dust lightly with flour.

Sift or blend together
   1½ cups all-purpose flour
   ½ teaspoon salt
   2 teaspoons baking powder

Cream
   ½ cup butter

Gradually blend in
   1 cup granulated sugar
   2 eggs
   1 teaspoon vanilla

Beat until light and fluffy.

Add sifted dry ingredients to creamed mixture alternately with
   ¾ cup milk

Make 3 dry and 2 liquid additions, combining lightly after each.

Turn into prepared pan.

Bake in 350° oven for 50 to 55 minutes, or until cake springs back when lightly touched.

Remove from pan and allow to cool.

Cumberland Blueberry Cake

Add ¼ teaspoon nutmeg to dry ingredients and fold 1 cup fresh blueberries into batter before baking. While still hot, cut in squares and serve upside down with Hot Honey-Butter Sauce (see page 121).

Butternut Spice Cake

This recipe is listed as Trumpour Cake in a handwritten family cook book that was passed along from mother to daughter. It was "company" cake and was served on the best pedestal cake plate, never iced, just dusted with fine sugar.

The difficulty with this cake was to gather the butternuts before the squirrels found them and then to enlist someone with time and patience to shell them and pry out the nutmeats. In years gone by, butternut trees were plentiful around the Bay of Quinte, in Ontario, where this recipe originated.

Preheat oven to 350° F.

Grease generously a 9-inch tube pan, plain or fluted.

Sprinkle bottom and halfway up sides of pan evenly with
   ½ cup finely chopped butternuts (pecans or walnuts)

Sift together
   2 cups pastry (soft wheat) flour
   1 teaspoon baking soda
   1 teaspoon cinnamon
   ½ teaspoon allspice
   ½ teaspoon nutmeg
   ½ teaspoon salt

Cream
   ⅔ cup butter

Blend in, beating until light and fluffy
   1⅓ cups lightly packed brown sugar

Beat in
   2 eggs

Stir dry ingredients into creamed mixture alternately with
   1 cup buttermilk or sour milk

Make 3 dry and 2 liquid additions, combining lightly after each.

Blend in
   ½ cup finely chopped butternuts (pecans or walnuts)

Turn gently into prepared pan.

Bake in 350° oven for 45 to 50 minutes, or until cake springs back when lightly touched. Cool in pan for 10 minutes.

Turn out on cake rack and cool completely. Leave upside down and sprinkle sifted icing sugar over cake before serving.

Christmas Cake

Plan on an October or November baking to have this rich dark fruit cake moist and flavourful for Christmastime. Many like to ice it with almond paste for a festive touch.

Preheat oven to 275° F.

Grease, line with brown paper and grease again an 8 x 8 x 3-inch fruit cake pan. Combine and allow to stand 2 hours or overnight

- **2 packages (2 ounces each) slivered blanched almonds**
- **2 packages (8 ounces each) candied cherries**
- **1 package (8 ounces) chopped mixed peel**
- **2 cups raisins**
- **1 cup currants**
- **1 cup chopped dates**
- **½ cup brandy**

Dredge fruit with
- **½ cup all-purpose flour**

Sift or blend together
- **2 cups all-purpose flour**
- **½ teaspoon baking soda**
- **1 teaspoon cloves**
- **1 teaspoon allspice**
- **1 teaspoon cinnamon**
- **½ teaspoon salt**

Cream
- **1 cup butter**

Gradually blend in
- **2 cups lightly packed brown sugar**
- **6 eggs**

Mix together
- **¾ cup molasses**
- **¾ cup apple juice**

Add sifted dry ingredients alternately with liquid. Make 4 dry and 3 liquid additions, combining lightly after each addition. Fold in floured fruit. Turn into prepared pan.

Bake in 275° oven for 3 to 3½ hours, or until cake tests done with a toothpick. Remove from pan and lift off brown paper. Cool cake completely and then wrap loosely in wax paper and store in an air-tight container.

Chocolate Custard Cake

The most valued recipe of all is one for a rich, dark, moist yet light chocolate cake such as this.

Preheat oven to 350° F.

Grease two 8-inch round layer cake pans. Line bottoms with wax paper or dust lightly with flour.

In a saucepan combine
- **3 squares unsweetened chocolate**
- **½ cup milk**
- **⅔ cup lightly packed brown sugar**
- **2 egg yolks**

Cook over low heat, stirring constantly, until thickened and smooth. Allow to cool.

Sift together
- **1¾ cups pastry (soft wheat) flour**
- **1 teaspoon baking soda**
- **1 teaspoon baking powder**
- **½ teaspoon salt**

Cream
- **½ cup butter**

Blend in, beating until light and fluffy
- **⅔ cup granulated sugar**

Mix together
- **¾ cup milk**
- **1 teaspoon vanilla**

Stir dry ingredients into creamed mixture alternately with liquid. Make 3 dry and 2 liquid additions, combining lightly after each. Stir in cooled custard.

Beat to form stiff but moist peaks
- **2 egg whites**

Fold into cake batter and beat by hand for 1 minute. Turn into prepared pans. Bake in 350° oven for 25 to 30 minutes, or until cake springs back when lightly touched.

Cool 5 minutes and remove from pans. Cool.

Spicy Crumb Cake

A cross between a cake and a coffee cake, crumb-topped cakes are favourites of long standing and are best when served warm and fragrant with spices.

Preheat oven to 350° F.

Grease a deep 8-inch square cake pan. Line bottom with wax paper or dust lightly with flour.

Blend together
1⅔ cups all-purpose flour
1¼ cups lightly packed brown sugar

Cut in until crumbly
½ cup shortening

Reserve one cup of this mixture.

Combine and add to remaining crumbs
¼ cup lightly packed brown sugar
1 teaspoon baking powder
½ teaspoon baking soda
½ teaspoon salt
½ teaspoon nutmeg
1¼ teaspoons cinnamon
pinch of cloves

Add
½ cup buttermilk or sour milk

Beat for 2 minutes at medium speed of electric mixer or 300 strokes by hand.

Add
¼ cup buttermilk or sour milk
1 egg

Beat for 2 additional minutes. Turn into prepared pan. Sprinkle with reserved crumbs.

Bake in 350° oven for 40 to 45 minutes, or until cake begins to pull away from sides of pan.

Elegant Light Fruit Cake

This is a fruit cake that does not require a ripening period, so if the festive season has arrived more quickly than you anticipated, this recipe is for you. Lovely to behold, easy to slice and delightful to eat, this cake will be a pleasure to serve to Christmas visitors.

Preheat oven to 300° F. Place pan of water in oven.

Grease thoroughly and line with heavy brown paper one set of tier pans (one 9 inch, one 7 inch, one 5 inch).

In a large bowl combine
2 cups ground almonds (commercial)
16 ounces red candied cherries
8 ounces green candied cherries
8 ounces diced citron peel
2 pounds bleached raisins
8 ounces diced candied pineapple
1 cup all-purpose flour

Cream together
1 cup butter
1 cup shortening

Gradually blend in
2⅔ cups granulated sugar

Then beat in
8 egg yolks
4 teaspoons almond flavouring

Beat until very light and fluffy.

Mix together
⅔ cup brandy
⅔ cup milk

Add to creamed mixture alternately with liquid
4½ cups all-purpose flour

Make 3 dry and 2 liquid additions, combining lightly after each.

Beat together to form stiff but moist peaks.
8 egg whites
1½ teaspoons cream of tartar

Fold into batter.

Lastly, fold in floured fruit mixture.

Bake in 300° oven for 2½ to 3½ hours, depending on size of pan. Bake until each cake tests done with a toothpick. Remove from pans and lift off paper. Cool.

Signal Hill Gingerbread

Named after the hill that overlooks the harbour of St. John's, Newfoundland, where many a keg of molasses has landed, this gingerbread is truly a cake rather than a bread, but what a delicious dessert it makes served with hot lemon sauce.

Preheat oven to 350° F.

Grease an 8-inch square cake pan. Line bottom with wax paper or dust lightly with flour.

Sift together into large mixer bowl
2 cups all-purpose flour
1½ teaspoons baking soda
½ teaspoon salt
½ cup granulated sugar
1 teaspoon ginger
1 teaspoon cinnamon

Add
  ½ cup shortening
  ¾ cup molasses
  1 egg
Beat for 2 minutes at medium speed of electric mixer or 300 strokes by hand.
Add
  1 cup boiling water
Beat for 2 additional minutes. Turn into prepared pan.

Bake in 350° oven for 50 to 55 minutes, or until cake springs back when lightly touched.

Jelly Roll

For the New Year's Yule log we included this jelly roll recipe, but for everyday use fill it with Lemon Filling (see page 107).

Preheat oven to 400° F.

Grease lightly a 15 x 10 x 1-inch jelly roll pan and line with wax paper.

Sift or blend together
  1 cup pastry (soft wheat) flour
  1 teaspoon baking powder
  ¼ teaspoon salt
Beat until thick and lemony
  4 eggs
  4 tablespoons water
Beat in
  1 teaspoon lemon juice
Add gradually
  1 cup granulated sugar
Beat until very thick.

Sift dry ingredients over egg mixture in 4 portions, folding in gently after each.

Turn into prepared pan.

Bake in 400° oven for 10 to 12 minutes.

Turn out immediately on a terry-cloth towel sprinkled with icing sugar. Remove wax paper and roll cake up in towel. Cool. Unroll, fill with jelly, jam or filling and re-roll.

Regina Mincemeat Cake

The flavour of this cake varies with the mincemeat used. Our homemade variety (see page 137) makes it especially pleasant.

Preheat oven to 350° F.

Grease two 9-inch round layer cake pans. Line bottom with wax paper or dust lightly with flour.

Sift together into large mixer bowl
  2 cups pastry (soft wheat) flour
  2½ teaspoons baking powder
  ½ teaspoon baking soda
  ½ teaspoon salt
  1 cup granulated sugar
Add
  ½ cup shortening
  ¾ cup buttermilk or sour milk
Beat for 2 minutes at medium speed of electric mixer or 300 strokes by hand.

Add and beat for 2 more minutes.
  ¼ cup buttermilk or sour milk
  2 eggs
  ¾ cup mincemeat
Turn into prepared pans. Bake in 350° oven for 30 to 35 minutes, or until cake springs back when lightly touched.

Cool 5 minutes and remove from pans.

Calgary Pumpkin Cake

This moist yet tender cake shows how well the early Canadians learned to adapt recipes for cooked pumpkin.

Preheat oven to 350° F.

Grease an 8-inch square cake pan. Line bottom with wax paper or dust lightly with flour.

Sift together into large mixer bowl
  1⅔ cups all-purpose flour
  1 teaspoon baking powder
  ¾ teaspoon baking soda
  ½ teaspoon salt
  1¼ cups granulated sugar
  1 teaspoon cinnamon
  ½ teaspoon allspice
Add
  ½ cup shortening
  ½ cup buttermilk or sour milk
Beat for 2 minutes at medium speed of electric mixer or 300 strokes by hand.
Add
  ¼ cup buttermilk or sour milk
  2 eggs
  1 teaspoon vanilla
  ⅓ cup canned pumpkin
Beat for 2 additional minutes. Turn into prepared pan.

Bake in 350° oven for 45 to 50 minutes, or until cake springs back when lightly touched.

Cool 5 minutes and remove from pan. Cool.

Maple Glazed Cake

The increasing market for maple syrup and maple sugar has prompted more Ontario farmers to tap their maple trees. Today, pipelines may carry the sap to the sugar house and modern processing takes place in shiny, hermetically-sealed evaporators. In general, the lighter the colour the finer is the quality of the syrup.

Preheat oven to 350° F.

Grease a 10-inch tube pan and dust lightly with flour.

Sift or blend together
3 cups pastry (soft wheat) flour
2½ teaspoons baking powder
½ teaspoon salt

Cream
1 cup butter

Blend in, beating until light and fluffy
2 cups granulated sugar
2 teaspoons maple flavouring

Add, one at a time, beating well after each addition
5 eggs

Stir dry ingredients into creamed mixture alternately with
¾ cup milk

Make 3 dry and 2 liquid additions, combining lightly after each.

Turn into prepared pan.

Bake in 350° oven for 60 to 65 minutes, or until cake springs back when lightly touched.

Cool 5 minutes and remove from pan.

Bring to a boil and simmer to 232° F. on a candy thermometer
1 cup maple syrup

Brush over warm cake.

Johnny Cake

Johnny Cake is thought to be a corruption of Journey Cake. Whatever the origin of the name, this delicious cornmeal cake served hot with New Brunswick maple syrup makes an excellent dessert.

Preheat oven to 350° F.

Grease thoroughly an 8-inch square cake pan.

Combine and set aside
1 cup cornmeal
½ cup milk

Cream
½ cup shortening

Gradually blend in
½ cup granulated sugar

Sift or blend together
1⅓ cups pastry (soft wheat) flour
2½ teaspoons baking powder
1 teaspoon salt

Add dry ingredients to creamed mixture alternately with
1 egg
1 cup milk

Blend in cornmeal mixture.

Bake in 350° oven for 40 to 45 minutes.

Serve hot, with maple syrup.

Maple Ginger Cake

This recipe was once made on a TV cooking show in Sydney, Nova Scotia, and as far as can be traced it has been popular both in the Maritimes and New England. This very fine-textured cake has a delicious spicy maple flavour.

Preheat oven to 350° F. Grease two 8-inch round layer cake pans. Line bottom with wax paper or dust lightly with flour.

Sift together into large mixer bowl
2 cups pastry (soft wheat) flour
1 teaspoon baking soda
1 teaspoon baking powder
¼ teaspoon salt
3 teaspoons ginger
2 teaspoons cinnamon
½ teaspoon cloves
½ teaspoon nutmeg

Add
½ cup shortening
⅔ cup lightly packed brown sugar
1 cup maple syrup
⅔ cup thick dairy sour cream

Beat for 2 minutes at medium speed of electric mixer or 300 strokes by hand.

Add
⅓ cup thick dairy sour cream
2 eggs

Beat for 2 additional minutes. Turn into prepared pans.

Bake in 350° oven for 30 to 35 minutes, or until cake springs back when lightly touched.

Cool 5 minutes and remove from pans. Cool.

Molasses Sponge Cake

This feather-light sponge from a bygone day deserves to be revived. We especially liked the hint of lemon in this recipe from a Toronto grandmother.

Preheat oven to 350° F.

Beat to form moist peaks
5 egg whites

Gradually beat in
¼ cup granulated sugar
½ teaspoon salt

Beat until very stiff and shiny.

Beat together until very light and fluffy
5 egg yolks
¼ cup granulated sugar

Beat in
½ cup table molasses
1 teaspoon grated lemon rind
2 teaspoons lemon juice

Sift in
¾ cup pastry (soft wheat) flour

Fold meringue gently into batter. Pour into an ungreased 9-inch tube pan.

Bake in 350° oven for 45 minutes.

Invert until cool, and then loosen edges and remove cake.

Pousse Café

As the name indicates, this feather-light dessert cake recipe comes from *la belle province.* Although not a traditional Quebec recipe it portrays the keen interest of modern French-Canadian homemakers in adapting recent recipes to suit their highly developed interest in fine cuisine.

Preheat oven to 350° F.

Grease thoroughly a fluted 2-quart ring mould. Dust lightly with flour.

Sift or blend together
2¼ cups pastry (soft wheat) flour
½ teaspoon salt
2½ teaspoons baking powder

Cream
¾ cup shortening

Gradually blend in
1½ cups granulated sugar
3 eggs
1 teaspoon vanilla
3 tablespoons cognac

Beat until light and fluffy.

Add dry ingredients to creamed mixture alternately with a mixture of
½ cup milk
½ cup light cream (10%)

Combine lightly after each addition.

Turn into prepared pan.

Bake in 350° oven for 45 to 50 minutes, or until cake springs back when lightly touched.

Remove from pan and allow to cool.

To serve, drizzle cake with a few drops of cognac and frost with sweetened whipped cream flavoured with instant coffee powder.

Revani

This Greek specialty, resembling a glazed cake, was demonstrated to the Vancouver home economists, one of whom sent in the recipe. Originally the baking powder was added to the orange juice, but we found the method below more dependable to ensure a light and fluffy cake.

Preheat oven to 350° F.

Grease a 9-inch square cake pan.

Beat
3 eggs

Gradually beat in
1 cup granulated sugar

Stir into beaten eggs
½ cup orange juice

Sift or blend together and add to egg mixture
1⅓ cups pastry (soft wheat) flour
2 teaspoons baking powder

Beat at high speed for 1 minute.

Pour into prepared pan.

Bake in 350° oven for 40 to 45 minutes, or until cake springs back when lightly touched.

Meantime, prepare syrup.

Boil to thickness of corn syrup (230° F. on a candy thermometer)
1 cup water
1 cup granulated sugar

Keep warm.

When cake is baked, cut at once into serving pieces. Pour syrup over cake and allow to stand for at least 2 hours before serving.

Broiled Topping

Through the years Canadians have preferred simple cake toppings such as this, or even just a light dusting with icing sugar.

Combine
- **¼ cup soft butter**
- **½ cup lightly packed brown sugar**
- **3 tablespoons cream or evaporated milk**
- **½ cup shredded coconut or chopped nuts**

Spread over top of warm cake.

Place cake under broiler, 6 inches from the heat, and broil for 2 to 3 minutes, or until topping bubbles and browns.

Basic Butter Icing

In Canada icing covers a cake and frosting is an American term — although some Canadians apply the word frostings to those fluffy confections made from egg whites.

Cream
- **¼ cup butter**

Gradually blend in
- **2 cups sifted icing sugar**

alternately with
- **1½ tablespoons milk or cream**
- **1 teaspoon vanilla**

Makes sufficient for top and sides of an 8- or 9-inch square cake.

Double the quantities for a layer cake.

Chocolate Butter Icing

Melt 1 square unsweetened chocolate and blend into butter.

Lemon Butter Icing

Replace milk with 1½ tablespoons lemon juice and 1 teaspoon lemon rind.

Butterscotch Icing

This buttery-good icing tops a spice cake to perfection.

In a saucepan combine
- **3 tablespoons butter**
- **3 tablespoons milk**
- **½ cup lightly packed dark-brown sugar**

Heat until sugar is dissolved.

Stir in
- **1⅔ cups sifted icing sugar**
- **½ teaspoon vanilla**

Beat until creamy.

Makes sufficient for top and sides of an 8- or 9-inch square cake.

Chocolate Fudge Icing

Beloved by children, chocolate fudge icing sets off a chocolate cake — and don't forget to let the youngsters scrape the pan.

In a saucepan combine
- **¾ cup granulated sugar**
- **½ cup cold water**
- **1 tablespoon corn syrup**

Cover, and bring to a boil.

Remove cover and continue cooking until a drop forms a soft ball in cold water (232° F. on a candy thermometer).

Cool to lukewarm without stirring.

Stir in
- **2 squares unsweetened chocolate, melted**
- **2 tablespoons butter**
- **1½ teaspoons vanilla**

Continue stirring until of good spreading consistency.

Makes sufficient for top and sides of an 8- or 9-inch square cake.

Double the quantities for a layer cake.

Fluffy Maple Frosting

This shiny frosting sets off to perfection the Maple Ginger Cake (see page 104).

Bring to a boil
- **1¼ cups maple syrup**

Beat to form stiff but moist peaks
- **2 egg whites**

Very gradually beat in hot syrup. Continue beating until very stiff and shiny.

If desired, beat in
- **¼ teaspoon maple flavouring**

Makes sufficient to fill and frost an 8- or 9-inch 2-layer cake.

Maple Sugar Icing

This icing really has that old-fashioned flavour.

Heat together until sugar melts
1 cup maple sugar
½ cup cream (18%)

OR

Heat
1½ cups maple syrup

until a drop forms a soft ball in cold water (232° F. on a candy thermometer).

Cool to lukewarm (110° F.) without stirring.

Beat until thick enough to spread.

If desired, fold in
½ cup chopped nuts

If mixture become too hard to spread, stir in a few drops of cream or milk. Makes sufficient for top and sides of an 8- or 9-inch square cake.

Icing Sugar Glaze

A simple glaze, primarily used for topping sweet yeast breads.

Mix together
¾ cup sifted icing sugar
1 tablespoon milk
¼ teaspoon almond flavouring

Spread on hot yeast breads.

Cream Filling

This old, reliable, but versatile filling has many uses — for cakes, as a pudding, or to spoon into baked tart shells.

Scald
1 cup milk

In a saucepan combine
1½ tablespoons cornstarch
¼ cup granulated sugar

Stir in scalded milk gradually. Cook over medium heat, stirring constantly, until thickened. Cover, and cook 2 minutes longer, stirring occasionally.

Stir a small amount of hot mixture into
1 slightly beaten egg (or 2 beaten egg yolks)

Then blend into remaining hot mixture.

Cook 1 minute longer, stirring constantly.

Remove from heat and blend in
1 tablespoon butter
½ teaspoon vanilla

Cool.

Makes sufficient to fill an 8- or 9-inch layer cake.

Chocolate Cream Filling

Increase sugar to ½ cup and add 1 square (1-oz.) unsweetened chocolate, broken in pieces, with the sugar.

Butterscotch Cream Filling

Substitute ½ cup lightly packed dark-brown sugar for granulated sugar.

Coconut Cream Filling

Blend in ⅓ cup shredded coconut with butter and vanilla flavouring.

Lemon Filling

Chocolate, spice or butter cake may be filled with this lemon smoothie, or, if you prefer, spoon it into baked tart shells.

In a saucepan combine
2 tablespoons cornstarch
½ cup granulated sugar
pinch of salt

Stir in gradually
1 cup boiling water

Cook over medium heat, stirring constantly, until thickened. Cover and cook 2 minutes longer, stirring occasionally.

Stir a small amount of hot mixture into
1 slightly beaten egg

Then blend into remaining hot mixture.

Cook 1 minute longer, stirring constantly.

Remove from heat and blend in
1 tablespoon butter
1 teaspoon grated lemon rind
3 tablespoons lemon juice

Cool.

Makes sufficient filling for an 8- or 9-inch layer cake.

*Desserts
and
Sauces*

Desserts

Our winter weather and perhaps our English heritage have contributed to the wonderful assortment of baked dessert recipes. These plus the glamorous ones for special occasions blended with others brought to this country by the newcomers, produced this assortment for your enjoyment.

Apple Crisp Northern Style

From Fort Smith, in the Northwest Territories, came this recipe for apple crisp that calls for dehydrated apples. Because fresh apples are available in Canadian cities all year round, we've given the recommended amount of fresh fruit. The crisp calls for honey, which reveals the proximity of Fort Smith to Alberta, the province that produces the most honey in Canada.

Soak overnight
2 cups dehydrated apples

in

2½ cups water

Simmer about 15 minutes, or until tender.

Preheat oven to 375° F.

Arrange in greased 6-cup deep baking dish, the drained apples OR
4½ cups peeled, cored and sliced apples

Drizzle with
½ cup liquid honey

Combine and pour over apples
2 teaspoons lemon juice
2 tablespoons water

Crumble together and sprinkle over apples
½ cup brown sugar
½ cup flour
½ cup rolled oats
3 tablespoons butter

Bake in 375° oven about 35 minutes, or until apples are tender.

Serve warm, with wedges of cheese or whipped cream.

Makes 6 servings.

Thornburry Apple Dumplings

This recipe came to Canada from England, and dumpling recipes are old enough to have arrived with the first settlers. That they continue in popularity testifies to their delicious flavour. You may prefer to use a Tea Biscuit dough (see page 29) rather than the pastry recommended in the recipe below.

Preheat oven to 375° F.

Lightly grease a large flat-bottomed baking dish.

Prepare Flaky Pastry (see page 170) and roll out to a 16 x 12-inch rectangle ⅛ inch thick. Cut into 6 squares.

Blend together
3 tablespoons butter
¾ teaspoon cinnamon
¾ teaspoon allspice
¾ teaspoon nutmeg
¼ teaspoon cloves
⅓ cup lightly packed brown sugar

Peel and core
6 medium apples

Cover outside of each apple with spice mixture. Place one apple on each pastry square.

Fill centre of each apple with
1 teaspoon crabapple jelly

Bring points of pastry together and seal. Place in prepared baking dish.

Bake in 375° oven for 30 minutes.

In a saucepan combine
1½ cups boiling water
1½ cups granulated sugar
3 tablespoons apple juice or water

Boil until sugar is dissolved.

Pour over baked apples and bake for 20 minutes longer, basting frequently.

Serve warm.

Makes 6 servings.

Apple Fritters

When testing this recipe, we thought we would just check it with a few wedges of apple but after the first mouthful we peeled and cut more apples until the last drop of batter was used.

Preheat 2-inch-deep fat to 375° F.

Mix together in a bowl to make a medium-thick batter that will cling to apples
- **1 cup pastry (soft wheat) flour**
  OR
- **⅞ cup all-purpose flour**
- **2 teaspoons baking powder**
- **½ teaspoon salt**
- **2 tablespoons granulated sugar**
- **1 egg, beaten**
- **½ cup milk (approximately)**
- **1 tablespoon oil or melted shortening**

Wash, peel, core and cut in ½-inch wedges
- **2 medium-sized tart apples**

Sprinkle with
- **2 tablespoons lemon juice**

Dip wedges in batter, using a fork.

Fry in preheated fat for about 3 minutes, or until lightly browned. Turn to brown evenly. Drain on cake rack set over absorbent paper.

Serve with roast chicken, or as a dessert with hot fruit sauce, maple syrup or whipped cream.

Makes 4 servings.

Annapolis Apple Pudding

Apples nestled beneath a cinnamon-flavoured light cake topping make this an all-Canadian favourite.

Preheat oven to 350° F.

Grease a 9-inch square baking dish.

Peel, core and slice and arrange in dish
- **6 medium-sized tart apples**

Sprinkle with
- **3 tablespoons granulated sugar**

Sift or blend together
- **1½ cups all-purpose flour**
- **3 teaspoons baking powder**

- **½ teaspoon salt**

Cream together
- **¼ cup shortening**
- **¾ cup granulated sugar**

Beat in
- **1 egg**

Add dry ingredients to creamed mixture alternately with
- **¾ cup milk or water**

Pour batter over apples.

Sprinkle with a mixture of
- **1 tablespoon granulated sugar**
- **1 teaspoon cinnamon**

Bake in 350° oven for 50 to 55 minutes, or until cake springs back when lightly touched.

Serve warm with Hot Honey-Butter Sauce (see page 121) or cream.

Makes 9 servings.

Baked Rice Pudding

Rice pudding was developed when the old coal stove was a part of every kitchen, with its oven always warm and ready to use for such desserts that owed their wonderful creaminess and flavour to long, slow cooking. We've given the modern-day recipe, but for the old-fashioned variety, combine ¼ cup rice, ½ teaspoon salt, ¼ cup sugar, 1 tablespoon butter, 3 cups milk and ½ teaspoon vanilla. Bake in 275° oven for three hours, stirring often during first hour.

Preheat oven to 325° F.

Grease a 1-quart casserole lightly.

Beat together
- **2 eggs**
- **2 cups milk**

Blend with
- **1 cup cooked rice**
- **½ cup lightly packed brown sugar**
- **⅓ cup raisins**
- **½ teaspoon salt**
- **few grains of nutmeg**

Turn into prepared casserole and set in a pan of hot water.

Bake in 325° oven for 1¼ hours, or until almost set. Stir once after first 30 minutes of cooking.

Makes 5 to 6 servings.

Blueberry Grunt

From New Brunswick we received this recipe with the comment "a quick and easy steamed dessert for summertime," indirectly indicating that even in summer, the evenings are cool enough to warrant a hot dessert. The sound of the pudding steaming led to the traditional name "grunt" for this kind of dessert.

In a saucepan with a tight-fitting cover combine
- **⅔ cup granulated sugar**
- **1 teaspoon cornstarch**
- **pinch of salt**

Stir in
- **1½ cups fresh blueberries**
- **1 teaspoon lemon juice (optional)**

Cook on top of range, stirring constantly, until mixture boils for about thirty seconds. Keep warm.

Sift or blend together
- **2¼ cups all-purpose flour**
- **4 teaspoons baking powder**
- **1 teaspoon salt**

With a pastry blender or two knives, cut in until crumbly
- **½ cup shortening**

Beat together and stir in
- **1 egg**
- **1 cup milk**

Mix lightly with a fork to make a soft, sticky dough. Drop by tablespoonfuls into hot blueberry mixture. Cover tightly, and simmer for 20 to 25 minutes.

Serve hot, spooning sauce over top.

Makes 6 to 8 servings.

Bishop's Pudding

Try as we might, the origin of the name "Bishop" proved too elusive. This moist and flavourful pudding, from Pointe Claire, Quebec, blends so well with the old-fashioned sauce, the recipe just had to be included.

Preheat oven to 350° F.

Grease a shallow 4-cup baking dish.

Beat until frothy
- **3 eggs**

Gradually beat in
- **1 cup granulated sugar**

Stir in
- **1 teaspoon salt**
- **1 cup chopped dates**
- **1 cup chopped walnuts**

Spread batter in prepared pan.

Bake in 350° oven for 45 minutes.

SAUCE

Simmer together
- **6 tablespoons granulated sugar**
- **¼ cup water**

Add, and simmer for a few minutes longer
- **2 tablespoons vinegar**
- **¼ cup butter**

Ladle hot sauce over hot pudding.

Makes 6 servings.

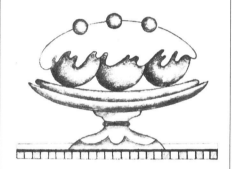

Cheese Blintzes

This Jewish dessert calls for those deliciously thin pancakes that are slightly lacy around the edges. The filling resembles the one the Ukrainians use for varenyky. The cosmopolitan combination makes a delightful dessert.

Prepare and cook French Pancakes 8 inches in diameter (see page 30).

Combine to a crumbly consistency
- **1 egg yolk**
- **1 pound cottage cheese**
- **2 tablespoons sugar**
- **½ teaspoon cinnamon**

Place rounded tablespoonfuls of filling in centre of each pancake and fold over like an envelope.

Bake to heat thoroughly, or fry in butter over low heat until golden brown.

Serve immediately, with sour cream if desired.

Makes 2 dozen.

113

Cottage Pudding

This fluffy, light cake when served warm with a hot chocolate, butterscotch or lemon sauce makes a delicious wintertime dessert. For a typical self-saucing cottage pudding try the maple variation below.

Preheat oven to 350° F.

Grease an 8-inch square cake pan.

Line bottom with wax paper or dust lightly with flour.

Sift or blend together
1½ cups all-purpose flour
½ teaspoon salt
2 teaspoons baking powder

Cream
⅓ cup shortening

Gradually blend in
1 cup granulated sugar
2 eggs
1 teaspoon vanilla

Beat until light and fluffy.

Add sifted dry ingredients to creamed mixture alternately with
¾ cup milk

Combine lightly after each addition.

Turn into prepared pan.

Bake in 350° oven for 50 to 55 minutes, or until cake springs back when lightly touched.

Serve warm with a sauce.

Makes 9 servings

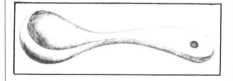

Maple Cottage Pudding

Grease a 9-inch square baking dish.

Bring to a boil
¾ cup maple syrup
¾ cup water

Pour into prepared baking dish.

Spoon Cottage Pudding batter on top.

Bake in 350° oven for 55 to 60 minutes, or until cake springs back when lightly touched. Serve hot, spooning sauce over top.

Christmas Pudding

From Stratford, Ontario, the home of the Shakespearean Festival, came this recipe for our traditional Christmas dessert.

Grease one 2-quart or two 1-quart moulds.

Sift or blend together
2 cups pastry (soft wheat) flour
2 teaspoons baking soda
½ teaspoon cinnamon

Combine
2 cups raisins
2 packages (8 ounces each) whole candied cherries
2 packages (8 ounces each) cut mixed peel
1½ cups currants

Sprinkle fruit with ½ cup flour mixture

Beat together
2 cups chopped suet (½ pound)
2 cups lightly packed brown sugar
2 eggs
⅓ cup molasses

Combine remaining flour mixture with
2 cups fine dry bread crumbs

Add dry ingredients to suet mixture alternately with
2 cups buttermilk or sour milk

Stir in floured fruit together with
½ cup slivered blanched almonds

Turn batter into prepared mould. Cover with wax paper and foil and tie tightly.

Steam for 3 to 4 hours. Turn out of moulds immediately and allow to cool.

To reheat for serving, return to mould, cover as before, and steam 1½ hours.

Crème Brûlée Canadienne

A classic French dessert that adapts to Canada's love for maple sugar. To translate the name to "burned cream" would cause this smoothly set custard to lose some of its appeal, and nothing should mar the elegance of this superb dessert.

Preheat oven to 325° F.

Heat in top of a double boiler
3 cups cream (18%)

Beat together
6 egg yolks
4 tablespoons granulated sugar

Gradually beat in hot cream.

Blend in
1 teaspoon vanilla

Pour into flat-bottomed 2-quart casserole and set in pan of hot water.

Bake, uncovered, in 325° oven for 45 to 50 minutes, or until set.

Sprinkle top with
⅓ cup finely grated maple sugar

Broil for 1 to 2 minutes, or until sugar melts.

Serve chilled.

Makes 6 to 8 servings.

Rhubarb Crisp

There are two schools of thought regarding "crisp" toppings. If you prefer the addition of rolled oats, refer to Apple Crisp Northern Style, on page 110. The toppings are interchangeable.

Preheat oven to 350° F.

Grease a shallow 8-inch square baking dish.

Arrange in dish
3 cups diced fresh or frozen rhubarb

Pour over top
⅓ cup corn syrup

Cream together
⅓ cup butter
1¼ cups lightly packed brown sugar

Stir in until crumbly
¾ cup pastry (soft wheat) flour
¼ teaspoon salt
¼ teaspoon cinnamon

Sprinkle over rhubarb.

Bake in 350° oven for 25 to 30 minutes, or until rhubarb is tender.

Serve with whipped cream, table cream or custard sauce.

Makes 5 to 6 servings.

Apple Crisp
Replace rhubarb and corn syrup mixture with 6 peeled, cored and sliced apples.

Cherry Crisp
Replace rhubarb with pitted fresh sour cherries and use the same amount of corn syrup.

Blueberry Crisp
Replace rhubarb and corn syrup mixture with 3¼ cups fresh blueberries.

Fresh Fruit Ice Cream

Anyone who has had the fun of licking the dasher as a reward for turning the crank, will know how truly scrumptious this ice cream is.

Heat in a double boiler or heavy saucepan until a film wrinkles over the top
1½ cups table cream (18%) or undiluted evaporated milk.

Stir in
½ cup granulated sugar
¼ teaspoon salt

Beat
4 egg yolks
and stir in a little hot cream, then slowly stir this into remainder of hot cream. Cook over boiling water, stirring constantly, until custard is as thick as corn syrup.

Stir in
1 teaspoon vanilla

Chill.

Fold in
2 cups heavy cream, whipped
1½ cups fresh berries or peaches, crushed

Pour into 2 refrigerator trays and freeze for about 3 hours.

Makes 1 quart.

Crank Freezer
Double recipe if desired. Place dasher in the freezing can. Pour ice cream mixture into can. Cover tightly. Pack a mixture of 8 parts crushed ice to 1 part coarse salt under and around the can right up to the top. Turn crank slowly for 5 minutes, then crank as fast as possible until ice cream is firm. Remove dasher. Cover can tightly including hole where dasher was. Pour off water. Pack around and on top of can with same ice-salt mixture. Cover with burlap bag or newspapers and blanket and let stand for 3 to 4 hours.

115

Irish Moss Blanc Mange

This recipe, typical of the Maritimes, was received from Prince Edward Island. Irish moss grows on rocks and ledges along the coast and is gathered at low tide and dried.

Wash thoroughly and soak for 15 minutes
¼ cup Irish moss
in
1½ cups cold water
Drain.

In top of a double boiler combine Irish moss with
1¾ cups milk
pinch of salt

Cook over boiling water for about 20 minutes, or until mixture thickens when dropped on a cold plate.

Strain milk mixture and blend in
1 teaspoon vanilla

Pour into jelly moulds and chill until firm.

Serve with cream and sugar or sliced fruit.

Makes 4 servings.

Maple Charlotte

From the Canadian Embassy in Moscow, just at the time when the maple sugar trees were being tapped here in Canada, we received this recipe for maple charlotte, which is an adaptation of charlotte russe.

Sprinkle
1 envelope unflavoured gelatine
over
¼ cup cold water
Add to
1 cup hot Canadian maple syrup

Stir and cook until gelatine is dissolved. Cool until consistency of unbeaten egg white.

Fold in
1 pint heavy cream, whipped

Line individual serving dishes with
lady fingers

Pour in syrup-cream mixture. Chill thoroughly.

Makes 6 to 8 servings.

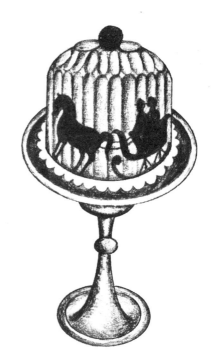

Maple Custard

Custard, to be Canadian, must have its maple sugar coating.

Preheat oven to 350° F.

Grease 6 custard cups lightly.

Melt in heavy frypan
½ cup maple sugar

Stir in
½ cup hot water

Cook gently until dissolved and syrup almost spins a thread (190° F. on a candy thermometer).

Pour syrup into prepared custard cups and tip to coat sides.

Scald together
2 cups milk
½ cup granulated sugar

Beat slightly
4 eggs
  OR
8 egg yolks

Gradually stir in milk mixture with
½ teaspoon vanilla

Strain, and pour into prepared custard cups. Set in pan of hot water.

Bake in 350° oven for 30 to 40 minutes, or until almost set.

Unmould when ready to serve.

Makes 5 to 6 servings.

St. Lawrence Maple Dumplings

This recipe for the traditional *grands-pères* of Quebec and the dumplings of the Maritimes came from East Farnham, Quebec. Newfoundlanders may substitute bakeapples, blueberries or partridgeberries for the maple syrup and increase the water to 1¾ cups. When hot, add sugar to taste, and then drop in the light dumpling batter. This recipe should delight all who hail from in and around the St. Lawrence, whether gulf or river.

In a wide saucepan bring to a boil
1 cup water
1¼ cups maple syrup

Meanwhile, sift or blend together
1½ cups pastry (soft wheat) flour
1 tablespoon sugar
3 teaspoons baking powder
½ teaspoon salt

With a pastry blender or two knives, cut in
¼ cup shortening

With a fork, stir in
½ cup milk

Stir only until moistened. Drop by tablespoonfuls into boiling syrup.

Sprinkle each mound with
chopped walnuts

Cover, and simmer without removing cover for 15 to 20 minutes.

Serve immediately.

Makes 6 servings.

Maple Soufflé

Let the guests wait for this special French-Canadian maple dessert, not vice versa.

Preheat oven to 300° F.

Boil for 7 to 8 minutes, or until thick
1 cup maple syrup

Beat to form soft peaks
4 egg whites

Gradually beat in a mixture of
½ cup sifted icing sugar
2 teaspoons baking powder

Gradually, pour hot syrup into egg whites, beating continuously.

Pour into 2-quart casserole.

Bake in 300° oven for 40 minutes.

Serve immediately.

Makes 6 to 8 servings.

Queen of Bread Pudding

Born of necessity, bread puddings were popular in pioneer days and undoubtedly journeyed here from England. This one merits present-day use, because it is sparked with flavourful jam and glamorized with meringue.

Preheat oven to 325° F.

Grease an 8-inch square baking dish.

Scald
4 cups milk

Pour over
3 cups cubed stale bread

Stir in
¾ cup granulated sugar
¼ teaspoon salt
3 egg yolks
1 whole egg
3 tablespoons butter, melted
½ teaspoon vanilla

Pour into baking dish and set in pan with 1 inch hot water in bottom.

Bake in 325° oven for 45 minutes, or until set.

Spread over top of hot pudding
½ cup jelly or jam

Beat to form soft peaks
3 egg whites

Gradually beat in
½ cup granulated sugar

Beat until stiff and shiny. Swirl this meringue over jelly.

Bake in 325° oven for about 20 minutes, or until lightly browned.

Makes 8 to 10 servings.

117

Regina Rhubarb Pudding

To be made anywhere in Canada when the rhubarb is pink and tender, this Saskatchewan recipe tops the rosy-hued fruit with a cake-type batter to produce a springtime dessert for family or company

Preheat oven to 350° F.

Grease a 1½-quart casserole.

Mix together and place in bottom of prepared casserole
   4½ cups rhubarb chunks
   1 cup granulated sugar

Sift or blend together
   1 cup all-purpose flour
   2 teaspoons baking powder
   ½ teaspoon salt

Blend together
   2 tablespoons butter
   2 tablespoons granulated sugar

Stir in dry ingredients alternately with
   ¼ to ½ cup cold water

Add sufficient water to make a soft dough.

Spoon over top of rhubarb.

Sprinkle on top of dough
   1 tablespoon sugar

Bake in 350° oven for 40 to 50 minutes, or until cake tests done.

Makes 4 to 5 servings.

Sauced Fruit Pudding

Puddings prove popular across Canada, from Newfoundland's figgy duff (a boiled raisin pudding) to shanty pudding of the West. The latter closely resembles this self-saucing pudding from New Brunswick.

Preheat oven to 375° F.

Grease a 6-cup casserole.

Sift or blend together
   1 cup all-purpose flour
   2 teaspoons baking powder
   2 teaspoons granulated sugar
   pinch of salt

With a pastry blender or two knives cut in until consistency of coarse meal
   2 tablespoons shortening

Stir in
   1 cup raisins
      OR

   ½ cup each of raisins and orange segments

With a fork, stir in
   ½ cup milk or orange juice
   1 teaspoon vanilla

Turn into prepared casserole.

Mix together and pour over batter
   1 cup lightly packed brown sugar
   2 tablespoons butter
   1¾ cups boiling water

Bake in 375° oven for 25 to 30 minutes, or until golden brown. Sauce will form in the bottom.

Serve warm with its own sauce.

Makes 4 servings.

Jemseg Strawberry Shortcake

Called Jemseg, after a town in the central area of New Brunswick where strawberries are cultivated, this strawberry shortcake proves popular throughout the country. For the cake-type shortcake lovers, use the Butter Cake recipe on page 100.

Preheat oven to 450° F.

Sift or blend together
   2¼ cups all-purpose flour
   4 teaspoons baking powder
   1 teaspoon salt
   ¼ cup granulated sugar

With a pastry blender or two knives, cut in until crumbly
   ½ cup butter or shortening

Stir in
   1 cup milk

Mix lightly with a fork to make a soft, slightly sticky dough.

Turn dough out on a lightly floured surface and knead gently 8 to 10 times. Roll out or pat to ½ inch thickness. Cut in 3-inch circles.

Bake on ungreased baking sheet in 450° oven for 12 to 15 minutes, or until light golden brown.

Cool, split in half and butter.

Fill with crushed fresh, sweetened strawberries allow ⅓ cup sugar for each cup fruit). Top with sweetened whipped cream and garnish with whole strawberries.

Makes 12 servings.

Wascana Suet Pudding

In earlier days, suet puddings were made in large quantities in November, buried under the snow (the freezer of the day), to be hastily retrieved when unexpected visitors arrived. Frequently, they were tightly covered and simmered with corned beef and cabbage or other boiled dinner. We've named it after the man-made lake of Regina, Saskatchewan, the capital city of the province with the most freezers per capita.

Grease two 5-cup moulds.

Sift together
   3 cups all-purpose flour
   1 teaspoon baking soda
   1 teaspoon cinnamon
   ½ teaspoon salt
   ½ teaspoon ginger
   ½ teaspoon cloves
   ½ teaspoon nutmeg
   ½ cup granulated sugar

Combine
   1 cup finely chopped suet
   1 cup molasses
   1 cup buttermilk or sour milk

Add sifted dry ingredients and mix thoroughly.

If desired, stir in
   1 cup raisins or currants

Fill prepared moulds ⅔ full, cover and steam for 3 hours.

Serve with Sterling Sauce (see page 120).

Makes 16 servings.

Trifle

This English import still continues as a popular dessert — perhaps because it uses up leftover cake in a glamorous dessert.

Scald together
   2 cups milk
   ½ cup granulated sugar

Beat until light
   3 eggs
      OR
   6 egg yolks

Gradually stir in milk mixture.

Return to saucepan and cook over low heat, stirring constantly, until custard coats a metal spoon.

Remove from heat and stir in
   ½ teaspoon vanilla

Chill.

Arrange in bottom of serving dish one layer of plain or spongecake pieces, sliced ¾ inch thick.

Sprinkle with
   ⅓ cup sherry or fruit juice

Spread with
   raspberry jam

Spoon soft custard over top. Chill.

Serve topped with whipped cream.

Makes 6 to 8 servings.

Pineapple Upside Down Cake

When the boys returned from overseas after the last war, many a Canadian mother was asked to bake a pineapple up-side-down cake and an apple pie. Both rank near the top in the list of most-popular desserts.

Preheat oven to 350° F.

Grease a 9-inch square cake pan.

Melt together and pour into pan
   2 tablespoons butter
   ¼ cup liquid honey

Arrange on top of honey
   9 slices canned pineapple
   9 maraschino cherries

Sift or blend together
   1½ cups pastry (soft wheat) flour
   ½ teaspoon salt
   2 teaspoons baking powder

Cream
   ⅔ cup butter

Gradually blend in
   ¾ cup granulated sugar
   2 eggs
   1 teaspoon vanilla

Beat until light and fluffy.

Add sifted dry ingredients to creamed mixture alternately with
   ⅔ cup milk

Combine lightly after each addition.

Turn into prepared pan.

Bake in 350° oven for 40 to 45 minutes, or until cake springs back when lightly touched.

Invert on serving platter and let stand for 5 minutes. Remove pan and allow to cool.

119

Vinarterta

Before there were schools in Iceland, students went to the Continent to study and of course picked up foreign customs and ideas. An example is this recipe from Manitoba where many Icelandic people settled: originally the multi-layered dessert was named for an opera that was playing in Vienna, but it eventually came to be Vinarterta, meaning Viennese torte.

Preheat oven to 375° F.

Grease six 9-inch round layer cake pans.

Sift or blend together
5 cups all-purpose flour
3 teaspoons baking powder

Cream
1 cup butter

Gradually blend in
1½ cups granulated sugar
3 eggs

Add dry ingredients to creamed mixture alternately with a mixture of
½ cup cream (10%)
1 teaspoon vanilla
1 teaspoon almond flavouring

Divide into 6 portions. Roll each out on a lightly floured surface and fit into prepared pan.

Bake in 375° oven for 12 to 15 minutes. Cool, and sandwich together with Prune Filling.

PRUNE FILLING

Simmer together until liquid is absorbed
2 pounds prunes
2 cups water

Remove stones and put prunes through a food grinder.

Stir in
2½ cups granulated sugar
1 teaspoon cardamom seeds, finely ground

Cook over high heat for 5 minutes, stirring constantly. Spread between cooled Vinarterta layers.

Ice with thin butter icing, letting it drip down sides of cake.

Prepare at least a day before, as it becomes pleasantly moist after standing.

Brandy Sauce

Here is a simple sauce for Christmas or suet pudding.

In a saucepan melt
¼ cup butter

Mix together and blend in
¼ cup flour
⅔ cup lightly packed brown sugar

Gradually blend in
1½ cups milk

Cook over medium heat, stirring constantly, until thickened.

Stir in
¼ cup brandy

Serve hot, on steamed or baked puddings.

Makes about 2 cups.

Sterling Sauce

The use of brown sugar makes this hard sauce a little sugary, but that's the way it is meant to be.

Cream
⅓ cup butter
Gradually beat in
¾ cup lightly packed brown sugar

Beat until mixture is very smooth and fluffy.
Beat in gradually
2 tablespoons heavy cream
2 teaspoons brandy

Chill thoroughly.
Serve on hot steamed or baked puddings.

Makes about 1 cup.

Foamy Sauce

Fluffy as snow, this sauce is a favourite for serving with Christmas pudding.

Beat until stiff but not dry
2 egg whites

Gradually beat in
1 cup sifted icing sugar

Blend in
¼ cup hot milk
1 teaspoon vanilla

Beat until thick and lemon-coloured
2 egg yolks

Beat in
¾ cup heavy cream

Fold into egg-white mixture.

Serve on steamed puddings.

Makes 2½ cups.

Hard Sauce

An American specialty, well-known in Canada, hard sauce melts delightfully on Christmas pudding. Our English friends know it as brandy or rum butter.

Cream
⅓ cup butter

Gradually add
1 cup sifted icing sugar

beating until fluffy.

Blend in
1 teaspoon vanilla
OR
1 tablespoon brandy, sherry or rum

Chill.

Serve cold, with hot baked or steamed puddings.

Makes 1 cup.

Hot Honey-Butter Sauce

From the province of beef and honey, Alberta, we received this scrumptious sauce recipe.

In a small saucepan mix together
½ cup cold water
1 tablespoon cornstarch

Stir in
½ cup honey
2 tablespoons butter

Cook over low heat, stirring occasionally, until sauce starts to boil and is thick and clear.

Add
few drops lemon flavouring

Serve hot, on cottage pudding, apple dumplings, steamed puddings, waffles or pancakes.

Makes about 1 cup.

Hot Rum Sauce

From Calgary, Alberta, we received this delicious sauce recipe, which we understand is served on hot apple pie in the Georgian Terrace dining-room on Macleod Trail.

In a saucepan blend together
1¼ cups lightly packed brown sugar
½ cup honey
pinch of salt
½ cup butter
¼ cup hot water

Bring just to the boiling point to melt butter.

Remove from heat and stir in
2 tablespoons rum flavouring
OR
⅓ cup rum

Spoon over individual servings of apple pie. Place under broiler for a few seconds until topping bubbles.

Serve immediately. Makes about 1¼ cups.

Cookies

We've tested recipes from the good old-fashioned teething cookies to modern no-bake confections, and we deem this selection of cookies to be representative of today's Canadian favourites.

Apricot Toasties

This recipe came into prominence as a winner in a Canadian recipe contest, and the cookies have retained their popularity through the intervening years.

Preheat oven to 375° F.

Grease a baking sheet lightly.

In a saucepan combine
   1 cup chopped dried apricots
   ½ cup water

Cover and cook together until soft, about 8 minutes. Cool.

Sift or blend together
   1¾ cups all-purpose flour
   2 teaspoons baking powder
   ½ teaspoon salt
Cream together
   1 cup shortening

   ½ cup granulated sugar
   ½ cup lightly packed brown sugar
   1 teaspoon vanilla
   ¼ teaspoon almond flavouring

Beat in
   1 egg

Beat until light and fluffy.

Stir in dry ingredients and cooled apricot mixture.

Drop batter from a teaspoon into
   1½ cups shredded coconut

and shape into balls. Place 1 inch apart on prepared baking sheet. Top each cookie with a whole almond.

Bake in 375° oven for 12 to 15 minutes, or until coconut is lightly toasted.

Makes about 6 dozen.

Chocolate Chip Cookies

Originating with our American cousins south of the border, these scrunchy chocolate-studded gems have been firmly adopted by Canadians and would be a strong contender for "Canada's favourite cookie."

Preheat oven to 375° F.

Grease a baking sheet lightly.

Sift or blend together
   1¼ cups pastry (soft wheat) flour
   ¼ teaspoon baking soda
   ½ teaspoon salt

Cream together
   ½ cup shortening
   ½ cup granulated sugar
   ¼ cup lightly packed brown sugar
   1 teaspoon vanilla

Beat in
   1 egg

Beat until light and fluffy.

Stir in dry ingredients.

Fold in
   1 package (6 ounces) chocolate chips
   ½ cup chopped walnuts

Drop batter from a teaspoon about 2 inches apart on prepared baking sheet.

Bake in 375° oven for 8 minutes, or until light golden brown.

Makes about 4 dozen.

Peanut Butter Cookies

An after-school treat and a lunch-box favourite, peanut butter cookies are always popular with children. They also keep well — if you can keep them!

Preheat oven to 350° F.

Grease a baking sheet lightly.

Sift or blend together
   1¼ **cups all-purpose flour**
   ¼ **teaspoon baking soda**
   ¼ **teaspoon salt**

Cream together
   ½ **cup butter**
   ½ **cup granulated sugar**
   ⅔ **cup lightly packed brown sugar**
   ⅔ **cup peanut butter**

Blend in
   1 egg

Stir dry ingredients into creamed mixture.

Shape dough into small balls and place about 3 inches apart on prepared baking sheet. Press with floured fork to flatten.

Bake in 350° oven for 12 to 15 minutes, or until golden brown.

Makes 4 to 5 dozen.

Skidaddle Ridge Drop Cookies

Skidaddle Ridge, New Brunswick, came by its name because it was a hide-out for draft dodgers. The "Skidaddlers" were Democrats who, not in sympathy with the Republican party during the American Civil War, "skidaddled" out of the country. Most of them returned home after the war, but many stayed to settle in New Brunswick and Southern Quebec.

These cookies are frequently packed in the lunch boxes carried by hunters of this region.

Preheat oven to 350° F.

Grease a baking sheet lightly.

Sift or blend together
   3 cups all-purpose flour
   1 teaspoon baking soda
   ½ **teaspoon salt**

Cream together
   ¾ **cup butter**
   1½ **cups lightly packed brown sugar**
   1 teaspoon vanilla

Beat in
   1 egg
   1 cup well-drained canned fruit cocktail

Stir in dry ingredients.

Fold in
   ½ **cup chopped walnuts**

Drop batter from a teaspoon about 2 inches apart on prepared baking sheet.

Bake in 350° oven for 10 to 12 minutes, or until golden brown.

Makes about 6 dozen.

Thimble Cookies

Thumbprint cookies, thimble cookies or Swedish tea rings — by whatever name you know them, it does not influence their tender goodness.

Preheat oven to 325° F.

Grease a baking sheet lightly.

Cream together
   ½ **cup butter**
   ⅓ **cup granulated sugar**

Blend in
   1 egg yolk
   ½ **teaspoon almond flavouring**

Stir in
   1 cup all-purpose flour

If necessary, chill dough. Shape into small balls.

Dip in
   1 slightly beaten egg white

Roll in
   1 cup finely chopped nuts

Place about 1 inch apart on prepared baking sheet. Make a depression in centre of each.

Bake in 325° oven for 5 minutes. Deepen depression, if necessary. Bake an additional 8 to 10 minutes, or until set.

Cool and fill depressions with
   jelly or jam

Makes 3 to 4 dozen.

Ginger Snaps

These Newfoundland cookies have the real old-fashioned "snap" to them and will make excellent gingerbread men, too, if dough is rolled a little thicker.

Preheat oven to 375° F.

Grease a baking sheet lightly.

Bring to a boil
- ¼ **cup water**
- ½ **cup molasses**
- ⅓ **cup shortening**

Cool.

Sift together
- 2 **cups all-purpose flour**
- ⅔ **cup granulated sugar**
- ½ **teaspoon baking soda**
- **pinch of salt**
- 1 **tablespoon ginger**
- ½ **teaspoon nutmeg**
- ½ **teaspoon cinnamon**

Stir dry ingredients into molasses mixture. Chill 1 hour.

Roll dough out on a lightly floured surface to ⅛ inch thickness. Cut with a cookie cutter. Place about 1 inch apart on prepared baking sheet.

Bake in 375 ° oven for 5 to 8 minutes, or until lightly browned.

Makes 6 dozen.

Hvorost — Butterfly Wings

Part of the enjoyment of recipes comes from the stories about where they originated. This recipe was given to one of our members by the daughter of a general in the Czar's army who fled to Shanghai. There the daughter was raised and was married to a Scotsman; they are now living in Vancouver.

Preheat deep fat to 375° F.

Beat
- 3 **egg yolks**

Stir in
- ⅓ **cup granulated sugar**
- ½ **cup cream (18%)**
- 2 **teaspoons vanilla**
- 2 **cups all-purpose flour**

Divide dough into 4 portions and roll it out very thinly.

Cut in diamond shapes with wheel cutter or knife. Slash centre of diamond and draw corners through and back.

Drop into preheated fat and fry until a light golden brown. Drain on absorbent paper.

Dust with
icing sugar

Store when cool.

Makes 4 dozen.

Lemon Biscuits

This recipe was taken from an old exercise book that contained recipes, accounts, budgets and governmental information including the following: "In the Dominion Parliament in Ottawa, the House of Commons has three parties — Reformers, Conservatives and Independents. The Reformers are in power now and their leader is Sir Wilfrid Laurier. Conservative leader, R. L. Borden."

Oil of lemon is an old-time ingredient that may still be purchased at the drug store. If you prefer, you may use the same amount of lemon flavouring.

Preheat oven to 375° F.

Grease a baking sheet lightly.

Sift or blend together
- 3¼ **cups all-purpose flour**
- ½ **teaspoon baking soda**
- **pinch of salt**

Mix together
- ¾ **cup butter, melted**
- 1¼ **cups granulated sugar**
- ¼ **teaspoon oil of lemon**

Beat in
- 2 **eggs**

Stir in dry ingredients.
If necessary, blend in additional flour to make a stiff dough.

Roll dough out about ⅛ inch thick on a lightly floured surface.

Cut into squares or cut with a cookie cutter and place about 1 inch apart on prepared baking sheet. Sprinkle with granulated sugar.

Bake in 375° oven for 10 to 12 minutes, or until golden brown.

Makes 4 to 5 dozen.

126

Maple Sugar Cookies

This tempting recipe has been passed down from the early days in Upper Canada, when cane sugar was scarce and maple sugar was a staple food. Nowadays maple sugar is a special treat.

Preheat oven to 350° F.

Grease a baking sheet lightly.

Sift or blend together
2 cups pastry (soft wheat) flour
1 teaspoon baking powder

Cream together
1 cup butter
1 cup maple sugar
½ cup lightly packed brown sugar

Blend in
1 egg
1 tablespoon water

Stir dry ingredients into creamed mixture.

Roll dough out about ⅛ inch thick on a lightly floured surface and cut with a floured 3-inch cookie cutter. Place about 1 inch apart on prepared baking sheet.

Bake in 350° oven for 5 to 8 minutes, or until golden brown.

Makes 6 dozen.

Oatmeal Cookies

Oatmeal, a traditional favourite of our Scottish ancestors, was a staple food in early pioneer days. These crispy wafers are from a hand-written book from Zorro Township, Ontario, the home of the famous tug-of-war team. Frequently two cookies are sandwiched together with a rich Date Filling (see page 131) but this tends to frustrate the baker as the 6 dozen cookies when paired shrink to 3 dozen.

Preheat oven to 375° F.

Grease a baking sheet lightly.

Sift or blend together
1¼ cups pastry (soft wheat) flour
½ teaspoon baking soda

Stir in
1¼ cups rolled oats

Cream together
¼ cup butter
¼ cup lard

½ cup lightly packed brown sugar

Blend in
¼ cup warm water

Stir dry ingredients into creamed mixture. Chill for 1 hour.

Roll dough out very thinly on lightly floured surface and cut with floured 3-inch cookie cutter.

Place on prepared baking sheet and sprinkle the centre of each cookie with a pinch of coloured sugar, if desired.

Bake in 375° oven for 5 to 8 minutes, or until golden.

Makes 6 dozen.

Ridged Oatmeal Cookies

Replace butter and lard mixture with ¾ cup butter and increase brown sugar to ⅔ cup. Shape into small balls and flatten with a floured fork. Bake as above.

Welsh Cakes

According to legend these are the cakes that King Alfred ruined while meditating on the affairs of his kingdom in the herdsman's cottage. Today the Welsh treasure this recipe for use on St. David's Day, the first day of March.

Preheat griddle or heavy frypan. Grease with unsalted fat.

Sift or blend together
2 cups all-purpose flour
3 tablespoons granulated sugar
¼ teaspoon baking powder

With a pastry blender or two knives, cut in until crumbly
½ cup butter

Stir in
½ cup currants

Beat
2 eggs
and add to other ingredients. Mix to a dough.

Roll dough out ¼ inch thick on a floured surface. Cut with a floured cutter. Bake on prepared griddle. Turn when golden brown.

Leave on griddle a few minutes to dry slightly. Sprinkle with granulated sugar while still warm.

Makes 3 dozen.

127

Shortbread

Shortbread and shortbread cookie recipes are handed down from mother to daughter, from generation to generation. The brown sugar version gives a slightly crunchier shortbread. The variation, from Prince Edward Island, was developed by combining the Scotch shortbread with the standard rolled cookies.

Preheat oven to 300° F.

Cream until very light
1 cup butter

Blend in
½ cup fruit sugar
OR
⅔ cup lightly packed brown sugar

Beat until light and fluffy.

Stir in gradually
2¼ cups all-purpose flour

Knead well to blend in last of flour. Chill for 30 minutes.

Roll dough out on lightly floured surface ¼ inch thick and cut into fancy shapes or squares, or roll into two circles ½ inch thick. Prick with a fork.

Bake on ungreased baking sheet in 300° oven for 18 to 20 minutes, or until set but not browned. Allow 1½ hours baking time for circles.

Scotch Cookies

Replace sugar with ¼ cup sifted icing sugar and ¼ cup lightly packed brown sugar and add ½ teaspoon vanilla. Roll dough out and cut into cookies. Bake as above.

Pyrizhky

This Polish, filled, pastry-type cookie was submitted by an Albertan from Edmonton, where many Poles and Ukranians settled. The original recipe called for breaking off small pieces of the chilled dough and rolling each into a flat circle. For convenience we've rolled the dough and cut with a cookie cutter.

Preheat oven to 375° F.

Grease a baking sheet thoroughly.

Cream
1 cup butter

Beat in
3 egg yolks
2 tablespoons thick dairy sour cream
1 teaspoon vanilla
¼ teaspoon salt

Beat until light and fluffy.

Stir in
2 cups all-purpose flour

Chill until firm enough to roll out.

Mix together
⅔ cup thick strawberry jam
½ cup chopped walnuts

Combine
⅓ cup finely chopped almonds
½ cup desiccated coconut

Beat until frothy
3 egg whites

Roll chilled dough out on a lightly floured surface. Cut with a 2½-inch cookie cutter. Place a little jam-walnut mixture in centre and fold over. Seal, shaping into a half circle. Dip in egg white and roll in almond-coconut mixture. Place on prepared baking sheet.

Bake in 375° oven until delicately browned.

Makes 5 dozen.

Antigonish Brownies

These scrumptious brownies satisfy lovers of the moist and chewy variety, since they have a thin layer of sauce in the middle.

Preheat oven to 350° F.

Grease an 8-inch square pan.

In a saucepan combine
⅓ cup undiluted evaporated milk
⅓ cup granulated sugar
2 tablespoons water
½ square unsweetened chocolate

Cook over medium heat, stirring constantly, until smooth. Set aside.

Cream
½ cup shortening

Gradually blend in
¾ cup granulated sugar
2 eggs
1 teaspoon vanilla
1½ squares unsweetened chocolate, melted

Mix together and blend into creamed mixture
⅓ cup all-purpose flour
½ teaspoon salt

Stir in
½ cup chopped nuts

Turn half of batter into prepared pan.

Spoon half of chocolate sauce over top. Cover with remaining batter.

Bake in 350° oven for 25 to 30 minutes.

Spread remaining chocolate sauce over top and sprinkle with
½ cup chopped nuts

Broil for 1 to 3 minutes, or until bubbly.

Cool in pan and cut into squares.

Makes 16.

Butter Mallow Brownies

An Oshawa member contributed this recipe for these moist and rich marshmallow-topped bars, but we understand the recipe came originally from Montreal.

Preheat oven to 350° F.

Grease an 8-inch square cake pan.

In a saucepan melt
⅓ cup butter

Blend in
1 cup lightly packed brown sugar
1 egg
1 teaspoon vanilla

Sift or blend together
¾ cup all-purpose flour
1 teaspoon baking powder
¼ teaspoon salt

Stir dry ingredients into butter mixture together with
½ cup chopped pecans

Spread batter in prepared pan.

Bake in 350° oven for 25 minutes.

Cut in half
20 marshmallows (approximately)

Place cut side down on top of hot cake. Press gently to flatten.

In a saucepan combine
1½ cups brown sugar

¼ cup butter
⅓ cup table cream (18%)
pinch of salt

Cover, and bring to a boil.

Remove cover and continue cooking until a drop in cold water forms a soft ball (238° F. on a candy thermometer).

Cool 5 minutes without stirring.

Beat in
1 teaspoon vanilla

Continue beating until of good spreading consistency.

Spread over marshmallows. Cool, and cut in bars.

Makes 24.

Cheddar Shorties

This versatile not-sweet cookie may start or finish the meal, depending on your whim. The English fondness for a savoury or cheese to follow the main course seems to have carried over into some of our customs.

Preheat oven to 400° F.

Grease a baking sheet lightly.

Sift or blend together
1 cup all-purpose flour
½ teaspoon paprika
¼ teaspoon dry mustard
pinch of cayenne

Cream
½ cup butter

Blend in gradually
2 cups (½ pound) shredded Canadian cheddar cheese

Stir in dry ingredients.

Shape into rolls about 1 inch in diameter. Wrap in wax paper and chill. Slice into ¼-inch slices and place about 1 inch apart on prepared baking sheet.

Brush with
milk

Sprinkle with
poppy seeds

Bake in 400° oven for 8 to 10 minutes, or until golden.

Makes 4 dozen.

Dutch Speculaas

This recipe comes from Dutch settlers on the Pitt Polder near Haney, British Columbia. Their version calls for one teaspoon of cloves, but we found this a trifle strong and have taken the liberty of reducing it.

Preheat oven to 350° F.

Grease a 9 x 13-inch cake pan.

Sift or blend together
   3¼ cups all-purpose flour
   1 teaspoon baking soda
   1 teaspoon nutmeg
   1 teaspoon ginger
   1 teaspoon allspice
   ½ teaspoon salt
   ¼ teaspoon cloves

Cream together
   1 cup butter
   1 cup lightly packed brown sugar
   1 cup granulated sugar

Beat in
   2 eggs

Beat until light and fluffy. Stir in dry ingredients. Turn into prepared pan.

Sprinkle with
   ½ cup sliced blanched almonds

Bake in 350° oven for 25 to 30 minutes, or until golden brown.

Makes 4 dozen.

Lemon Squares

An old cookbook, prepared by the Ladies Auxiliary of an Eastern Townships' church in the province of Quebec, yielded this recipe which we have up-dated slightly. The tangy lemon flavour proves to be most refreshing.

Preheat oven to 375° F.

In a saucepan combine
   ½ cup granulated sugar
   2 egg yolks
   1 tablespoon grated lemon rind
   3 tablespoons lemon juice
   2 tablespoons butter

Cook, stirring frequently, until thickened. Set filling aside to cool.

Cream together
   ½ cup butter
   ½ cup lightly packed brown sugar

Blend in until crumbly
   1½ cups pastry (soft wheat) flour

Press into bottom of ungreased 9-inch square cake pan.

Bake in 375° oven for 14 to 16 minutes.

Spread with cooled filling.

TOPPING

Beat until stiff but still moist
   2 egg whites

Gradually beat in
   ⅓ cup granulated sugar

beating until very stiff and shiny.

Fold in
   2 cups desiccated coconut

Spread over filling.

Return to oven and bake for 15 minutes longer, or until golden brown.

Cool, and cut into squares.

Makes 20.

Nanaimo Bars

A version of these no-bake bars developed in the Canadian kitchens of a well-known food company, was christened by them "Nanaimo bars" after the city of that name on Vancouver Island. Nanaimo (from sne-ny-mo, a local Indian term for a loose confederation of five bands) started as a Hudson Bay Trading Post in 1849.

Grease a 9-inch square cake pan.

In a saucepan combine
   ½ cup butter
   ¼ cup granulated sugar
   5 tablespoons cocoa
   1 egg
   1 teaspoon vanilla

Cook over medium heat, stirring constantly, until smooth and slightly thickened.

Stir in
   1⅔ cups fine graham wafer crumbs
   1 cup desiccated coconut
   ½ cup chopped walnuts

Press into prepared pan.

Cream
   ¼ cup butter

Beat in gradually
2 cups sifted icing sugar
1 egg

Spread over crumb mixture and chill for about 15 minutes.

Over hot water, melt together
4 squares semi-sweet chocolate
1 tablespoon butter

Spread on top and chill. When set, cut into squares.

Makes 20.

Pink Snow Squares

From before the days of packaged marshmallows, this recipe from Moncton, New Brunswick, proves almost as simple as melting the purchased confection.

Preheat oven to 325° F.

Cream together
⅔ cup butter
⅓ cup lightly packed brown sugar

Stir in
1⅓ cups all-purpose flour

Press into ungreased 9 x 12-inch pan.

Bake in 325° oven for 20 minutes, or until golden brown.

Soften
2 envelopes unflavoured gelatine
in
½ cup cold water

In a saucepan combine
2 cups granulated sugar
½ cup water

Bring to a boil and boil for 2 minutes. Stir in softened gelatine. When gelatine is dissolved, remove from heat and whip at high speed of electric mixer until stiff.

Blend in
½ cup chopped maraschino cherries
½ cup chopped toasted almonds
1 teaspoon almond flavouring

Spread over baked pastry and cool.

Cut into squares with a moistened knife.

Makes 4 dozen.

Date Squares

Known in our Western provinces as matrimonial cake, this recipe combines a luscious date filling between layers of crunchy oatmeal. Serve dainty squares for afternoon tea or larger ones for dessert.

Preheat oven to 350° F.

Grease an 8-inch square cake pan.

DATE FILLING

In a saucepan combine
2 cups chopped dates
¾ cup corn syrup
½ cup water
½ teaspoon vanilla
1 to 2 tablespoons lemon juice

Bring to a boil and simmer until thickened and soft. Set aside to cool.

Mix together
1⅓ cups all-purpose flour
1⅓ cups lightly packed brown sugar

Stir in
½ teaspoon baking soda
1⅓ cups rolled oats

With a fork, blend in
⅔ cup butter, melted

Stir until crumbly.

Press half of crumb mixture into prepared pan. Spread with cooled date mixture. Cover with remaining crumbs and pat down until smooth.

Bake in 350° oven for 30 to 35 minutes, or until light golden brown.

Cool, and cut into squares.

Makes 16.

Candy

Selected for their particular relationship to our country, these candy recipes just had to be included. Modern homemakers use a thermometer to take the guesswork out of candy making, but should you not be so equipped, this table will be an excellent guide.

TEMPERATURES AND TESTS FOR SYRUP AND CANDIES			
Temperature of Syrup at Sea Level (indicating concentration desired)			
Product	**degrees F.**	**Test**	**Description of Test**
Syrup . . . . 230 to 234		Thread	Syrup spins a 2-inch thread when dropped from a fork or spoon.
Fondant Fudge . . . . 234 to 240 Panocha		Soft ball	Syrup when dropped into very cold water forms a soft ball that flattens on removal from water.
Caramels . . . . 244 to 248		Firm ball	Syrup when dropped into very cold water forms a firm ball that does not flatten on removal from water.
Divinity Marshmallows . . 250 to 266 Popcorn balls		Hard ball	Syrup when dropped into very cold water forms a ball that is hard enough to hold its shape, yet plastic.
Butterscotch Toffees . . . . 270 to 290		Soft crack	Syrup when dropped into very cold water separates into threads that are pliable and not brittle.
Brittle Glacé . . . . 300 to 310		Hard crack	Syrup when dropped into very cold water separates into threads that are hard and brittle.
Barley sugar 320		Clear liquid	The sugar liquefies.
Caramel 338		Brown liquid	The liquid becomes brown.

Maple Butterscotch

Maple butterscotch brings fond memories of old-time "sugaring off" parties, where the maple sap was boiled until it "threaded" in cold water then drizzled over white snow in lacy taffy twirls.

In a saucepan combine

- **1 cup granulated sugar**
- **⅔ cup maple syrup**
- **⅓ cup butter**
- **½ cup water**

Bring to a boil and cook without stirring, until a drop in cold water separates into pliable threads (285° F.).

Turn into buttered 8-inch square pan. Mark into squares while still soft. Break when cold.

Maple Fudge

The early French settlers learned of the delights of maple syrup from the Indians, who slashed the bark of the maple trees and trapped the sap in a hollowed-out log.

The use of maple syrup in this fudge gives a creamy confection that is easy to make.

Grease an 8-inch square pan.

In a saucepan bring to a boil

- **2 cups maple syrup**
- **¾ cup cream (10%)**
- **2 tablespoons butter**

Boil, uncovered, until a drop in cold water forms a soft ball (236° to 238° F.).

Cool to lukewarm without stirring (110°). Beat until creamy. Turn into buttered 8-inch pan. Cut into squares.

Pulled Molasses Taffy

In French Canada pulled taffy traditionally commemorates November 25th, the feast day of St. Catherine, the patron saint of unmarried girls. Origin of the custom is attributed to Marguerite Bourgeoys, the founder of the Congregation of the Sisters of Notre Dame, who is said to have made some taffy for her pupils. Even today in Montreal, known in early days as Ville Marie de Montréal, the Sisters teach candy making in their home economics classes on November 25th.

Butter a jelly roll pan thoroughly.

In a large saucepan bring to a boil, stirring until sugar is melted
2 cups lightly packed brown sugar
2 cups molasses
1 tablespoon butter
2 tablespoons vinegar
½ cup water

Continue boiling, without stirring, until a drop in cold water separates into threads (260° F. on a candy thermometer).

Stir in
½ teaspoon baking soda

Turn into buttered pan. With a metal spatula, fold over from edges until cool enough to handle.

With buttered hands, pull quickly, folding taffy back on itself.

When colour begins to lighten, twist, continuing to pull as long as possible. Twist into lengths and cut into pieces. (If taffy becomes too hard to pull, warm in the oven for a few minutes).

Wrap individual pieces in wax paper.

Candy Apples

Traditionally candy apples have been associated with Halloween, but what mother-in-the-suburbs can cope with making enough for the fifty to seventy-five characters who appear at the front door? Better to make these juicy confections for a select group of favourite children of any age.

Grease a baking sheet lightly.

Wash and remove stems from
8 medium-sized apples

Firmly insert in stem end a wooden meat skewer or stick.

In a saucepan combine
2 cups granulated sugar
⅔ cup light corn syrup
1 cup water

Cook, stirring, until sugar dissolves.

Cover, and bring to a boil. Wipe inside of pan with moistened cheesecloth. Boil uncovered and without stirring until a few drops in cold water separate into hard brittle threads (300° F. on a candy thermometer).

Blend in
½ teaspoon cinnamon
6 to 8 drops of red food colouring

Remove from heat. Tip saucepan and dip apples in syrup, turning to coat evenly. Place, stick up, on prepared baking sheet to harden.

Fredericton Walnut Toffee

This brittle toffee was traced to a cook book printed in London, England, in 1735. The book, or at least the recipe, must have been brought to this country by the English settlers; for it has become a Christmas Day favourite in the area around Fredericton, New Brunswick.

Butter a 9-inch square pan thoroughly.

Spread in pan
½ cup walnut pieces

Mix together in heavy frypan
1⅓ cups lightly packed brown sugar
1 cup butter

Cook over medium heat (keep mixture bubbling), stirring constantly, for 12 minutes.

Pour toffee mixture quickly over nuts.

Sprinkle over hot toffee
3 squares semi-sweet chocolate, grated (or one chocolate bar broken in pieces)

As chocolate melts, spread until smooth.

Sprinkle with
chopped nuts

Chill, and break into pieces.

133

Preserves

Our native fruits and vegetables just beg to be prepared and tucked into jars to enliven winter menus whether as jam, jelly or pickles. In general, Canadians use more preserved food and prepare more in the home than our American neighbours.

For successful jam and jelly making, select fruits known to be good jelly makers and fruit that is a little underripe, because the pectin content is higher at this time.

Pectin Test For Jellies

Combine in a small dish 1 tablespoon juice that has been dripped through a jelly bag with 2 tablespoons rubbing alcohol. Let stand 30 seconds and pour out into a saucer. If one jelly-like clot forms, the juice contains sufficient pectin to make good jelly using 1 cup sugar to 1 cup juice. If two or three jelly-like clots form, the juice contains sufficient pectin to make good jelly using ¾ cup sugar to 1 cup juice. If many small clots form, the juice contains insufficient pectin and requires concentration by boiling the juice until a good pectin test is obtained.

WARNING: Rubbing alcohol is a poison. Immediately after observing the pectin test pour the sample down the drain and wash the dish.

Jelly Test

To detect when the jelly has been boiled sufficiently, dip up the boiling syrup with a large metal spoon. Holding the spoon well above the kettle, allow the syrup to run off the side of the spoon back into the pan. When the syrup no longer runs in a steady stream but separates into two distinct streams of drops which finally flow or "sheet" together, the jelly stage has been reached.

Bread and Butter Pickles

As the name implies, fresh bread and butter is the perfect accompaniment to these crunchy cucumber slices, but they are wonderful with sandwiches and cold meats.

In a crock or bowl combine
- **16 cups thinly sliced pickling cucumbers**
- **½ cup coarse salt**
- **7 cups sliced onions**
- **1 cup sweet red pepper strips**

Cover with ice cubes. Let stand 2 or 3 hours, or until cucumbers are crisp and cold. Add more ice if necessary. Drain.

In a large preserving kettle combine
- **4 cups white wine vinegar**
- **6 cups granulated sugar**
- **1½ tablespoons celery seeds**
- **2 tablespoons mustard seeds**
- **1½ teaspoons turmeric**
- **½ teaspoon white pepper**

Bring liquid quickly to a boil and boil 10 minutes. Add cucumber-onion mixture and bring to the boiling point.

Pack at once in sealers and store in a cool place for 1 month before using.

Makes 8 to 9 pints.

South Essex Chili Sauce

The aroma of homemade chili sauce simmering on the range is second only to bread baking in the oven and is a most familiar scent in the early fall. This recipe comes from Leamington, in Essex County, Ontario, which is considered the largest tomato growing area in Canada.

Peel and chop
18 large ripe tomatoes

Remove seeds and chop
6 large green peppers

Wrap loosely in cheesecloth
3 tablespoons mixed pickling spice

In a large saucepan or preserving kettle combine tomatoes and peppers with
4 medium onions, chopped
¾ cup granulated sugar
3 tablespoons salt
3 cups mild vinegar

Add spice bag and bring to a boil, stirring frequently. Simmer, stirring occasionally, for about 1 hour, or until thickened.

Remove spice bag during last 15 minutes of cooking.

Pack in sealers and seal.

Makes 7 pints.

Montrose Pickled Baby Corn

We have named this specialty from Waterloo County after a village of the region, West Montrose, that has one of the few remaining covered bridges in the province of Ontario. The thrifty Mennonite homemakers developed the recipe many years ago to use the sucker or third cob on field corn which is about 3 to 4 inches long and ½ inch in diameter at the base end.

Cover with boiling water and simmer for 5 minutes
1 quart baby ears of corn (husked)

Drain. Arrange corn in sterilized jars, packing well.

In a saucepan combine
1½ cups white vinegar
½ cup water
¾ cup granulated sugar
1½ teaspoons pickling salt

Tie together loosely in cheesecloth
1 tablespoon mixed pickling spices
1 tablespoon celery seed

Add cheesecloth bag to saucepan and bring to a boil. Simmer 5 minutes and remove bag. Pour hot liquid over corn, filling jars. Seal and store for at least 2 weeks before serving.

Makes 2 pints.

Mincemeat

To start a controversial discussion amongst good cooks, just ask whether mincemeat should contain meat. In Canada, in early days, ground meat was an essential ingredient, but English mincemeat does not contain meat—hence the controversy. On one thing both groups agree, that mincemeat pie should be served in the Christmas season.

In a large saucepan cook until browned
2 cups (1 pound) ground beef
Stir in
2 cups (1 pound) chopped suet
2 cups raisins
2 cups currants
6 cups grated apple (6 to 7 apples)
2 cups lightly packed brown sugar
2 cups granulated sugar
⅔ cup molasses
1½ teaspoons salt
2 teaspoons nutmeg
2 teaspoons cinnamon
2 teaspoons cloves
1 package (8 ounces) chopped candied citron
¾ cup cider vinegar

Bring to a boil and cook for 10 minutes.
Stir in
1 cup brandy

Pack in sterilized sealers.

Makes 4 pints.

Pickled Orange Slices

This novel garnish can be prepared well in advance to await the arrival of the Rice Lake Duckling with Orange Sauce (see page 80).

In a saucepan combine
6 oranges

Add
water to cover

Boil for 1 hour, or until tender.
Change water once. Then add
2 teaspoons salt

Drain. Cut oranges into ½-inch-thick slices. Insert in rind of each slice
3 whole cloves

Mix together in a saucepan
2 cups granulated sugar
¼ cup corn syrup
1 cup malt vinegar
2 cups water
12 bruised coriander seeds
2 cardamom pods
1 (4-inch) cinnamon stick

Boil for 5 minutes. Add orange slices and boil for 15 minutes.

Pack in sterilized sealers, and use as required.

Pickled Peaches

You'll love the spicy aroma of the syrup as it simmers gently with the peach-packed sealers standing by.

Dip peaches in boiling water and then in cold water to loosen skins.

Peel
6 pounds peaches (about 25 medium)

Peel peaches and stick in each one
2 whole cloves

Cover peaches with a mixture of
2½ quarts (12½ cups) water
3 tablespoons vinegar

In a large preserving kettle combine
9 cups granulated sugar
5 cups white vinegar
1½ cups water

Tie together in cheesecloth and add
1 piece whole dried ginger
3 (3-inch) cinnamon sticks

Bring to a boil and add drained peaches.

Cover, and boil for about 10 minutes, or until tender.

Let stand overnight with a plate on top to keep peaches under surface of liquid.

Pack peaches in hot sterilized sealers.

Bring syrup to a boil and simmer, uncovered for 5 minutes. Remove spice bag. Pour over peaches, filling each jar to overflowing. Secure top.

Serve with turkey, duck, pork or veal.

Makes 6 to 7 pints.

Magnetawan Rhubarb Relish

From an Ontario summer resort on Lake Cecebe, on the Magnetawan River System, we received this rhubarb relish recipe with the notation "We make our season's supply in June and serve it with meat or chicken all summer."

In a large saucepan combine
10 cups rhubarb chunks
8 cups granulated sugar
2 cups cider vinegar
2 teaspoons cinnamon
2 teaspoons allspice
1 teaspoon cloves

Bring to a boil and cook, uncovered, for about 1¼ hours, or until thick. Stir occasionally to prevent sticking. If necessary, tint with red food colouring.

Pack in sealers.

Serve with chicken, ham or cold meats.

Makes 3 pints.

Tomato Butter

This Ontario recipe can be traced back four generations from mother to daughter and daughter-in-law and can rightly be considered a pioneer recipe. Tomato butter is used as a spread but is usually preferred as an excellent accompaniment to meats.

Scald, peel and mash finely
10 pounds tomatoes

Pour
1 pint (2½ cups) cider vinegar
over the tomatoes and let stand overnight.

Next day, place tomatoes in a colander. Drain and reserve liquid.

Make a syrup of
3 pounds granulated sugar
1½ cups reserved liquid
¼ teaspoon pepper
1 tablespoon salt

Wrap loosely in cheesecloth and add to syrup
1 tablespoon whole allspice
1 (3-inch) cinnamon stick

Add the drained tomatoes to the syrup.

Cook slowly until the mixture is thick.

Remove spice bag. Ladle into sterilized jars and seal.

Makes 3 to 4 pints.

Bakeapple Jam

Bakeapples or cloudberries are yellow in colour, shaped like blackberries and have a delicious flavour. They grow low down in bogs in Newfoundland and Labrador.

Strangers confuse them with baked apples and are surprised when berries are served. It is said that when the French landed on the shore of Newfoundland they said of this unknown fruit "What is this berry called" or "*Baie qu'appelle.*"

Wash and weigh berries.

Mix berries and sugar together in a bowl.

For each
1 pound bakeapples

Use
¾ pound granulated sugar

Allow to stand overnight.

Next morning bring to a boil and boil gently for 20 minutes, or until a spoonful when chilled quickly has desired consistency.

Ladle into sterilized jars. Seal while hot with a thin layer of melted paraffin.

Makes about 10 (6-ounce) jars.

Blueberry Jam

Wild blueberries are harvested commercially in the Atlantic Provinces, Quebec and Ontario, and cultivated blueberries are grown in British Columbia. This popular fruit is quite versatile and is used in many dessert and cake recipes. Eskimos relish blueberries preserved in fish oil, but the more southerly residents of Canada prefer them made into jam with sugar.

Wash and stem about 1½ quarts fresh blueberries.

Measure
6 cups blueberries

In a large saucepan or preserving kettle combine with
2 tablespoons lemon juice
1 tablespoon grated lemon rind
¼ teaspoon cinnamon
2 cups granulated sugar

Bring to a boil and boil, uncovered, for 5 minutes, or until a spoonful when chilled has desired consistency. Stir frequently.

Ladle into sterilized jars. Seal while hot with a thin layer of melted paraffin.

Makes about 10 (6-ounce) jars.

Rhubarb Ginger Preserve

This Alberta recipe reflects a Chinese influence in the use of preserved ginger. The reddish, juicy stalks of rhubarb, though technically recognized as a perennial vegetable, are welcomed and cooked as "fruit" from early spring to late fall.

In a bowl or crock combine and allow to stand overnight
   6 cups rhubarb
   6 cups granulated sugar
   ½ cup lemon juice
   1 tablespoon grated lemon rind

The next morning transfer mixture to a large saucepan.

Bring to a boil and cook, uncovered, for about 1 hour, or until thickened.

Stir in
   ¼ cup chopped preserved ginger

Simmer for 5 minutes longer.

Ladle into hot sterilized jars. Seal while hot with a thin layer of melted paraffin.

Makes about 12 (6-ounce) jars.

Saskatoon and Rhubarb Jam

Saskatoon berries grow in coulees, bluffs and open woodlands of the Prairie Provinces. In the early days, settlers of the area depended on these berries for almost their entire fruit supply. Experimental work today indicates that Saskatoons are worthy of orchard culture and they have been shipped for sale in Vancouver stores. These sweet purple berries blend well with tart rhubarb in this richly coloured jam.

Wash, stem and mash
   6 cups Saskatoon berries

Wash and finely dice rhubarb and measure
   4 cups diced rhubarb

In a saucepan combine rhubarb with
   ½ cup water

Bring to a boil and simmer, covered, until soft.

Stir in mashed Saskatoons and bring to a boil.

Meanwhile, warm
   6 cups granulated sugar

Stir warmed sugar slowly into hot fruit.

Bring to a boil and boil, uncovered, for 10 minutes, or until a spoonful when chilled quickly has desired consistency. Stir frequently.

Ladle into sterilized jars. Seal while hot with a thin layer of melted paraffin.

Makes 8 to 10 (8-ounce) jars.

Seville Marmalade

Save a little time in February, after the Seville oranges arrive, for making a batch of marmalade. The rich, tangy flavour of these oranges makes a superbly flavoured preserve. Incidentally the word marmalade originally came from the Portuguese word *marmelo* meaning quince, but nowadays it commonly refers to the preserve made from oranges and sugar.

Halve from stem to blossom end and slice very thinly (including rind)
   12 Seville oranges
   3 large sweet oranges
   2 lemons

Measure prepared fruit and for each cup of fruit add
   2¼ cups water

Cover and let stand for 24 hours. Bring to a boil and simmer uncovered for 1½ hours. Allow to stand overnight.

Measure 4 cups fruit mixture and add
4 cups granulated sugar

Bring to a boil and cook, uncovered, for 1 hour, or until a spoonful when chilled quickly has desired consistency (220° F. on a jelly thermometer).

Ladle into sterilized jars. Seal while hot with a thin layer of melted paraffin.

Repeat with additional fruit mixture until all has been cooked. (By cooking in small batches the marmalade will have a better colour.)

Makes about 40 (6-ounce) jars.

Sunshine Strawberry Jam

In the Gaspé area this method of making strawberry jam is referred to as "quick jam" because of the short cooking time required. The whole berries are suspended in a rich jelly and despite the unorthodox method of preserving this is an amazingly successful recipe.

Wash, stem and hull about 2 quarts fresh strawberries.

Measure
4 cups strawberries

In a large saucepan or preserving kettle combine with
4 cups granulated sugar
2 tablespoons lemon juice

Bring to a boil and boil, uncovered, for 8 to 10 minutes, or until a spoonful when chilled has almost desired consistency. Stir frequently.

Pour into shallow containers. Cover with glass or plastic wrap, but prop up to allow evaporation. Set in sun, stirring occasionally. When thick enough (2 or 3 days) ladle into sterilized jars. Seal with a thin layer of melted paraffin.

Makes about 6 (6-ounce) jars.

Apple Butter

The crisp days of autumn signal the arrival of apple cider and subsequently, large kettles of apple butter waft their spicy aroma in kitchens across the country.

Some say the early German settlers brought the recipe to Canada and others attribute it to English arrivals. The important thing is that, in a country renowned for the high quality of its apples, the people prize this spicy spread.

Wash and quarter (do not peel or core) sufficient apples to give
8 cups quartered apples

In a large saucepan or preserving kettle combine apples with
4 cups apple cider

Bring to a boil and simmer until very soft.

Press through colander or strainer.

In a large saucepan combine apple purée with
1¾ cups granulated sugar
1 teaspoon allspice
1 teaspoon ground cinnamon
½ teaspoon cloves

Cook until thickened to desired consistency, stirring frequently. Pour into hot sterilized sealers.

Makes 2 pints.

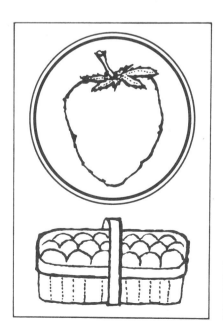

Spiced Crabapple Jelly

One early Canadian cookbook suggests that if you have a large family to cook for there is little use in making crabapple jelly in small quantities. The recipe goes on to give directions for making a kettle-full each day and ends with the observation that "You will be surprised to see how much can be made and with very little trouble." If you do not subscribe to making wholesale quantities, try this recipe.

Wash and remove blossom ends and stems from
1 basket (6 quarts) crabapples
Combine in a large saucepan with enough water to cover.

Bring to a boil and simmer, uncovered, for 20 minutes, or until mushy.

Strain through jelly bag overnight.

Measure
5¼ cups crabapple juice

In a saucepan combine with
½ cup white vinegar

Tie in cheesecloth and add
1 (4-inch) cinnamon stick (broken)
1 tablespoon whole cloves

Bring to a boil and boil, uncovered, for 3 minutes. Remove spice bag.

Stir in slowly
5 cups granulated sugar

Bring to a boil and boil, uncovered, about 25 minutes, or until a spoonful when chilled quickly has desired consistency. Stir frequently.

Ladle into sterilized jars. Seal while hot with a thin layer of melted paraffin.

Makes about 8 (6-ounce) jars.

Damson Jelly

The small rounded damson plum makes a delicious tangy jelly, just with sugar and water. In the late fall, baskets of damsons appear in farmers' markets in the large Ontario centres and they require very little preparation — no cutting, seeding or chopping. The taste is reminiscent of the wild Canada plum.

Wash, remove stems and measure
15 cups damson plums (5 pounds)

In a large saucepan combine with
6 cups water

Bring to a boil and cook, uncovered, for 15 minutes, or until damsons are soft. Crush. Continue cooking until very juicy (about 5 minutes longer).

Strain through jelly bag overnight. Test juice for pectin (see page 136). Measure juice into a large saucepan.

For each cup of juice stir in
1 cup granulated sugar

Bring to a boil and boil, uncovered, for 10 minutes or until a spoonful when chilled quickly has the desired consistency (220° F. on a jelly thermometer). Stir frequently.

Ladle into sterilized jars. Seal while hot with a thin layer of melted paraffin.

Makes about 10 (6-ounce) jars.

Grape Jelly

Autumn in the Niagara Peninsula brings the annual Grape Festival, when the crowning of a Festival Queen culminates an old-fashioned parade in St. Catharines, Ontario. For best grape jelly, select slightly underripe fruit; some say to wait till after the first frost. Thrifty homemakers use the juice that drips through the cloth for the jelly and then add water to the pulp and squeeze to make grape juice.

Wash and stem about
6 quarts fresh Concord grapes

In a large saucepan or preserving kettle combine with
1 cup water

Bring to a boil and cook, uncovered, for 15 minutes, stirring occasionally.

Strain through jelly bag. Allow juice to stand overnight in refrigerator. Measure juice, being careful not to use sediment.

Combine

4 cups grape juice

With

3½ cups granulated sugar

Bring to a boil and boil, uncovered, for 20 minutes, or until a spoonful when chilled quickly has desired consistency.

Ladle into sterilized jars. Seal while hot with a thin layer of melted paraffin.

Repeat until all juice has been made into jelly.

Makes about 16 (6-ounce) glasses.

Green Pepper Jelly

The abundance of homegrown green peppers and the Canadian custom of serving tart jellies with meat and poultry led to this Ontario favourite. Sweet red peppers may replace green peppers, if preferred.

Put through food grinder
8 medium-sized green peppers

Measure pulp and juice and combine 2 cups of it in a saucepan with
5½ cups granulated sugar
1 cup white wine vinegar

Heat to the boiling point and set aside for 15 minutes. Then strain through sieve or jelly bag (the latter for slightly clearer jelly).

Mix strained juice with
⅓ cup lemon juice

Bring to a boil, stirring constantly.

Stir in
1 bottle liquid fruit pectin
½ teaspoon green food colouring

Bring to a full rolling boil and boil for 1 minute, stirring constantly. Remove from heat, skim off foam and pour quickly into sterilized jars. Seal while hot with a thin layer of melted paraffin.

Makes 6 to 7 (6-ounce) jars.

High Bush Cranberry Jelly

The high bush cranberry is fairly common in prairie woodlands, parts of the Gaspé, and northern Ontario. The berries are an orange-red colour with a single, somewhat flattened seed and have a distinctive, slightly "gamy" aroma. The fruit, being generally high in pectin, makes excellent jelly and was a standby of prairie settlers for serving with poultry or meat. These jelly and catsup recipes from Saskatchewan are both prepared from one batch of fruit.

Stem and wash

high bush cranberries (slightly underripe)

Place in a large saucepan or preserving kettle. Add just enough water to be visible through the fruit. Bring to a boil and simmer until soft.

Strain through jelly bag overnight. Reserve pulp for cranberry catsup. Test juice for pectin (see page 136). Measure juice into a large saucepan.

For each cup of juice stir in

1 cup granulated sugar

Bring to a boil and boil, uncovered, for 10 minutes, or until a spoonful when chilled quickly has desired consistency (220° F. on a jelly thermometer). Stir frequently. Ladle into sterilized jars.

Seal while hot with a thin layer of melted paraffin.

HIGH BUSH CRANBERRY CATSUP

Press pulp (from making high bush cranberry jelly) through a coarse seive to remove seeds and skin.

In a large saucepan combine
3 cups cranberry pulp
4 cups granulated sugar
1 cup vinegar
1 teaspoon salt
1 teaspoon cloves
2 teaspoons cinnamon
1½ teaspoons black pepper

Bring to a boil and boil, uncovered, for 5 minutes, or until the desired consistency. Stir frequently.

Pour into hot sterilized sealers.

Makes 2 pints.

143

Vegetables

Cooking of vegetables, as with corn on the cob, routinely consists of gentle simmering in water until tender, draining and serving with a dollop of butter and a dash of seasoning or perhaps a cream sauce. The following regionally popular recipes increase the scope of these nourishing and colourful dinner partners.

Corn on the Cob

As Canadian and as widespread as our national motto *A Mari Usque Ad Mare* — From Sea to Sea.

Fill a large kettle with sufficient water to cover the corn. Bring to a rolling boil.

Add
1 to 2 teaspoons sugar

Husk and remove the silk from
fresh cobs of corn

Plunge into the rapidly boiling water. When water returns to a boil, cook for 3 to 5 minutes, or until tender.

Serve hot, with salt, pepper and butter.

Baked Corn Pudding

Indian corn or maize is so thoroughly entwined with our Canadian heritage that this all-purpose vegetable and staple grain is taken for granted. Endless ways were devised by the settler's wife for using fresh corn, dried corn, cornmeal and flour to achieve diet variety. Serve this flavourful corn casserole with hot or cold roasted meats and for company, assemble ahead of time, refrigerate and bake when needed.

Preheat oven to 350° F.

Butter a 9-inch square baking dish.

In a saucepan melt
3 tablespoons butter

Add
2 tablespoons chopped onion
1 tablespoon chopped green pepper

Stir and cook over medium heat for 5 minutes.

Blend in
⅓ cup all-purpose flour

Stir in
1½ cups milk

Cook over medium heat, stirring constantly, until thickened. Remove from heat.

Combine
2 slightly beaten eggs
2 cups cream-style corn
1½ teaspoons salt
1 teaspoon granulated sugar
pinch of pepper

Gradually blend cream sauce into egg and corn mixture. Pour into prepared baking dish.

Set in a pan of warm water and bake in 350° oven for 50 to 60 minutes, or until set.

If desired, before baking top with
1 cup buttered soft bread crumbs

and sprinkle with
¼ cup grated cheddar cheese

Makes 6 to 8 servings.

Corn Fritters

This recipe comes from Yorks restaurant in Victoria County, New Brunswick, near Andover, where generous-sized fritters are served with the province's excellent maple syrup. To serve as a meat accompaniment, drop smaller spoonfuls into the hot fat.

Preheat shortening in deep fryer to 375° F.

Blend or sift together
1⅓ cups all-purpose flour
1½ teaspoons baking powder
½ teaspoon salt

Combine and stir in
2½ cups cream-style corn
1 egg, well beaten

Drop heaping tablespoonfuls into preheated deep fat. Fry for 5 minutes, turning to insure even browning. Drain on absorbent paper. Keep warm in a 300° oven until all are cooked.

Makes 18.

Fiddleheads

Fiddleheads, the edible frond of the ostrich fern, are found in quantity in the St. John River Valley in New Brunswick. Since being nationally marketed in frozen form, they have become a Canadian specialty and a gourmet vegetable. The pioneer housewife considered them a good springtime tonic and served them to the family, as she did other greens, boiled with salt pork or bacon.

The name fiddlehead describes the appearance of this delicacy, and the flavour resembles a combination of asparagus and broccoli. They are served hot with butter or with a cheese or hollandaise sauce. Also served cooked, chilled and marinated in French dressing for salads or a starter course.

Remove brown sheath and scales of fiddleheads and if stem is crisp leave attached to the head.

Wash in several changes of lukewarm water and then soak in salted cold water for 30 minutes. Drain.

Cook in boiling water (about 1 cup to 2 pounds fiddleheads) for 10 to 15 minutes, or until sharp-tined fork will pierce the stalk.

Drain and add
2 tablespoons butter
1 teaspoon vinegar or lemon juice
½ teaspoon salt
pinch of pepper

Makes about 4 servings.

RICH CHEESE SAUCE

In a double boiler combine
1 cup cream (10%)
2 egg yolks, well beaten
⅓ cup grated Canadian process cheese

Set over hot water (not boiling) and stir until cheese melts and sauce is thickened. Serve with seasoned fiddleheads.

Makes 1¼ cups.

Yorkton Nachynka

Nachynka traditionally means stuffing for poultry, but this recipe indicates the adaptability of the Ukrainian immigrants to foods available on the Canadian prairies. This blending of the old country and the new produces a delicately flavoured cornmeal spoon bread that we have named after the largest Ukrainian settlement in Saskatchewan.

Preheat oven to 350° F.

In a saucepan fry together until onion is transparent
⅔ cup finely sliced onion
3 tablespoons butter
1 cup cornmeal

Stir in and heat
3 cups milk

Beat together
3 eggs
1 cup cream (10%)
1 teaspoon granulated sugar
1 teaspoon salt
1 teaspoon vanilla
a few grains of cinnamon

Blend into cornmeal mixture and cook, stirring constantly, until thickened. Pour into a 1½-quart casserole.

Bake in 350° oven for 30 to 45 minutes, or until brown on top.

Makes 6 servings.

Kitchener Kartoffel Kloesse

The German settlers brought to Canada their potato dumplings, and the Acadians from the Moncton, New Brunswick, region adopted the recipe as their own. Called *poutine râpée*, this dish is traditionally served with sugar and molasses during the New Year's festivities. In the Acadian version, the potato mixture is wrapped around diced salt pork. From Kitchener, Ontario, came this slightly different dumpling for serving as a vegetable.

Peel, wash and finely grate
4 medium potatoes

Wrap in a clean tea towel and press to extract as much water as possible.

Combine in a mixing bowl with
1 cooked mashed potato
¼ cup all-purpose flour
¾ to 1 teaspoon salt
1 egg, well beaten

Form into dumplings about 2 inches in diameter. Drop into 2 quarts boiling salted water. Cover and cook for 20 to 25 minutes.

Makes 6 to 8 dumplings.

ONION SAUCE

In a saucepan melt
2 tablespoons butter

Add and sauté until transparent
2 medium Spanish onions, coarsely chopped

Stir in
1 cup milk
¼ teaspoon salt

Simmer until onion is soft. Spoon over dumplings.

Spinach au Gratin

Cooked fresh spinach may replace the frozen spinach in this flavourful casserole. In some areas of Ontario the hardy spinach proves to be a valuable second crop for the farm vegetable garden. Even the first snowfall seems to protect it as it stays fresh and green for late fall harvesting.

Cook according to package directions
2 packages (12 ounces each) frozen spinach
OR
2 packages (10 ounces each) frozen chopped broccoli

Drain thoroughly in a colander or strainer.

In a saucepan melt
3 tablespoons butter

Blend in
3 tablespoons all-purpose flour

Mix together
½ cup boiling water
2 chicken bouillon cubes

and combine with
1 cup milk

Gradually stir this liquid into butter-flour mixture.

Cook over medium heat, stirring constantly until thickened.

In a buttered 1½-quart casserole arrange half the spinach.

Top with half of
¼ cup drained, sliced canned mushrooms

Spread half the sauce on top.

Repeat with a layer of spinach, a layer of mushrooms and then the remainder of cream sauce.

Sprinkle on top
½ cup soft bread crumbs
1 tablespoon grated Parmesan cheese

Bake in preheated 350° oven for 25 minutes.

Makes 6 servings.

Succotash

This old-fashioned side dish began as a combination of cooked beans and cooked fresh corn, cut from the cob. Each locality of the older settled areas has its own recipe developed to suit the tastes of the people and the locally grown foods. Salt pork slices are often included and the type of bean used varies greatly — dried pea or navy beans, green limas, green string beans and shelled green beans. The corn cob is often cooked with the beans to "cook out the sweetness." The following recipe follows this practice and is traditional in the Annapolis Valley of Nova Scotia.

Husk and silk
12 large ears of corn

Slice kernels thinly from the cobs, scraping thoroughly.

Place the corn cobs in a large saucepan together with
1 cup shelled green beans
1½ pints boiling water

Cook for 30 minutes, or until beans are quite tender. Remove corn cobs, cool and scrape a second time. Add corn kernels to cooked beans and liquid and cook 10 minutes.

Stir in
1 cup cream (10%)
3 tablespoons butter
1 teaspoon salt
¼ teaspoon pepper

Reheat and season to taste. Serve very hot in side dishes.

Makes 8 to 10 servings.

Quick Succotash

The more modern version using frozen or canned vegetables.

In a saucepan combine
1½ cups hot cooked, drained green lima beans
1½ cups hot cooked, drained whole kernel corn

Stir in
2 tablespoons butter
½ cup cream (10%)
1 teaspoon salt
pinch of pepper

Heat until butter is melted and cream is just beginning to boil. Season to taste.

Makes 6 servings.

Glazed Squash Rings

Squash is one of the few vegetables that has its origin in North and Central America as well as Peru. Belonging to the pumpkin and gourd family and commonly grown by the Indians, squash was much appreciated by the explorers and settlers of our country.

This recipe comes from sunny southern Alberta where "all types of squash grow to an enormous size."

Preheat oven to 375° F.

Wash and cut crosswise, into ½-inch rings
2 acorn squash

Arrange in a single layer in a shallow baking pan. Add water to the depth of ¼ inch. Cover with foil and steam in 375° oven for 10 minutes.

Combine in a saucepan
½ cup corn syrup
¼ cup orange juice
1 tablespoon grated orange rind
2 tablespoons butter

Bring mixture to a boil and remove from heat. Drain the squash rings and sprinkle with salt and pepper. Pour the hot glaze over the rings and return to the oven.

Bake for 30 minutes longer, basting frequently, until the squash is tender.

Makes 4 to 6 servings.

Herb Scalloped Tomatoes

Home canning (using cans and necessary closure equipment) has been a unique and important part of farm economy in Ontario and Quebec. With the advent of the freezer, many farm-grown foods for home use are processed by freezing, with the exception of tomatoes which are still canned. The rural housewife with a year's supply of canned tomatoes on hand, together with her urban counterpart using store-bought tomatoes, have a readily available source for menu variety. Here's a favorite supper dish using canned tomatoes to serve with either hot or cold meats.

Preheat oven to 375° F.

In a medium saucepan melt
3 tablespoons butter

Add
2½ cups small bread cubes
1½ teaspoons instant minced onion
½ teaspoon basil leaves
1 teaspoon parsley flakes

Toss bread, onion and herbs with butter.

To
1 can (19-ounces) or 2½ cups tomatoes

Stir in
1 teaspoon granulated sugar
½ teaspoon salt

Arrange alternate layers of tomatoes and bread cubes in a buttered shallow 4-cup casserole ending with bread cubes.

Bake, uncovered, in 375° oven for 20 minutes.

Place under broiler to brown the topping, if desired.

Makes 4 servings.

Stuffed Tomatoes

Imagine cooking without tomatoes, and yet only about 130 years ago they began to gain acceptance as an edible food on this continent. Use the magnificent large tomatoes of August for stuffing with this lightly curried rice for an elegant dish.

Preheat oven to 400° F.

Wash and slice off tops from
6 large firm tomatoes

Scoop out pulp, leaving shells ¼-inch thick. Drain.

Combine
¼ cup chopped tomato pulp
2 tablespoons finely chopped green pepper
1 tablespoon finely chopped onion
1 tablespoon finely chopped parsley
¾ teaspoon salt
½ to ¾ teaspoon curry powder
1½ cups hot cooked rice
3 tablespoons melted butter

Fill tomato shells with rice mixture and place in shallow baking pan.

Bake in 400° oven for 20 to 25 minutes.

Makes 6 servings.

Scalloped Turnip and Apples

An 1889 cook book notes that turnip contains little nutritive value and should be avoided by persons with weak digestion. However, early settlers in Virginia (1612) discovered that their turnip crop helped to alleviate the scurvy from which they had suffered during the first years in the new land. By 1833, turnips were grown extensively in Upper Canada, having been a luxury item in the early settlement. The mild, mellow flavour of today's yellow table turnip has contributed greatly to its increased popularity, and in the following recipe it is teamed with apples for an unbeatable combination.

Preheat oven to 350° F.

Peel, dice and cook in water
1 large turnip

Drain and mash turnip, adding
1 tablespoon butter

Peel, core and slice sufficient apples to give
1½ cups apple slices (about 2 apples)

Toss apples with
¼ cup lightly packed brown sugar
pinch of cinnamon

Arrange alternate layers of mashed turnip and sliced apples in a greased 2-quart casserole, beginning and ending with turnip layer.

Mix together until crumbly
⅓ cup all-purpose flour
⅓ cup lightly packed brown sugar
2 tablespoons butter

Sprinkle over top of casserole.

Bake in 350° oven for 1 hour. Serve hot.

Makes 6 to 8 servings.

Finnish Turnip Loaf

A traditional dish served with Christmas dinner in Finnish-Canadian homes. This turnip loaf may be assembled in advance and baked as required.

Preheat oven to 375° F.

Peel, dice and cook in boiling salted water
1 (2-pound) turnip (6 cups diced)

Cook for 15 to 20 minutes, or until tender. Drain and mash. Add

1 teaspoon granulated sugar
pinch of pepper
pinch of nutmeg
½ cup cream (10%)
2 eggs, slightly beaten

Blend thoroughly and turn into buttered 6-cup casserole.

Toss together
¼ cup soft bread crumbs
1 tablespoon melted butter

Sprinkle over casserole.

Bake in 375° oven for 55 to 60 minutes. Serve hot.

Makes 6 to 8 servings.

Wild Rice and Mushroom Casserole

Wild rice traditionally accompanies game and game birds and is a delicacy that has become better known in the last two decades. The rice, a grain of an aquatic grass, grows in the marshes of Rice Lake, Ontario, Lake Winnipeg, Manitoba, and other northern lakes. The Indians harvest wild rice in the Autumn.

Although a staple grain of many Indian tribes living in the marshy areas, there is little recorded evidence that the early settlers used these long grey-black needles as a food.

Grease a 1½-quart casserole.

Wash thoroughly and soak for 30 minutes
1 cup wild rice

Drain.

In the top of a double boiler combine the wild rice with
¼ teaspoon thyme
¼ teaspoon basil leaves
½ teaspoon salt

Mix to dissolve and add
3 cups boiling water
3 beef bouillon cubes

Cover and cook over boiling water for 45 minutes, or until tender, stirring occasionally.

Preheat oven to 350° F.

In a frypan melt
¼ cup butter

Add and cook until transparent
⅓ cup finely chopped onion

Push to one side of pan, add more butter (about ¼ cup) and brown lightly
¾ pound sliced fresh mushrooms

Combine rice and a little of remaining liquid with sautéed onions and mushrooms. Season to taste and place in casserole. Dot with butter and bake in 350° oven for 20 to 25 minutes. Serve from casserole.

Makes 4 to 6 servings.

Specialties

These bite-sized morsels to start the dinner are designed for today's entertaining and we have selected the most popular, most suitable ones.

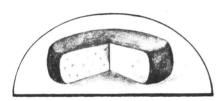

Angels on Horseback

It's the classic name for these hot hors d'oeuvres, perhaps because they taste so good.

Preheat oven to 450° F.

Drain
1 pint shucked (shelled) small oysters

Cut in half
12 thin slices side bacon

Wrap each piece of bacon around an oyster and secure with a toothpick.

Place in shallow baking dish or on broiler rack.

Bake in 450° oven for 10 to 15 minutes, or until bacon is crisp.
     OR
Broil 4 inches from heat for 7 minutes, or until bacon is crisp, turning once.

Makes 24.

Bacon Dip

To show off one of the finest Canadian products, bacon, here is a modern dip for potato chips.

Fry until crisp
4 slices bacon

Drain, reserving drippings. Crumble bacon in small pieces.

Cream
1 package (8 ounces) cream cheese

Blend in until fluffy
3 to 4 tablespoons bacon drippings
5 to 6 tablespoons thick dairy sour cream

Stir in chopped bacon with
2 tablespoons finely chopped onion
1 tablespoon chopped parsley
¼ teaspoon salt
pinch of pepper

Let stand to develop flavour.

Makes 1 cup.

Crab Bouchées

These delectable morsels may be stuffed with many different kinds of fillings for serving as an appetizer. We particularly liked this version using British Columbia crab meat.

Preheat oven to 375° F.
Grease a baking sheet lightly.

In a saucepan bring to a boil
1 cup water

Blend in
½ cup butter

Add all at once
1 cup all-purpose flour
¼ teaspoon salt

Beat vigorously until mixture leaves the sides of the pan. Remove from heat.

Cool slightly.

Add, one at a time, beating until smooth after each addition
4 eggs

Beat until glossy. If necessary, chill dough.

152

Drop by teaspoonfuls on prepared baking sheet, at least 2 inches apart.

Bake in 375° oven for 25 to 30 minutes, or until light and dry.

Allow to cool, away from drafts. Slit sides and fill.

FILLING

Fry until tender
3 ounces mushrooms, sliced

in
2 tablespoons butter
few drops lemon juice

Combine with
¾ cup flaked crab meat
2 hard-cooked eggs, chopped
2 teaspoons parsley
salt and pepper

Makes 3 to 4 dozen bouchées.

Cheese Fondue Continental

Continental because this recipe reminds us of the cheese fondue served in a Quebec City restaurant of that name. It's deep-fried to a crispy golden brown on the outside and a meltingly soft goodness on the inside.

Preheat deep fat to 375° F.

Cut in pieces, 2 inches square by ½ inch thick
1 pound old Canadian cheddar cheese

Sift or blend together
1½ cups all-purpose flour
½ teaspoon baking powder
½ teaspoon salt

Blend in
2 eggs

Add
1 cup light beer

or sufficient to give a smooth batter the consistency of slightly whipped cream.

Dredge cheese blocks with
flour

Dip in batter, coating well.

Fry cheese, a few pieces at a time, in 375° fat until golden brown.

Drain on absorbent paper.

Serve hot.

Cheese Straws

Bits of left-over pastry have traditionally made tangy morsels on baking day by being rolled with some shredded cheese. The pre-packaged grated process or cheddar cheese proves a tempting timesaver today.

Preheat oven to 450° F.

Prepare half of Flaky Pastry recipe (see page 170).

Roll out into a rectangle on a lightly floured surface.

Cover half of dough with
¼ cup grated old Canadian cheddar cheese

Sprinkle with
paprika

Fold over and pinch edges together. Fold over again, pinching edges.

Roll out about ¼ inch thick. Cut in 4 x ½-inch strips. Twist and place on un-greased baking sheet.

Bake in 450° oven for 8 to 10 minutes, or until crisp and golden brown.

Hot Cheese Tartelettes

These tiny appetizer tarts, from Toronto, may be all ready to fill and bake at the last moment for party serving.

Preheat oven to 450° F.

Prepare Flaky Pastry (see page 170). Roll out dough and line 3 dozen tiny tart pans.

Beat slightly
3 egg whites

Stir in
1½ cups shredded Canadian cheddar cheese
1 tablespoon minced onion
2 teaspoons Worcestershire sauce
1 teaspoon paprika
1 teaspoon dry mustard
½ teaspoon salt

Spoon into prepared shells.

Bake in 450° oven for 10 minutes, or until golden.

Makes 3 dozen.

153

Crab Cocktail Sauce

The Alaska king crab grows to an enormous size and is found only in the cold northern waters of the Pacific. The canneries process only the legs to produce excellent crab meat. Serve it with this delicious seafood sauce.

Mix together
1 tablespoon mayonnaise
3 tablespoons catsup
2 teaspoons lemon juice
1 teaspoon prepared horseradish
¼ teaspoon prepared mustard
¼ teaspoon Worcestershire sauce
2 drops Tabasco sauce

Chill.

Cretons

Cretons is the French-Canadian word for potted meat which is similar to *pâté de foie gras,* and the touch of allspice in this recipe gives a delicious flavour.

In a large saucepan melt slowly until crispy
1 pound leaf lard, peeled and diced

Strain, reserve residue and return fat to saucepan.

Stir into fat
3 pounds ground lean pork
3 medium onions, diced
2½ cups boiling water

Bring to a boil and simmer, covered, for 2 hours.

Stir in leaf lard residue and
2½ teaspoons salt
¼ teaspoon pepper
½ teaspoon allspice

Simmer, uncovered for 2 hours longer.

Turn into moulds that have been rinsed in cold water. (The fat will rise to the surface and harden when cold, sealing the meat.)

Chill, and serve with brown bread or crackers.

Makes about 6 cups.

B.C. Smoked Salmon

One of the greatest Canadian delicacies, smoked salmon is fully cooked and ready for serving cold, sometimes with caviar, a little lemon juice or horseradish cream and thin slices of brown bread.

Solomon Gundy

A very old recipe, this appetizer is typical of the Lunenburg County area.

Thoroughly clean and remove skin from
2 salt herrings

Fillet and cut in 2-inch pieces.

Soak in cold water for 5 hours, changing water frequently. Drain.

Heat
sufficient vinegar to cover herring

Remove from heat and stir in
1 tablespoon granulated sugar
pinch of pepper

Allow to cool.

Pour over herring and add
1 onion, sliced

Let stand for a few hours.

Serve squares of marinated herring on slices of raw onion set on a cracker or on toast and garnish with
pickled red pepper strips

154

Pigs in Blankets

Tiny little sausages may be wrapped in either pastry or tea biscuit dough to make these exceedingly popular appetizers.

Preheat oven to 450° F.

Cook
½ pound cocktail sausages
OR
regular sausages, cut in three

Prepare half of Tea Biscuit dough (see page 29).

Divide dough in half and roll out into a rectangle. Cut in 2-inch squares and spread with
prepared mustard

Place a cooked sausage on each square of dough. Roll up diagonally and seal. Place on baking sheets.

Bake in 450° oven for 10 minutes, or until golden.

Serve hot.

Makes about 32.

Soups

Many of these originated with the wood stove, when it was a simple thing to keep the soup pot bubbling away merrily. We've updated some of the recipes, but others just had to be included because of their regional popularity.

Old-Fashioned Split Pea Soup

Dried peas still continue as a winter staple and this is the English-Canadian counterpart to French-Canadian pea soup.

Pick over and wash
2 cups (1 pound) green split peas

In a large kettle combine with
12 cups cold water

Bring to a boil, cover and remove from heat.

Let stand 1 hour.

Wrap loosely in cheesecloth
4 whole cloves
1 bay leaf

Add to kettle with
1 ham bone, fat removed
1 cup finely chopped onion
1 cup finely diced celery
½ cup finely diced carrots
2 beef bouillon cubes

Bring to a boil. Cover, and simmer gently 1½ to 2 hours, or until peas are soft.

Remove ham bone and spice bag.

Purée soup in a blender or press through a sieve, and reheat in soup kettle with finely diced ham from bone.

Season to taste, using approximately 1 tablespoon salt, ¼ teaspoon pepper, and a pinch of savory. (Amount of salt will vary with the variety of ham.)

Makes 8 to 10 servings.

Muk-Luk Mardi-Gras

Muk-Luks are the gaily-decorated knee-·high Eskimo boots, and Edmonton, the capital city of Alberta, has adopted the name for their recently inaugurated Mardi-Gras Festival. It seems only fitting to call this soup, prepared from beans, the basic food of settlers and prospectors, after the festival of the gateway city to the North-land.

Soak for four hours or overnight
1 cup small white beans
in
8 cups cold water

Bring to a boil and simmer for 1 hour, or until beans are tender.

Fry until crisp
3 strips bacon, chopped

Stir in and allow to brown
1 teaspoon flour

Add bacon to beans along with
1 medium onion, finely chopped

Simmer for 2 hours.

Season with
½ teaspoon salt
pinch of pepper

Makes 4 to 6 servings.

Le Bouilli De Chez Nous

A certain sign of summer, this *bouilli*, from Quebec, contains the tender young vegetables at their ·most flavourful best. The threading of the beans together, facili-tates serving and is an ingenious trick of the French-Canadian homemaker.

In a large saucepan melt
¼ cup shortening or chicken fat

Rub skin of
1 (5- to 6-pound) chicken

with
1 whole nutmeg

Brush inside and out with
3 tablespoons cognac or cider vinegar

and season with
salt, pepper and thyme

Brown chicken on all sides in melted fat.

Add sufficient water to cover and add
1 piece (1 pound) salt pork
2 large onions, chopped
½ cup finely chopped celery leaves
1 tablespoon salt
¼ teaspoon savory

Cover, and simmer for 1 to 1½ hours, or until chicken and pork are almost tender.

Add
1 young cabbage, cut in 8 sections
10 new carrots
10 small onions
12 new potatoes

Thread together in serving portions
2 pounds fresh wax beans

Add to saucepan with
1 teaspoon salt

Cover. Bring to a boil and simmer for 20 minutes, or until vegetables are tender.

To serve, arrange chicken in centre of platter and surround with vegetables, removing thread, if desired.

SAUCE

Melt
½ cup butter

Stir in
3 tablespoons cognac
½ cup chopped parsley
¼ cup chopped chives or green onions

Makes 6 to 8 servings.

Cheese Soup

Cheese soup recipes abound throughout the country. This smooth-as-silk version with a flavour of onion came from Toronto, but should you prefer the more traditional variety, replace the milk with chicken broth and do not strain before serving.

Fry until transparent
2 large onions, chopped

in
3 tablespoons butter

Stir in until blended
2 tablespoons all-purpose flour

Gradually add
1 can (10 ounces) condensed beef bouillon

Cook until thickened, stirring constantly.

Add and simmer for 15 minutes
3 cups milk

Strain.

Stir in until smooth
3 cups grated process cheese

Reheat and serve immediately.

Makes 4 servings.

Clam Chowder

In the Maritimes chowder is an important item on the menu. Incidentally, the word chowder comes from the French *chaudière* meaning iron pot, which makes us think that the word originated in Eastern Canada.

Fry in a large heavy saucepan
¼ pound salt pork, diced
OR
4 slices side bacon, finely diced

Drain the crisp pork or bacon and reserve drippings.

Cook in pork drippings until transparent but not browned
1 onion, finely diced

Add
3 to 4 potatoes, diced
1½ cups boiling water
1 cup canned tomatoes, if desired

Bring to a boil and reduce heat. Cover, and cook for 10 minutes, or until potatoes are just tender.

Drain and reserve liquid from
2 cans (10 ounces each) clams
OR
1 pint fresh clams in liquor

Measure clam liquor and add sufficient milk to make
4 cups liquid

Add to cooked potatoes and heat slowly just to the boiling point.

Stir in drained clams and crisp pork or bacon together with
½ cup cream (18%)
1 teaspoon salt
1 teaspoon celery salt
pinch of pepper
2 teaspoons butter

Reheat just to boiling point and season to taste.

Serve garnished with paprika or parsley.

Makes 8 to 10 servings.

Fish Chowder

158

The Maritimers would be lost without their chowders, and now that the rest of Canada is learning to cherish them, you'll want this recipe.

Cut into bite-sized pieces
1 pound fillets, fresh or smoked

In large saucepan melt
2 tablespoons butter or other fat

Cook in melted fat until tender
1 medium onion, sliced
½ cup diced celery

Add
2 cups diced potatoes
½ cup sliced carrots
2 cups boiling water
1 teaspoon salt
pinch of pepper

Cover, and simmer for 10 minutes, or until vegetables are tender. Add fish and cook for 10 minutes longer.

Add
2 cups milk

Reheat, but do not boil.

Makes 6 servings.

Onion Soup au Gratin

A recipe that no doubt came from France; but it must have been some years ago as it is thoroughly integrated into our national cuisine.

In a heavy saucepan heat
¼ cup butter

Add
1½ cups sliced Bermuda onions

Cover, and brown very slowly, stirring occasionally until onions are a deep, even brown, (about 30 minutes).

Remove from heat and add
1 garlic clove, finely chopped
2 teaspoons flour
½ teaspoon salt
¼ teaspoon pepper
4 cups consommé

Return to heat and stir until it comes to a boil. Reduce heat and simmer, covered, for 20 minutes.

Sprinkle with
¾ cup grated Parmesan cheese

Preheat oven to 300° F.

Oven toast
4 thick slices French bread

When ready to serve put bread in the bottom of 4 individual soup bowls and fill with soup.

Sprinkle top with
¼ cup grated Parmesan cheese

Place under broiler to melt and slightly brown the cheese.

Makes 4 to 6 servings.

Soupe Aux Pois Classique

French-Canadian pea soup has become popular throughout the country and this version carefully follows the traditional method.

Wash and drain
1 pound dried green peas

Combine in large pot with
½ pound salt pork
2¾ quarts (13¾ cups) water
3 medium onions, finely chopped
2 carrots, cut in cubes
2 to 3 bay leaves
1 handful chopped celery leaves
¼ cup finely chopped parsley
1 teaspoon savory

Bring to a boil and boil for 2 minutes. Remove from heat and let rest for 1 hour. Bring to a boil again, lower heat and let simmer for 1½ hours, or until peas are cooked.

Stir in
1 tablespoon salt
½ teaspoon pepper

Serve.
If purée is preferred put through a colander, meat grinder or blender.

Makes 8 servings.

P.E.I. Potato Soup

Named after our island province which is noted for the high quality of its potatoes, this soup provides a happy compromise between that made with meat stock by the homesteaders and the modern cream of potato soup.

Cook together in covered saucepan for 25 minutes, or until tender

- **3 to 4 medium potatoes, quartered**
- **3 cups boiling water**
- **1 teaspoon salt**

(Part chicken or beef stock may be used instead of all water.)

Drain, reserve liquid and press potatoes through a sieve.

Combine in a large saucepan liquid from potatoes with

- **1 can (16 ounces) undiluted evaporated milk**
- **1 tablespoon grated onion**
- **3 tablespoons butter**
- **pinch of pepper**

Heat, but do not boil. Stir in sieved potatoes. Reheat and add water if necessary. Season to taste.

Stir in

- **½ cup grated cheese**

Heat until cheese melts.

Serve garnished with chopped parsley.

Makes 6 servings.

Red River Scotch Broth

The Earl of Selkirk, after three attempts, finally succeeded in establishing a settlement of Scots on the Red River, in Manitoba. The story of the hardship and tragedy of the first two groups to arrive so far from other settlements provides a fascinating chapter in Canadian history. It seems most fitting to name this traditional Scottish soup after this early settlement.

Soak overnight or for 2 hours in sufficient water to cover

- **⅓ cup pot or pearl barley**

Trim off all the fat and cut in 2-inch pieces

- **3 pounds stewing lamb**

In a large saucepan combine meat and lamb bones with

- **8 cups cold water**
- **2 teaspoons salt**
- **¼ teaspoon pepper**

Bring to a boil and skim.

Stir in

- **½ cup chopped onions**

Wrap loosely in cheesecloth and add

- **1 bay leaf, crushed**
- **2 whole cloves**

Cover and simmer about 45 minutes. Remove spice bag and bones, if desired.

Skim fat from broth, preferably by cooling overnight, or until fat hardens.

Drain barley and stir into broth. Bring to a boil. Cover and simmer 45 minutes.

Stir in

- **½ cup chopped onion**
- **½ cup diced turnip**
- **½ cup diced celery**
- **½ cup diced carrots**
- **½ cup diced potato**

Bring to a boil and simmer for 30 minutes, or until vegetables, meat and barley are tender. Add salt and pepper to taste.

Serve garnished with chopped parsley.

Makes 6 servings.

160

Salads

Very few salad recipes are to be found in early hand-written "receipt" books for the simple reason that salads as we know them are a twentieth century innovation. However, many of the vegetables used in today's salads were served raw and fresh in season, with vinegar, sugar and seasonings.

Cook books published in the 1880's include chapters on salads, but the choice was pretty much limited to chicken, potato, cabbage and oyster salads. The latter must have been very reasonable because one recipe calls for "50 small oysters" (for 6 servings). By the 1900's, moulded salad recipes appear in cook books, — usually tomato aspic — with the promotion of this new use for gelatine. Other unusual salad ingredients called for were sweetbreads, tongue, shad roe and for a breakfast salad "musk melon" served ice cold with salt, pepper, lemon juice and olive oil.

Pickled Cabbage

Some early cook books call it cold slaw and some kohl slaw — a German preparation of cabbage. There are cabbage slaws (or salads) for everyone — hot or cold; finely shredded or coarsely shredded; thin dressings or creamy ones.

Combine
½ cup cider vinegar
½ cup granulated sugar
¼ cup water
¼ teaspoon celery seeds
1 teaspoon salt
freshly ground pepper

Stir to dissolve sugar and salt. Taste the mixture and, depending upon the strength of the vinegar, add sugar, water and seasonings as necessary. Do not heat the mixture.

Pour the seasoned vinegar mixture over
4 cups shredded cabbage

Toss thoroughly.

Refrigerate for 24 hours before serving.

For variation add to the cabbage
1 cup grated carrots
1 cup grated cucumber
¼ cup finely chopped onion

Makes 6 servings pickled cabbage.

Makes 10 servings with added vegetables.

Hot Cabbage and Ham Salad

This is a modern version of hot kohl slaw, using commercial French dressing and ham in place of pork or bacon and a dressing.

Heat in a frypan
¾ cup bottled French- or Italian-type salad dressing

Add
4 cups coarsely shredded cabbage
3 tablespoons sliced green onions
½ teaspoon salt
pinch of pepper
¼ teaspoon dillweed (optional)
1 cup diced cooked ham

Stir gently to combine. Cover, and simmer for 10 to 12 minutes, or until cabbage is just tender.

Serve immediately. Good with crusty rolls and corn on the cob.

Makes 4 servings.

Fisherman's Treat

Fresh or frozen scallops from the Digby area of Nova Scotia are available all year to provide wonderful seafood dishes, both hot and cold. In this unusual salad, scallops are teamed with cooked potatoes, green beans and a well-seasoned dressing.

In a saucepan combine
2 cups water
2 tablespoons lemon juice
½ teaspoon salt
1 bay leaf
1 teaspoon instant minced onion

Bring to a boil and add
1 pound fresh or frozen (thawed) scallops

Reduce heat, cover and simmer for 5 minutes. Drain and cut scallops in halves or quarters, depending on size.

Cook until tender
4 to 5 medium potatoes

Cool, and slice ¼ inch thick.

Cook until just tender
1 cup fresh or frozen cut green beans

Marinate for at least 2 hours the scallops, potatoes and beans separately in a small amount of oil and vinegar dressing (avoid using a red or tomato-base dressing). Keep in refrigerator.

Combine scallops, potatoes and beans with a mixture of
1 cup mayonnaise
½ cup thick dairy sour cream
¼ cup chopped green onions
¼ cup chopped parsley
½ teaspoon dried dillweed
1 tablespoon horseradish
1 cup thinly sliced celery

Toss gently and arrange in lettuce-lined serving bowl. Garnish with cherry tomatoes or tomato wedges and lemon slices.

Makes 8 servings.

161

Moulded Beet Salad Ring

Jellied salads at one time often suffered from being too bland, but their visual appeal was so great that most community "socials" would have been considered a dismal flop without them.

Jellied salads, whether fish, fowl, fruit or vegetable, are the darlings of today's buffet table and are favoured by the hostess, as they may be prepared in advance.

Soften
2 envelopes unflavoured gelatine
in
½ cup cold water

Drain and reserve liquid from
2 cans (14 ounces each) diced beets

Finely chop the beets and measure 3 cups. Set aside until needed.

Measure into a saucepan
1½ cups beet liquid

Blend in
½ cup granulated sugar
1½ teaspoons salt
½ cup white vinegar

Bring to a boil, add the softened gelatine and stir until dissolved. Remove from heat. Chill until slightly thickened.

Fold in chopped beets with
1¼ cups finely diced celery
1 tablespoon finely chopped onion
2 tablespoons prepared horseradish

Pour into an oiled 6-cup ring mould or 8 individual moulds. Chill until set, preferably overnight for the large mould. To serve, unmould on salad greens and fill centre with cottage cheese (use a small glass comport if you have one the right size). Serve with cucumber mayonnaise.

Makes 8 to 10 servings.

Spiced Fruit Mould

Gay and colourful for buffet serving.

Soften
2 envelopes unflavoured gelatine

in
½ cup canned pineapple juice

Combine in a saucepan
3 cups canned pineapple juice
½ teaspoon whole cloves
½ teaspoon whole allspice
2 sticks cinnamon

Bring to a boil, reduce heat and simmer for 5 minutes. Remove spices, add softened gelatine and stir until dissolved.

Add
1 tablespoon lemon juice

Cool mixture and chill until it begins to thicken.

Fold in
2½ cups well-drained whole, diced or sliced fruit

Pour into a 6-cup mould and chill until firm, preferably overnight.

Suggested fruit combinations: diced unpeeled apples, diced celery, chopped walnuts; OR sliced peaches, green seedless grapes, red grapes, halved and seeded; OR crushed pineapple, fresh blueberries; OR diced pears, orange segments, 2 tablespoons chopped preserved ginger.

To serve, unmould on serving plate and garnish with fresh fruit in season (melon balls, raspberries, etc.) mint sprigs or watercress.

Serve with Creamy Orange Dressing or mayonnaise. Good with cold meats or poultry. Makes 8 servings.

CREAMY ORANGE DRESSING

Blend
¼ cup mayonnaise
1 package (4 ounces) cream cheese

Add
2 tablespoons liquid honey
2 tablespoons orange juice
1 tablespoon grated orange rind
¼ teaspoon salt
½ cup thick dairy sour cream

Combine until well blended.

Makes 1¾ cups.

Hot German Potato Salad

Hot potato salad, also called Dutch or German indicating the origins of the recipe, is a popular supper dish often accompanied by homemade head cheese and pickled cabbage. In the following recipe, bacon has replaced the crisp pieces of fried salt pork.

Cook until just tender
6 medium potatoes

Peel and slice while still hot (there should be 6 cups sliced potatoes) and keep warm in serving dish.

Cook until crisp
¼ pound side bacon, cut in pieces

Remove bacon, drain and add to the potatoes.

In
¼ cup of the bacon fat

gently fry
¼ cup sliced green onions or finely chopped cooking onions

Add
⅓ cup vinegar
⅓ cup beef broth or water
1 tablespoon granulated sugar
½ teaspoon salt
½ teaspoon celery salt
freshly ground pepper

Bring to a boil, pour over the potatoes and bacon and toss lightly to combine ingredients. Top with chopped parsley and paprika. Serve the salad hot.

Makes 6 servings.

Quinte Salad

This is a thoroughly modern salad despite the name Quinte, which implies United Empire Loyalists, antiques and historical sites (Bay of Quinte area in Ontario).

In a large bowl combine
2 cups diced cooked chicken
¾ cup diced cooked ham

¾ cup Swiss-style cheese, diced or in strips
2 hard-cooked eggs, chopped
1 cup finely diced celery
3 tablespoons thinly sliced green onion
1 tablespoon chopped green pepper
1 tablespoon chopped pimiento

Blend together
⅔ cup mayonnaise
¼ teaspoon poultry seasoning
¼ teaspoon dry mustard
1 tablespoon lemon juice or vinegar

Pour over meats and vegetables. Toss gently and season to taste. Refrigerate until needed.

To serve, toss with about
3 cups crisp shredded lettuce

Add more mayonnaise if necessary.

Serve in a lettuce-lined bowl and garnish with tomato wedges and radish roses.

Makes 4 to 6 servings.

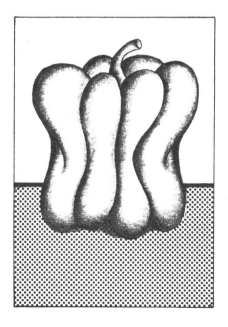

Tossed Green Salad à la Flemming

Today's popular tossed green salad is none other than grandmother's "spring greens" in a more sophisticated version. It is no longer a seasonal salad since choice fresh greens and vegetables are readily available all year.

This version of tossed salad, from New Brunswick, is attributed to H. J. Flemming, when he was Premier of that province. The recipe, a favourite of Mr. Flemming's, was publicized during National Salad Week.

In a salad bowl combine
1 cup shredded young spinach leaves
1 cup shredded lettuce
1 cup grated carrots
½ cup chopped parsley

Other vegetables such as chives, sliced green onions or snipped dandelion leaves may be added.

Combine
2 tablespoons vegetable oil
2 tablespoons vinegar
2 teaspoons granulated sugar
¼ teaspoon salt
freshly ground pepper

Add to salad and toss gently.

Makes 3 to 4 servings.

BASIC FRENCH DRESSING

Combine in jar or decanter with tight fitting lid
¾ cup vegetable oil
¼ cup vinegar
1 teaspoon salt
1 teaspoon sugar
½ teaspoon paprika
¼ teaspoon dry mustard

Shake until well blended.

Chill and shake each time before using.

Makes 1 cup.

White Salad for Weddings

One of the most popular salads in the 1930's was the make-ahead or twenty-four hour salad that appeared at innumerable social festivities — teas, showers, card parties and club meetings. Today it is often served at weddings.

In a large mixing bowl gently combine
2 cups drained canned white cherries, halved and pitted
2 cups drained pineapple tidbits
2 cups seedless green grapes
1 cup diced banana
1 cup sliced almonds, toasted
2 cups small marshmallows

Refrigerate.

In the top of a double boiler combine
2 eggs, well beaten
   OR
4 egg yolks
2 tablespoons granulated sugar
½ cup light cream (10%)
½ teaspoon finely grated lemon rind

Gradually add
3 tablespoons lemon juice

Cook over boiling water, stirring constantly, until thickened. Chill.

Fold in
1 cup heavy cream, whipped

Pour over fruit mixture and combine gently. Refrigerate 24 hours before serving. Do not freeze.

Serve in lettuce cups, garnished with silver dragées and cress.

Makes 10 servings.

Winnipeg Dandelion Salad

In early settlements, especially where land was not cleared sufficiently to provide the settler's wife with a kitchen garden, cooked or raw dandelion greens were a welcome change from the monotonous winter diet.

If you have a source of dandelion greens (not sprayed with weed killer), select and wash the small tender leaves before flowering takes place.

Wash and crisp
4 cups dandelion greens

Hard cook and cool
3 eggs

Fry until crisp
3 slices side bacon

Drain and crumble, reserving fat.

Dice 2 of the eggs and combine in a salad bowl with dandelion greens and bacon.

Add sufficient dressing to moisten.

Toss and arrange a "daisy" garnish on top made with the remaining hard-cooked egg.

DRESSING

Combine in a saucepan
2 tablespoons bacon fat
2 tablespoons all-purpose flour

Gradually add
2 cups warm water
¼ cup vinegar
2 tablespoons sugar

Cook over medium heat until mixture is thickened, stirring constantly. Stir a little of the hot mixture into
1 beaten egg

Return to saucepan and cook for 3 minutes longer, continuing to stir.

Season to taste with onion salt, curry powder, mustard or pepper. Chill.

To make the "daisy": sieve egg yolk onto centre of salad. Cut egg-white halves into 6 strips each and arrange these petals around the yellow centre.

Makes 4 to 6 servings.

Beverages

We skipped tea, coffee and cocoa, the most commonly prepared beverages, in order to present a more varied selection. We're certain you'll warm the pot when making tea and allow the tea to steep in a little boiling water for a few minutes before adding the rest of the boiling water — to produce a good "cuppa."

Okanagan Apple Punch

Apples are among the many fruits grown on the slopes of the famous Okanagan Valley, in British Columbia. This recipe for punch uses apple juice processed from these apples and is combined with spices, lemon juice, tea and ginger ale.

In a saucepan combine
- **1 cup water**
- **½ cup granulated sugar**
- **4 to 5 whole cloves**
- **⅓ stick of cinnamon**

Boil for 10 minutes. Strain.

Combine with
- **1½ cups strong tea**
- **¼ cup lemon juice**
- **1 can (48 ounces) apple juice**

Chill.

Just before serving stir in
- **1 cup ice water**
- **1½ cups ginger ale**

Makes 20 (4-ounce) servings.

Newfoundland Blueberry Wine

Place in a large kettle
- **2 quarts blueberries**
- **4 quarts boiling water**

Bring to a boil. Strain and measure.

For each gallon (20 cups) juice stir in
- **6 cups granulated sugar**

Boil for 5 minutes. Cool and add

- **3 cups prunes**

Place in crock or jar. Cover with cheesecloth and let stand for 2 months.

Strain, bottle and cork.

Muskoka Cranberry Cocktail

We've named this spicy hot beverage "Muskoka" because there is a large cranberry marsh near Gravenhurst, in the heart of the Muskoka district of Ontario.

In the bottom part of a 6-cup coffee percolator place
- **2⅓ cups water**
- **1 cup jellied cranberry sauce (broken up)**
- **1 cup pineapple juice**
- **¼ cup lightly packed brown sugar**
- **1 tablespoon butter**

Place in percolator basket or in cheesecloth bag
- **pinch of salt**
- **pinch of nutmeg**
- **pinch of cinnamon**
- **pinch of allspice**
- **4 whole cloves**

Assemble percolator and allow to complete regular coffee cycle, or percolate gently for 6 to 8 minutes.

If desired, add a few drops red food colouring. Serve hot .

Makes 6 (6-ounce) servings.

Dandelion Wine

From rural Alberta and Newfoundland came recipes for this old-time favourite.

Pour
- **1 gallon boiling water**

over
- **3 quarts dandelion blooms**

Let stand overnight. Strain.

Stir into liquid
- **juice of 3 lemons**
- **juice of 1 orange**
- **3 pounds granulated sugar**

Boil for 30 minutes. Cool.

Spread
- **1 slice toast**

with
- **½ yeast cake**

Add to liquid.

Let stand for 4 weeks, or until fermentation ceases. Bottle and cork well.

Lemonade

Many a Canadian as a child memorized this recipe to make on a hot sunny day and sell for a penny a glass on the city streets.

Cut in half and squeeze the juice from
6 lemons

Cut each rind half in four.

Combine lemon juice, pulp and rind with
2 pounds granulated sugar
1½ ounces citric acid

Cover with
1½ quarts (7½ cups) boiling water

Stir until sugar is dissolved. Allow to cool. Strain and pour into sterilized jars. Store in a cool place.

When serving, dilute 1 part syrup with 1 part water.

Makes 6 pints syrup.

Maple Leaf Cocktail

This national cocktail uses two locally produced products — rye and maple syrup.

Combine
2 parts rye whisky
1 part (or more) lemon juice
1 part maple syrup

Shake thoroughly with crushed ice just long enough to chill without diluting.

Strain.

Serve in chilled cocktail glasses with
twist of lemon peel

Pioneer Wild Raspberry Vinegar

Many a Canadian longs for just one glass of this old-time wild raspberry vinegar.

Place in an earthenware jar
2 quarts raspberries
1 quart cider vinegar

Cover, and let stand for 48 hours.

Drain off liquid from berries and pour over
1 quart raspberries

Let stand for 48 hours.

Repeat again with another
1 quart raspberries

Let stand for 48 hours.

Strain through a wet jelly bag until all juice is extracted.

Measure juice and for each cup stir in
1 cup granulated sugar

Boil slowly for 5 minutes. Skim. Let stand for 15 minutes.

For each cup juice stir in
2 ounces brandy

Bottle and seal.

When serving, dilute 1 part syrup with 3 parts water. Garnish with fresh mint.

Makes about 4 pints syrup.

Rhubarb Cocktail

Undoubtedly one of the reasons rhubarb grows so well in most settled areas of Canada can be attributed to our climate. Rhubarb develops a rich red colour under moderate temperatures, but in hotter weather this fades to an unappetizing green.

The tangy flavour of this recipe from Nova Scotia makes it a marvelous refresher.

Cut in chunks
5 pounds rhubarb

In a large saucepan combine with
2 tablespoons grated lemon rind
3 quarts water

Bring to a boil and simmer until rhubarb is tender.

Stir in
⅓ cup lemon juice

Strain through a cloth. Makes about 13 cups juice.

Stir into juice
3 cups granulated sugar

Bring to a boil. Pour into sterilized jars and seal. Store in a cool place.

Makes about 7 pints.

Rudi's Egg Liqueur

Popular in Holland and Germany, this beverage is made to be served during the Christmas season. It is a recent arrival to this country and has been named after the young German who shared the recipe with us. Vanilla sugar may be purchased in some food shops, or, if you prefer, slit a vanilla bean and bury it in some sugar.

Beat together
10 egg yolks
1 envelope (⅓ ounce) vanilla sugar

Place in a saucepan
1 quart milk
2¼ cups granulated sugar

Bring to a boil, stirring constantly until sugar is dissolved. Remove from heat. Stir some of hot milk into beaten egg yolks and then stir egg yolks into hot mixture.

Return to medium heat and, stirring constantly, reheat until first bubbles appear. Do not boil.

Cool custard mixture.

Thoroughly blend in
12 to 16 ounces alcohol

Pour into sterilized bottles. Soak new corks in boiling water to moisten and cork bottles. Store on sides in cool dark place to age for 2 weeks before using. Can be stored indefinitely.

Serve in small liqueur glasses with after-dinner coffee.

Makes about 3 pints.

Canadian Wine

Lief Ericson, who is reported to have discovered the eastern shores of the North American continent, found such a luxuriant growth of wild vines, some of which were undoubtedly wild grape, that he named his discovery Vineland. Starting with the French, early colonists planted European grape vines and attempted to make wine both from these and from the wild grapes found in abundance.

Today more than 20,000 acres of grapes are under cultivation in the Niagara Peninsula and about 60% of the crop goes into the production of wines. Many new varieties of special wine-making grapes have been planted in recent years, some imported from Europe and others developed through patient research in experimental vineyards here. The result has been a steady improvement in the calibre of Canadian wines — some have won international acknowledgements of their quality.

Wine varies according to the kind of grape from which it comes, and according to the method of production. Many wines are blended, which is an art requiring great skill and a thorough knowledge of wines.

Almost all wines belong to one of four principal classes:

1. Appetizer wines, which are served before a meal to stimulate the appetite, range from 15% to 20% in alcoholic content. They may be served at room temperature or cooled. Both sherry and vermouth are popular appetizer wines and both are produced by Canadian wineries.

2. Table wines contain less than 14% of alcohol. The white table wines are light bodied and have a delicate flavour. They should be served lightly chilled and generally with fish, chicken, eggs and light meats. Red table wines are usually dry and have a more robust flavour. They are served at room temperature or lightly chilled with roasts, steaks, game and other hearty meats. Rosé is a pink wine, dry to medium-sweet in flavour, and may be served with most foods. Some have a light effervescence and are described as "crackling". Rosé should be lightly chilled before serving.

3. Dessert wines are sweet with an alcoholic range from 16% to 20%. Port, muscatel and sweet sherry are examples.

4. Sparkling wines are light and bubbly and have an alcoholic content of less than 14%. Most sparkling wines, such as champagne and sparkling burgundy, are corked and should be stored on their side. They may be served at any time with any food and should be thoroughly chilled.

Canada does not produce "vintage" wines (wines of a particular year that have varying quality). Climatic conditions in the Niagara Peninsula are relatively stable so that the grapes are of good, even quality each year. To produce a consistently good product, Canadian wine makers blend the wines of three or four years' production.

Pastries

Pie, as we know it, is a North American specialty and the most popular dessert in Canada. The many different varieties show off our native foods to advantage and we found the regional differences fascinating.

Flaky Pastry

In Ontario, where soft winter wheat is grown, homemakers generally use pastry flour for most of their baking. Prairie cooks rely on all-purpose flour made from the hard spring wheat of the West. In British Columbia, the Maritimes and Quebec both types of flour are widely used — so our national pastry recipe gives the recommended amount of each flour.

Blend together
2 cups pastry (soft wheat) flour
OR
1¾ cups all-purpose flour
¾ teaspoon salt

Using a pastry blender or two knives, cut in until very fine
⅓ cup shortening or lard

Then cut in until the size of peas
⅓ cup shortening or lard

Stir in lightly with a fork, a tablespoon at a time,
4 to 5 tablespoons cold water

Use just enough water to make a dough that will cling together and clean easily from the bowl.

Divide in half. Roll each portion out on a lightly floured surface, rolling from the centre of the dough to the outside edge. (This will keep it round in shape.)

Extra pastry may be wrapped tightly in plastic wrap or wax paper and stored in refrigerator.

Makes sufficient pastry for one 9-inch 2-crust pie, or two 9-inch pie shells or 12 to 14 medium-sized tart shells.

Butter Pastry

To some Canadians, butter is an essential ingredient in pastry. In this version we try to have the best of both worlds.

Measure into a bowl
2 cups pastry (soft wheat) flour
OR
1⅔ cups all-purpose flour

With a pastry blender or two knives, cut in until the consistency of coarse meal
¼ cup shortening

Then cut in until the size of small peas
½ cup butter

Stir in with a fork, a tablespoon at a time,
3 to 5 tablespoons cold water

Add water only until dough almost clings together. Wrap in wax paper and chill.

Makes sufficient pastry for one 2-crust pie or 2 pie shells.

Klondike Never-Fail Pastry

Versions of this never-fail or refrigerator pastry may be found right across the country. This one, from Paradise Valley near Edmonton, Alberta, differs by calling for a small amount of brown sugar. We've named it Klondike, since Edmonton was a starting point for the well-known Yukon gold rush and the name itself means to many the cold northland — hence a refrigerator pastry.

Mix together
- **5½ cups all-purpose flour**
  OR
- **6⅓ cups pastry (soft wheat) flour**
- **1½ teaspoons salt**
- **1 teaspoon baking powder**
- **3 tablespoons brown sugar**

With a pastry blender or two knives, cut in
- **1 pound lard or shortening**

Continue cutting until the consistency of coarse meal with a few larger pieces. Break into a measuring cup and beat slightly
- **1 egg**

Add
- **1 tablespoon vinegar**

Fill cup to ¾ mark with
- **cold water**

and blend together with a fork.

With a fork, gradually stir liquid mixture into flour mixture. Add only enough liquid to make dough cling together.

Wrap tightly in wax paper and chill until ready to use.

Makes about three 9-inch double-crust pies or six 9-inch pie shells.

Sweet Pastry For Tarts

European settlers in Saskatchewan devised this sweeter pastry recipe to suit their tastes.

Blend together
- **2 cups pastry (soft wheat) flour**
  OR
- **1⅔ cups all-purpose flour**
- **3 tablespoons granulated sugar**
- **½ teaspoon salt**

With a pastry blender or two knives cut in until the consistency of coarse meal
- **¼ cup butter**

Cut in until the size of small peas
- **½ cup butter**

Beat slightly
- **1 egg**

With a fork, stir egg into flour mixture. Wrap tightly in wax paper and chill.

Makes sufficient pastry for one 2-crust pie or 2 pie shells.

Butter Tarts

Recipes for butter tarts appeared in cook books printed sixty to seventy years ago, and they seem to have been as nationally popular as they are today.

To prevent butter tarts from bubbling over, stir as little as possible.

Prepare sufficient pastry to line 15 medium-sized muffin cups. Do not prick.

Preheat oven to 375° F.

Pour boiling water over
- **½ cup raisins or currants**

Let stand 5 minutes and drain.

Stir together
- **¼ cup soft butter**
- **½ cup lightly packed brown sugar**

Blend in
- **1 cup corn syrup**
- **2 slightly beaten eggs**
- **1 teaspoon vanilla**
- **1 teaspoon lemon juice**

Stir in drained raisins.

Fill pastry-lined muffin cups ⅔ full.

Bake in 375° oven for 15 to 20 minutes, or until pastry is golden.

Do not allow filling to bubble.

Makes 15.

Lemon Cheese Tart Filling

Lemon cheese, butter, curd or whey are names that are commonly used for this type of rich filling for tarts. It keeps very well in the refrigerator.

Beat with a fork until blended
- **2 eggs**

Stir in
- **6 tablespoons lemon juice**
- **2 tablespoons grated lemon rind**
- **1 cup granulated sugar**

Add
- **¼ cup butter**

Cook in heavy saucepan over low heat until thick, resembling the consistency of soft custard.

Pour into jar. Cool. Store in refrigerator. When ready to use, spoon into baked tart shells.

Makes sufficient for 15 tarts.

Maple Pecan Tarts

Ontario adapts Quebec's sugar pie in this recipe. All maple syrup may be used if you have a plentiful supply. As with butter tarts, stir as little as possible to prevent the filling bubbling over during baking.

Prepare sufficient pastry to line 2 dozen medium-sized tart pans or muffin cups.

Preheat oven to 425° F.

Stir to combine
½ cup maple syrup
½ cup corn syrup

Beat slightly
2 eggs

Stir in
½ cup granulated sugar

and then syrup mixture.

Arrange in tart shells
1 cup pecan halves

Pour syrup mixture on top, filling ⅔ full.

Bake in 425° oven for 13 to 16 minutes, or until pastry is golden.

Makes 2 dozen tarts.

Old-Fashioned Molasses Tarts

This recipe came originally from Joe Batt's Arm on Fogo Island, which is at the entrance to Notre Dame Bay off the coast of Newfoundland. Sometimes instead of tarts the same pastry is used to make a pie or "tart." (Some Newfoundlanders use the English terminology and speak of a tart when referring to a dessert pie.) Serve with clotted cream or whipped cream.

Preheat oven to 425° F.

Sift or blend together
1½ cups all-purpose flour
½ teaspoon allspice
½ teaspoon cinnamon
pinch of cloves
pinch of salt

With a pastry blender or two knives, cut in
½ cup shortening

With a fork, stir in
¼ cup molasses

Blend in
2 to 3 tablespoons cold water

Roll dough out on a lightly floured surface. Cut with a floured cookie cutter and line about 2 dozen small-sized muffin cups.

Fill tart shells ⅔ full with
partridgeberry or blueberry jam

Bake in 425° oven for 12 to 15 minutes, or until brown.

Makes 2 dozen tarts.

Toronto Pie

The *Home Cook Book*, published in Toronto in 1879, included a recipe for Toronto pie. Although continuing as a family favourite, the name slipped into disuse during the intervening years. A delicate, hot-milk sponge cake split and filled with raspberry jam, Toronto pie belongs to the same family as Boston cream pie.

Preheat oven to 350° F.

Grease a 9-inch round layer cake pan and line with wax paper.

Combine
½ cup scalded milk
2 tablespoons butter

Sift or blend together
1 cup pastry (soft wheat) flour
1¼ teaspoons baking powder
¼ teaspoon salt

Beat until very light and fluffy
2 eggs

Gradually beat in
⅔ cup granulated sugar
¼ teaspoon vanilla

With mixer at high speed beat for one minute. Fold in dry ingredients and then stir in hot milk mixture. Turn into prepared pan.

Bake in 350° oven for 30 to 35 minutes, or until cake springs back when lightly touched.

Cool in pan. When almost cool, loosen edges and remove from pan. Split into two layers, sandwich together with raspberry jam and sprinkle top with granulated sugar or icing sugar.

Alberta Honey Apple Pie

The spicy honey flavour blends well with the apples and the glaze adds a festive touch, in this pie from Alberta.

Preheat oven to 450° F.

Prepare sufficient pastry for a 2-crust 9-inch pie. Roll out half the dough, line pie plate and trim. Roll out top crust.

Peel, core and slice thinly
6 medium-sized apples

Turn into pastry-lined pie plate.

Mix together
1 tablespoon cornstarch
1 teaspoon cinnamon
½ teaspoon salt
3 tablespoons brown sugar

Blend in
3 tablespoons butter
⅓ cup honey

Pour over apples.

Cover with top crust. Seal and flute edges. Slit or prick top crust.

Bake in 450° oven for 15 minutes, or until pastry is golden. Reduce heat to 350° and bake for 25 to 30 minutes longer, or until fruit is tender.

Mix together and spread over top
¼ cup brown sugar
¼ cup honey
2 tablespoons all-purpose flour
2 tablespoons soft butter
¼ cup chopped walnuts

Return to oven for 10 minutes.

Old-Fashioned Apple Pie

At one time apples were buried in sand-filled barrels to retain their freshness all winter long. Now, as then, they swell the crust of this time-honoured version of apple pie.

Preheat oven to 450° F.

Prepare sufficient pastry for a 2-crust 9-inch pie. Roll out half the dough, line pie plate and trim. Roll out top crust.

Mix together
1 tablespoon flour
1 cup maple sugar or lightly packed brown sugar
½ teaspoon cinnamon
pinch of nutmeg

Combine with
7 or 8 large tart apples, peeled, cored and sliced

Turn into pastry-lined pie plate.

Dot with
1 tablespoon butter

Cover with top crust. Seal and flute edges. Slit or prick top crust.

Bake in 450° oven for 15 minutes, or until pastry is golden. Reduce heat to 350° and bake for 40 to 45 minutes longer, or until fruit is tender.

If desired, serve with Hot Rum Sauce (see page 121).

Fresh Berry Pie

From the partridgeberries of Newfoundland to the salal berries of British Columbia our land is "just the berries." We've tested this recipe with the more common fruits such as raspberries, blueberries, Saskatoon berries and blackberries, and we hope it will serve at least as a guide for using other berries.

Preheat oven to 450° F.

Prepare sufficient pastry for a 2-crust 9-inch pie. Roll out half the dough, line pie plate and trim. Roll out top crust.

Mix together
¼ cup all-purpose flour
¾ cup granulated sugar
pinch of salt

Combine with
4¼ cups berries

Turn into pastry-lined pie plate.

Dot with
1 tablespoon butter

Cover with top crust. Seal and flute edges. Slit or prick top crust.

Bake in 450° oven for 15 minutes. Reduce heat to 350° and bake for 50 to 55 minutes longer, or until filling is thickened and fruit is tender.

Note: If using strawberries, increase sugar to 1 cup.

Frozen Berry Pie

Designed for berries frozen without sugar, this simple pie brings to the table all year round the fresh berries of our land.

Preheat oven to 450° F.

Prepare sufficient pastry for a 2-crust 9-inch pie. Roll out half the dough, line pie plate and trim. Roll out top crust.

Mix together
> 1¾ **cups granulated sugar**
> ¼ **cup cornstarch**

Combine with
> 1 **package (20 ounces) or 4½ cups frozen berries, unthawed**

Turn into pastry-lined pie plate.

Dot with
> 2 **tablespoons butter**

Cover with top crust. Seal and flute edges. Slit or prick top crust.

Bake in 450° oven for 20 minutes. Reduce heat to 350° and bake for 50 to 65 minutes longer, or until filling is thickened.

Homespun Pie

This recipe from Nova Scotia indicates the ingenuity of the early homemakers to adapt recipes to utilize readily available foods, thus producing regional Canadian specialties. This pie closely resembles mincemeat pie, but is much more economical and has a tangy flavour all its own.

Preheat oven to 450° F.

Prepare sufficient pastry for a 2-crust 9-inch pie. Roll out half the dough, line pie plate and trim. Roll out top crust.

Combine in 4-quart saucepan
> 3 **cups grated raw potato**
> 2 **cups grated raw apple**
> 2 **cups raisins**
> 2 **cups lightly packed brown sugar**
> ½ **cup mixed peel**
> ½ **cup molasses**
> ½ **cup vinegar**
> 3 **cups hot water**
> 1½ **teaspoons salt**
> 2 **teaspoons nutmeg**
> 2 **teaspoons cinnamon**
> 3 **tablespoons butter**

Simmer slowly over low heat for about 30 minutes, or until thick. Watch carefully as it burns readily.

This makes sufficient for 4 pies.

Remainder may be sealed hot in sterilized jars for future use.

Turn 4 cups filling into pastry-lined pie plate. Cover with top crust. Seal and flute edges and slit or prick top crust.

Bake in 450° oven for 10 minutes, or until pastry is golden. Reduce heat to 350° and bake for 30 minutes longer.

Mincemeat Pie

There is an old story about the farmer's wife who made, baked and froze her pies during the winter months. When asked how she knew which pie was which she replied that she marked the pie top with T. M. — meaning T'is Mince and T'aint Mince. There's no doubt about this filling — T'is Mince!

Preheat oven to 450° F.

Prepare sufficient pastry for a 2-crust 9-inch pie. Roll out half the dough, line pie plate and trim. Roll out top crust.

Turn into pastry-lined pie plate
> 4 **cups mincemeat (see page 137)**

Cover with top crust. Seal and flute edges and slit or prick top crust. Bake in 450° oven for 15 minutes, or until pastry is golden. Reduce heat to 350° and bake for 30 minutes longer.

Serve hot, and, if desired, with Hot Rum Sauce (see page 121).

Niagara Peach Pie

Fruit growers in the Niagara Peninsula are watching with apprehension the slow but definite industrialization of their precious orchards and farms. Peaches and other fruits were grown in the Niagara area as early as 1790, introduced, it is believed, by Count de Boussaye, a French emigré. Mrs. Simcoe mentions in her diary the orchard behind the Lieutenant Governor's official residence and how they enjoyed fruits all summer long.

Preheat oven to 450° F.

Prepare sufficient pastry for a 2-crust 9-inch pie. Roll out half the dough, line pie plate and trim. Roll out top crust.

Mix together
⅔ cup granulated sugar
3 to 4 tablespoons cornstarch

Combine with
4½ cups sliced, peeled, fresh peaches (about 8)

Turn into pastry-lined pie plate.

Dot with
2 tablespoons butter

Sprinkle with
1 tablespoon lemon juice

Cover with top crust. Seal and flute edges and slit or prick top crust. Bake in 450° oven for 15 minutes. Reduce heat to 350° and bake for 50 to 55 minutes longer, or until filling is thickened.

Raisin Pie

Here is a standard 2-crust raisin pie that really needs no introduction. Some devotees chop the raisins to enhance the flavour.

Preheat oven to 450° F.

Prepare sufficient pastry for a 2-crust 9-inch pie. Roll out half the dough, line pie plate and trim. Roll out top crust.

Simmer together for 10 minutes
2 cups seedless raisins
2 cups water

Mix together and gradually stir into raisins
½ to ⅔ cup granulated sugar
2 tablespoons flour
pinch of salt

Blend in
½ teaspoon vanilla
1 tablespoon butter
1 tablespoon lemon juice (optional)

Cool. Turn into pastry-lined pie plate.

Cover with top crust. Seal and flute edges and slit or prick top crust.

Bake in 450° oven for 15 minutes, or until pastry is golden. Reduce heat to 350° and bake for 25 to 30 minutes longer.

Rhubarb Pie

At one time called "pie plant," rhubarb has been a favourite for pies in Canada since it was first brought to this country from Europe. Modern growing of rhubarb in well-sheltered heat-controlled buildings during the winter means that it first appears on the market in January, and not until July does the last of the outdoor variety disappear.

Preheat oven to 450° F.

Prepare sufficient pastry for a 2-crust 9-inch pie. Roll out half the dough, line pie plate and trim. Roll out top crust.

Mix together
⅓ cup all-purpose flour
1 to 1½ cups granulated sugar

Combine with
4 cups cut rhubarb (1-inch pieces)

Turn into pastry-lined pie plate.

Dot with
1 tablespoon butter

Cover with top crust. Seal and flute edges and slit or prick top crust.

Bake in 450° oven for 15 minutes, or until pastry is golden. Reduce heat to 350° and bake for 40 to 45 minutes longer, or until fruit is tender and bubbly at centre.

Traditional Custard Pie

Many ideas exist for preventing the bottom crust of custard pies from becoming moist. We prefer high temperature baking for the first few minutes, and it's a good idea to bake the pie near the bottom of the oven.

Preheat oven to 450° F.

Prepare sufficient pastry and line a 9-inch pie plate. Trim, flute edge, but do not prick.

Scald
2½ cups milk

Beat slightly
3 eggs

Stir in
⅓ cup granulated sugar
¼ teaspoon salt

Gradually stir in scalded milk.

Add
1 teaspoon vanilla

Strain into pie shell.

Sprinkle with
few grains of nutmeg

Bake in 450° oven for 10 minutes. Reduce heat to 325° and bake for 30 to 40 minutes longer, or until filling is almost set. Cool.

Homestead Pie

The name reflects the origin of this recipe, for in these early homes the spices, butter and dried fruits were carefully hoarded to make this special-occasion pie.

Preheat oven to 450° F.

Prepare sufficient pastry and line a 9-inch pie plate. Trim, flute edge, but do not prick.

Cream together
½ cup butter
1 cup lightly packed brown sugar

Beat in
4 egg yolks
1 teaspoon vanilla

Blend together and stir in
½ cup pastry (soft wheat) flour
1 teaspoon cinnamon
½ teaspoon allspice
½ teaspoon nutmeg

Stir in
1 cup cream (18%)
½ cup chopped dates
½ cup raisins
½ cup coarsely chopped pecans

Turn into unbaked pie shell.

Bake in 450° oven for 15 minutes, or until crust is golden. Reduce heat to 350° and bake for 30 to 35 minutes longer, or until almost set.

Cool. Top with meringue, if desired.

Molasses Pie

When Newfoundlanders talk of molasses pie, they refer to a very simple mixture of 1 cup molasses and 1 egg blended together and baked in an unbaked pastry shell until the filling sets.

In Quebec variety abounds and no one seems to be able to resolve the controversy of whether *ferlouche* or molasses pie should be thickened with egg, flour or cornstarch, and whether or not to add raisins. Our version follows the Quebec custom of cooking the filling first.

Preheat oven to 425° F.

Prepare sufficient pastry and line a 9-inch pie plate. Trim, flute edge and prick. Bake in 425° oven for 10 to 12 minutes, or until golden. Cool.

In a saucepan combine
⅓ cup cornstarch
½ cup lightly packed brown sugar

Stir in
½ cup table molasses
1½ cups water
1 tablespoon grated lemon rind
pinch of nutmeg

Cook over medium heat, stirring constantly, until thickened. Cover, and cook for 2 minutes longer, stirring occasionally.

Cool to lukewarm and turn into prepared pie shell. Chill.

Serve topped with whipped cream

Schnitz Pie

The first Mennonite community in Canada was at Twenty Mile Creek, on Lake Ontario, and subsequent arrivals journeyed beyond Hamilton into central Ontario to settle in what was then bush. Even today a leisurely drive through Waterloo County shows to advantage the prosperous farms that these industrious and God-fearing people carved out of the wilderness. Although they still dress simply and travel by horse and carriage, their communities have grown in size and prosperity due to their agricultural skills.

Most of the womenfolk excel in cooking, relying on sight and touch rather than actual recipes. For this reason, we particularly prize this schnitz pie recipe. Formerly the apple slices, or as they say *apfel schnitz*, were dried for longer storage, but now fresh apples are used.

Preheat oven to 450° F.

Prepare sufficient pastry and line a 9-inch pie plate. Trim, flute edge, but do not prick.

Beat with a rotary beater until smooth
   3 tablespoons flour
   ¾ cup granulated sugar
   1 cup thick dairy sour cream

Arrange attractively in pie shell
   5 cups peeled apple quarters

Pour sour cream mixture over top.

Bake in 450° oven for 15 minutes, reduce heat to 350° and bake for 35 to 40 minutes longer, or until fruit is tender and filling set.

Sprinkle over hot pie
   ¼ cup lightly packed brown sugar

Broil for 2 to 3 minutes, or until sugar is melted.

Serve warm.

Elmira Peach Pie

This delightful combination of sugar, sour cream and fresh peaches comes from Elmira, Ontario, in Waterloo County. This region is largely populated by descendants of German immigrants of the Mennonite and Amish faiths who are noted for their honesty, industry and their wonderful food.

Preheat oven to 450° F.

Prepare sufficient pastry and line a 9-inch pie plate. Trim, flute edge, but do not prick.

Beat with a rotary beater until smooth
   ⅓ cup all-purpose flour
   ½ cup granulated sugar
   1 cup thick dairy sour cream

Arrange flat edge down in concentric circles in pie shell
   5 cups quartered, peeled peaches (about 9)

Pour sour cream mixture over top.

Bake in 450° oven for 15 minutes. Reduce heat to 350° and bake for 30 to 35 minutes longer, or until filling is set.

Sprinkle over hot pie
   ¼ cup lightly packed brown sugar

Broil for 2 to 3 minutes, or until sugar is melted.

Serve warm.

Pumpkin Pie

Pumpkin pie varies with each region in Canada — in the Eastern Townships some like a touch of molasses while some demand that it be served with maple syrup. We decided to sit on the fence with regard to white or brown sugar.

Preheat oven to 450° F.

Prepare sufficient pastry and line a 9- or 10-inch pie plate. Trim, flute edge, but do not prick.

Beat together
   2 eggs
   1 cup milk
   1 can (14 ounces) or 1½ cups pumpkin
   ½ teaspoon salt

Mix together and stir into pumpkin mixture
   1⅓ cups lightly packed brown sugar
   OR
   1 cup granulated sugar
   1 teaspoon cinnamon
   ½ teaspoon ginger
   ½ teaspoon nutmeg
   ¼ teaspoon cloves

Pour into pie shell.

Bake in 450° oven for 10 minutes. Reduce heat to 350° and bake for 45 to 50 minutes longer, or until almost set.

Shoofly Pie

Shoofly pie originated with the German settlers, who served it as a breakfast coffee cake. Similar to the lassy tart of Newfoundland, which calls for molasses, egg and soft bread crumbs, this particular recipe came from Quebec—we wonder whether it travelled there from Nova Scotia, Pennsylvania or Waterloo County, Ontario, or whether it was a heritage of the United Empire Loyalists of German origin who settled in Quebec after 1776.

Preheat oven to 450° F.

Prepare sufficient pastry and line a 9-inch pie plate. Trim, flute edge, but do not prick.

Combine
⅓ cup molasses
⅓ cup honey
1 cup boiling water

Blend together until crumbly
⅓ cup butter
¾ cup lightly packed brown sugar
¾ cup all-purpose flour

Sprinkle one third of crumb mixture in pie shell. Pour half of liquid mixture on top.

Sprinkle on top
½ cup raisins
½ cup chopped walnuts

Repeat crumb layer and then remaining liquid.

Top with remainder of crumbs.

Bake in 450° oven for 15 minutes. Reduce heat to 350° and bake for 25 to 30 minutes longer, or until set.

Serve slightly warm, with pouring cream or whipped cream.

Modern Sugar Pie

This recipe comes from the Eastern Townships of Quebec and it results in a perfectly smooth, fuller sugar pie than customary. Perhaps its simplicity combined with the excellent results account for its popularity in Sherbrooke and the surrounding countryside.

Preheat oven to 425° F.

Prepare sufficient pastry and line a 9-inch pie plate. Trim, flute edge, but do not prick.

In the top of a double boiler combine
1½ cups corn syrup
1 cup condensed milk

Heat over boiling water for 5 minutes, or until blended.

Pour into prepared pie shell.

Sprinkle with
½ cup pecan halves

Bake in 425° oven for 10 minutes. Reduce heat to 350° and bake for 20 to 25 minutes longer, or until filling bubbles in the centre.

Quebec Sugar Pie

Quebec sugar pie has as many versions as cooks but tradition demands that the filling be somewhat thin in consistency and, because of its richness, that the depth of filling be much less than for pies in general.

Nowadays the maple sugar version denotes that spring is on the way.

Preheat oven to 375° F.

Prepare sufficient pastry and line a 9-inch pie plate. Trim, flute edge, but do not prick.

Bring to a boil over low heat
2 cups lightly packed brown sugar
OR
2 cups soft maple sugar, chopped
1 cup heavy cream

Cook, stirring slowly, for 10 minutes, or until thickened.

Remove from heat and stir in
½ cup chopped nuts

Cool. Pour into prepared pie shell.

Bake in 375° oven for 30 to 35 minutes.

Cool. Filling will set when cold.

Butterscotch Pie

Fond memories of good old-time butterscotch pie prompted the development of this simplified recipe calling for dark-brown sugar, thus eliminating the caramelizing of the sugar.

Preheat oven to 425° F.

Prepare sufficient pastry and line a 9-inch pie plate. Trim, flute edge and prick. Bake in 425° oven for 10 to 12 minutes, or until golden. Cool.

Scald
2¾ cups milk

In a saucepan combine
- **¼ cup cornstarch**
- **1¼ cups lightly packed dark-brown sugar**
- **½ teaspoon salt**

Gradually add scalded milk. Cook over medium heat, stirring constantly, until thickened. Reduce heat, cover and cook for 2 minutes longer, stirring occasionally.

Stir a small amount of hot mixture into
- **3 slightly beaten egg yolks**

then blend into remaining hot mixture. Cook for 2 minutes longer, stirring constantly.

Remove from heat and blend in
- **2 tablespoons butter**
- **1 teaspoon vanilla**

Cool to lukewarm and pour into prepared pie shell.

If desired, top with meringue of
- **3 egg whites**
- **¼ teaspoon cream of tartar**
- **⅓ cup granulated sugar**

Return to 400° oven for 5 minutes, or until meringue is golden.

Cool at room temperature.

Lemon Meringue Pie

The name should prove sufficient enticement to try this favourite. In early days, when lemons were in short supply, vinegar replaced some of the lemon juice. Today we enjoy the full lemon flavour.

Preheat oven to 425° F.

Prepare sufficient pastry and line a 9-inch pie plate. Trim, flute edge and prick. Bake in 425° oven for 10 to 12 minutes, or until golden. Cool.

Reduce oven heat to 400°.

In a saucepan combine
- **½ cup cornstarch**
- **1 cup granulated sugar**
- **¼ teaspoon salt**

Gradually add
- **3 cups boiling water**

Cook over medium heat, stirring constantly, until thickened. Cover and cook for 2 minutes longer, stirring occasionally.

Stir a small amount of hot mixture into
- **3 slightly beaten egg yolks**

then blend into remaining hot mixture. Cook one minute longer, stirring constantly.

Remove from heat and blend in
- **1 tablespoon butter**
- **¼ teaspoon vanilla**
- **1 tablespoon grated lemon rind**
- **½ cup lemon juice**

Cool to lukewarm and turn into prepared pie shell.

Top with a meringue of
- **3 egg whites**
- **¼ teaspoon cream of tartar**
- **⅓ cup granulated sugar**

Return to 400° oven for 5 minutes, or until meringue is golden.

Cool at room temperature.

Maple Syrup Pie

Three quarters of the maple products in Canada come from the province of Quebec and the other quarter from New Brunswick and Ontario.

In this recipe, typical of Quebec, both flour and eggs set the syrup to a custardy smoothness during baking.

Preheat oven to 400° F.

Prepare sufficient pastry and line a 9-inch pie plate. Trim, flute edge, but do not prick.

Beat slightly
- **2 eggs**

Mix together and blend in
- **1 cup lightly packed brown sugar**
- **2 tablespoons flour**

Stir in
- **1 cup maple syrup**
- **2 tablespoons butter, melted**
- **½ cup coarsely chopped nuts**
- **1 teaspoon vanilla**
- **pinch of salt**

Pour into prepared pie shell.

Bake in 400° oven for 35 to 40 minutes, or until filling is set.

Cool.

Canadian Menus

Although its story has never been told before the recipes in this cook book demonstrate conclusively that we do have a Canadian cuisine. But a Canadian cook book which merely assembled these recipes would only give part of the picture. The way that these foods are grouped together and served as meals, whether breakfast, lunch or dinner, completes the story of our national cuisine.

In this section, therefore, we have placed five regional menus: British Columbia, the Prairie Provinces, Ontario, Quebec, and the Atlantic Provinces; special-occasion menus for Christmas Eve, New Year's Day, Easter Sunday, and Dominion Day, and a menu for a Saturday night family supper.

Saturday Supper

Clam Chowder

Glazed Back Bacon

Baked Beans with Tomato Butter

Coleslaw

Shediac Brown Bread   Oatmeal Brown Bread

St. Lawrence Maple Dumplings

OR

Applesauce with Spicy Crumb Cake

British Columbia Dinner

Crab Meat Bouchées

Okanagan Apple Punch

Stuffed Fraser River Salmon

Tartar Sauce

Mashed Potatoes   Herb Scalloped Tomatoes

Spiced Fruit Mould

Pulla   Capilano Rye Bread

Trifle

Nanaimo Bars   Hvorost

Prairie Dinner

Muk-Luk Mardi-Gras Bean Soup

Winnipeg Goldeye with Lemon Wedges

Salt Broiled Steaks

Yorkton Nachynka   Buttered Carrots

Dandelion or Tossed Green Salad

Versatile Muffins   Hot Bannock

Alberta Honey Apple Pie

Ontario Dinner

Hot Cheese Tartelettes

Piquant Honey Chicken

Magnetawan Rhubarb Relish

Steamed Wild Rice   Scalloped Turnip and Apples

Sliced Tomatoes

Early Ontario Sour Cream Biscuits
OR
York County Corn Bread

Fresh Fruit Ice Cream   Butternut Spice Cake

Canadian White Wine

Quebec Dinner

Onion Soup au gratin
Les côtelettes de porc Charlevoix
Pommes de terre en robes des champs
Buttered spinach
Pain sur la sole
(French bread)
Modern Sugar Pie
Homemade Wine

East Coast Supper

Soused Herring
P.E.I. Potato Soup
Corned Beef and Cabbage
Bread and Butter Pickles
Corn Fritters
Trappers Bread   Abegweit Oatcakes
Annapolis Apple Pudding
OR
Old-Fashioned Molasses Tarts
Newfoundland Blueberry Wine

Christmas Eve Buffet

Canadian Sherry
Cretons
Ontario Spiced Beef
Cold Sliced Turkey
Tourtière
South Essex Chili Sauce   Bread and Butter Pickles
Holubtse
Moulded Beet Salad Ring   White Salad
Dutch Kringle Bread   100% Whole Wheat Bread
Bonavista Fruit Bread
Bûche de Noël
Christmas Cake   Scotch Cookies
Maple Leaf Cocktail

New Year's Dinner

Muskoka Cranberry Cocktail

Roast Turkey with Old-Fashioned Stuffing

Green Pepper Jelly

Parsley Potatoes

Mashed Turnips   Buttered Peas

Celery and Carrot Sticks

Christmas Pudding with Foamy Sauce

Mincemeat Pie

Fredericton Walnut Toffee

Easter Dinner

Grapefruit Baskets

Baddeck Scotch Eggs

Glazed Ham with Pickled Peaches

Baked Potato   Asparagus Tips

Pickled Cabbage

Paska   Greek Easter Bread

Rhubarb or Lemon Meringue Pie

Canadian Sparkling Rosé

Dominion Day Patio Party

Solomon Gundy

Rhubarb Cocktail

Cold Sliced Peasant's Coulibiac

OR

Barbecued Spareribs

Montrose Pickled Baby Corn

OR

Spiced Crabapple Jelly

Potato Chips   Tomatoes Stuffed with Curried Rice

Sliced Cucumbers in Sour Cream

Sourdough Bread   Blueberry Muffins

Jemseg Strawberry Shortcake

OR

Butter Tarts

Canadian Cheese and Crackers

Lemonade

Cooking Terms

Bake —To cook by dry heat, usually in an oven.

Barbecue — To roast slowly on a rack or spit, over coals or a free flame, or to serve highly seasoned sauce.

Baste — To spoon a liquid over a solid is to baste it as in roasting of meats, when hot fat is spooned over.

Beat — To make a mixture smooth or to introduce air with a brisk lifting motion. (See Eggs).

Blend — To stir until each ingredient has lost its own identity.

Boil — To heat a liquid until it bubbles rapidly.

Braise — To brown floured and seasoned meat, etc. with fat in a frypan and then add a little liquid and simmer, covered.

Broil — To cook by exposing surfaces of food to dry heat. Used for tender meat, young poultry or fish.

Browned flour — Flour that has been cooked until golden in an ungreased heavy pan. Use twice the amount of browned flour to thicken gravy as regular flour.

Cream — To stir and beat until soft and fluffy.

Cut in — Usually used when cutting firm fat into a dry mixture of flour, etc. May be done (1) with a wire pastry blender, each wire of which cuts through the fat or (2) with two knives used scissor fashion. Cut cleanly, sharply, without twisting, reducing fat to size indicated.

Dot with — To arrange small portions of a solid ingredient (generally butter) over surface.

Drain — (1) To completely pour off such liquid as water, juice, etc., from solids. (2) To place fried food on paper towelling or other absorbent paper, to remove the fat from the surface of the food.

Dredge — To sprinkle food evenly and generously.

Drippings — The fat which melts from meat, during roasting, broiling or frying.

Eggs — To Beat to Given Degree — If whole eggs are to be beaten "slightly" that means just until whites and yolks are sufficiently intermingled that neither can be seen alone. If to be beaten "well," yolks and whites together should be beaten with a rotary beater (electric or hand-turned) until very light — lots of air beaten in. To Separate — Over a bowl, crack shell of egg on one side with a knife, then with thumbs, pull half the shell. Slip yolk from one half shell to the other to drain off all the white possible. Should you get a tiny streak of yolk in the white, use a piece of shell to remove it cleanly.

Egg Whites — To Beat Stiff — In several recipes it says to beat egg whites "to form stiff but moist peaks". This means to beat them until they hold their shape and the bowl could be turned upside down without the whites slipping out. The surface of the beaten whites must still be glossy.

Fold — Generally used with regard to combining whipped cream or stiffly beaten egg white with another mixture. The purpose is to blend it in without losing any of the air incorporated in the whipped cream or beaten egg white. With a rubber spatula or wooden spoon (upside down), touching bowl all the time, carry spatula or spoon down one side, across the bottom of bowl and up the opposite side turning to have right or other side up. Turn bowl slightly and repeat until no blobs of egg white or whipped cream are visible.

Fricassee — To cook by braising.

Fry — To cook food with fat. (1) Panfrying calls for just a little fat to prevent food from sticking. (2) Deep-frying is to immerse and cook plain or coated food in deep fat at suitable temperature.

Glaze — A film over the surface of food such as a syrup or sugar glaze on ham, a thickened transparent sweet coating over fruit in pies and tarts, or a clear coating formed on candied fruits and nuts.

Grind — To reduce to particles in meat grinder or food blender.

Knead — A folding over and pressing together of dough to make it more elastic. Generally used for yeast doughs and some quick breads. Lift one half of dough with fingertips and fold over to give a double thickness; then press together with heels of the hands. Give dough a quarter turn and repeat.

Marinate — To steep a solid food for a time in a flavourful liquid.

Meringue — Beaten egg white into which sugar or syrup has been beaten.

Mince — To grind or chop very fine.

Pare — To cut off the outside covering.

Pastry Cloth — A piece of canvas used as a surface for rolling out pastry, cookie doughs and tea biscuit so that the dough itself absorbs a minimum amount of flour.

Peel — To strip off the outside covering.

Plump — To cover raisins with boiling water and let stand 2 to 3 minutes.

Poach — To cook gently in simmering liquid.

Pot Roast — To brown meat on all sides with high heat and then finish cooking in covered pan with small amount of liquid.

Roast — To cook tender meat or poultry by dry heat in the oven using an uncovered pan.

Rise, Rising — When yeast dough is set in a warm place (90° F.) to permit the yeast to form a gas which permeates the dough thus increasing the volume.

Sauté — To brown or cook in a small amount of fat (see Fry).

Scald — To make hot, but not to the point of boiling. Liquid has reached "scalding point" when bubbles form a ring against side of pan, but do not appear across surface of liquid.

Seasoning — Salt is the primary seasoning for food — used to bring out natural flavours of all other ingredients. For additional flavour, add pepper, mustard and any other spices, herbs, onion (and all its kin, from delicate chives to pungent garlic), salts that have been given the special flavour of celery, onion, garlic, etc., vinegars of various flavours and bottled sauces.

Simmer — To cook over gentle heat just below boiling point.

Soufflé — A very airy mixture consisting of very lightly beaten egg. It may be baked, in which case it must be served immediately it comes from the oven.

Steam — To cook food in a covered perforated container set over a pot of boiling water.

Stew — To cook gently in liquid.

Stir — To mix food materials with a circular motion to secure a uniform consistency.

Stock — The liquid in which meat, fish, poultry or vegetables have been cooked.

Yeast — This is a tiny living plant that grows under proper conditions, producing carbon dioxide gas to make a dough rise. It is more readily purchased as active dry yeast which consists of tiny beige-coloured pellets. Compressed fresh yeast is available in cake form. For best results soften dry yeast in sweetened water at 100°F. To substitute fresh yeast for active dry yeast, use one yeast cake for each envelope of dry yeast and do not sweeten the water which should be at 80°F.

Whip — To beat rapidly to produce expansion due to incorporation of air, as applied to heavy cream, eggs and gelatine dishes.

MEASURING LIQUID INGREDIENTS

Liquid measuring cups have the cup line a little below the rim so that a cup of liquid will not spill over. Place the measuring cup on the table. Pour in liquid until, if you stoop to see the mark at eye level, the liquid is at the required line. To measure a spoonful of liquid, lift what the spoon will normally hold — it will be more than level. (There are 12 tablespoons liquid to a cup but 16 tablespoons dry measure.)

MEASURING DRY INGREDIENTS

Dry measuring cups have the line right at the rim.

Flour — Spoon flour directly from canister or bag into dry measuring cup until full to overflowing. With a straight-edged spatula or knife, push off the flour that rises above the rim. (Cups in fraction sizes can be measured in the same way.)

Granulated Sugar — Follow the same method as for flour.

Brown Sugar — All recipes in this book call for 'lightly-packed' brown sugar. Spoon brown sugar into dry measuring cup, pressing down lightly to be sure there are no hollows underneath. Level off in the usual way. When turned out of the cup the sugar should hold its shape, but crumble if lightly touched.

Other Dry Ingredients — Some products, such as baking powder, baking soda and cocoa, have a tendency to pack down in their containers. To measure, stir the product to loosen, then lift a spoonful and level off in the usual way.

MEASURING FAT

Solid Fat — The simplest method is to press the butter, shortening or lard into a dry measuring cup. Press down firmly to be sure there are no air spaces. Remove from cup. Fat may be measured by the water-displacement method. Fill liquid measuring cup to 1/3 or 1/2 cup level with cold water. Drop fat into water, making certain it is completely immersed, until water level is at the 1 cup mark. If you started with 1/3 cup water, you have 2/3 cup fat; if you started with 1/2 cup water, you have 1/2 cup fat.

Liquid Fat — Measure the same as any other liquid.

Note: If the recipe reads 1 tablespoon butter, melted — the butter would be measured before melting. If it reads 1 tablespoon melted butter the butter would be measured after melting.

ALL-PURPOSE FLOUR vs PASTRY FLOUR

If you use an all-purpose flour and the recipe calls for pastry (soft wheat) flour; use 6/7 of the measurement.

If you use a pastry (soft wheat) flour and the recipe calls for all-purpose flour; use 7/6 of the measurement.

Note: For best results use all-purpose flour in those recipes that call for yeast.

SUBSTITUTIONS

Ingredients	Equivalent to
1 cup butter	= 1 cup margarine
1 cup granulated sugar	= 1-1/3 cups lightly packed brown sugar
1 square unsweetened chocolate	= 3 tablespoons cocoa + 1 tablespoon fat
1 cup buttermilk OR sour milk	= 1 tablespoon vinegar or lemon juice + sweet milk to make 1 cup (let stand 5 minutes)

Index

187